THE CO-PRESIDENCY
OF BUSH AND CHENEY

Shirley Anne Warshaw

STANFORD POLITICS AND POLICY
An imprint of Stanford University Press
Stanford, California

Stanford University Press
Stanford, California

Printed in the United States of America on acid-free, archival-quality paper

Library of Congress Cataloging-in-Publication Data

Warshaw, Shirley Anne, 1950-
The co-presidency of Bush and Cheney / Shirley Anne Warshaw.
p. cm.
Includes bibliographical references and index.
ISBN 978-0-8047-5818-5 (cloth : alk. paper)
1. United States--Politics and government--2001- 2. Cheney, Richard B.
3. Bush, George W. (George Walker), 1946- 4. Cheney, Richard B.--Influence.
5. Vice-Presidents--United States. 6. Executive power--United States. I. Title.
E902.W376 2009
973.931092--dc22   2009006217

Typeset by Bruce Lundquist in 10/15 Sabon

Contents

Acknowledgments

THE JOURNEY TO UNDERSTAND how deeply engaged Vice President Dick Cheney was in the Bush presidency involved support from the many people who helped me research, write, and edit this book. I began the research in 2006, using a cadre of students of mine at Gettysburg College. This dedicated group of students worked tirelessly as we followed the trail of Cheney's involvement in domestic, economic, and national security policy and then began systematically to interview members of the Bush campaign (both before and after Dick Cheney was added to the ticket), and members of the Bush-Cheney White House. This group was led by Kat Atwater and then Rachel Burg, both of whom spent endless hours organizing material, scheduling interviews, directing student researchers, and finding the missing pieces as we built our case on the role that Cheney played in decision making. The Gettysburg student group included Lauren Meehan, Owen Carhart, Denista Koleva, Aaron Lawson, Cassie Sanford, Shaina Wright, Jean Schumacher, Patrick Murphy, Liz Kocienda, Kristin Makar, Bill Lamb, Mike Hollander, Keith Hinder, and Matt Arscott.

Gettysburg College, which has always supported my research into presidential decision making, provided me with a research sabbatical and funding. Ken Mott, my colleague in the Department of Political Science, and Patti Lawson, Jerold Wikoff, and Kendra Martin in the Communications Office of Gettysburg College, and Joe Lynch in the Alumni Office, have worked with me at every stage of the project and provided invaluable insights.

Many of my colleagues across the nation have reviewed the manuscript, as have many friends in Washington, D.C., each of whom has offered excellent criticisms and ideas, which have been incorporated into the final product. I am especially indebted to Bradley Patterson, an expert on White House staffing, who hammered out numerous ideas with me on the operations of the president's and vice president's staffs.

Once the book went into production, my extraordinary editor, Stacy Wagner, provided tireless guidance. Both Susan Wels and Peter Dreyer, whose careful and thoughtful editing sharpened the organization of each chapter, significantly enhanced the book. Stanford University Press constantly championed this book to challenge the nation's knowledge of the unprecedented power that Vice President Cheney wielded in crafting national policy. Dick Cheney was not just the vice president, but in reality the unelected co-president of the United States.

Finally, my deepest gratitude goes to my family, who were by my side as the light stayed on late into the night through many drafts of each chapter. My husband, Allen Warshaw, would often read chapters and suggest ideas to expand points that I was making. My three sons, Chris, Andy, and Bobby, who have very busy lives of their own, also provided ideas both for and against points I was making. It takes a village to write a book, with family, friends, colleagues, and people one hardly knows standing by your side. For this, I am deeply grateful.

Shirley Anne Warshaw
Gettysburg, Pennsylvania
December 2008

THE CO-PRESIDENCY
OF BUSH AND CHENEY

CHAPTER I

Introduction

T HROUGHOUT NOVEMBER 2000, the nation and world awaited a final decision as America's two presidential candidates, Al Gore and George W. Bush, battled past election day for the coveted prize of the Oval Office. One hundred million votes were cast, without a clear winner, in the most controversial and hotly contested election in over a hundred years. This is the part of the story that we know.

There is another part of the story, however, that did not receive media attention, which remained under the public radar. This story has only recently begun to trickle out, in bits and pieces that may no longer shock, but should certainly infuriate us. While the candidates, their lawyers, and the state of Florida itself were in the spotlight between November and December, Dick Cheney was hard at work in the quiet of his McLean, Virginia, office. And he was up to nothing less than crafting his future role as the most powerful vice president in history. As transition director for a Bush-Cheney administration, Cheney spent hours assembling personnel, creating governing strategies, and effectively beginning his tenure as what I call a co-president, weeks before the Supreme Court announced its decision.[1] The shared presidency of George W. Bush and Dick Cheney began on election night, November 7, 2000, and continued for the next eight years.

Cheney, with his lengthy service in both the executive and legislative branches of government, exerted more influence than any vice president in history—and more than any vice president will have in future administrations. He and Bush created the first co-presidency in America's history: a division of labor, based on their separate spheres of interest and influence. Bush managed his faith-based agenda, moved forward his compassionate conservatism, and served as the public face of the administration. Cheney managed the larger portfolio of economic, energy, and national security policy and worked to expand the power of the presidency.

Cheney's ascendancy did not involve the stealing or hijacking of power, as some have suggested. Rather, Bush handed his vice president a significant role in the administration. This extraordinary delegation of power stemmed in part from the experience of his father, George H. W. Bush, who had served as Ronald Reagan's vice president. Reagan's staff never trusted George H. W. Bush, a Reagan rival in the 1980 Republican Party primaries, and permitted him little influence over White House policy making.

Not surprisingly, George W. Bush wanted to ensure that his own vice president would play a significant role in his administration— although co-president was not the one he originally envisioned. That role emerged during the course of the transition, which Cheney managed, and Bush quickly became comfortable with the division of labor. Dick Cheney, in fact, was one of the few people in the political world with the depth of experience to plan and execute such an expansion of power for the vice president. Cheney had breadth and depth across the federal government, in both the executive and legislative branches. His career in the executive branch spanned four administrations: under Richard Nixon, he had worked for Donald Rumsfeld in the Office of Economic Opportunity; under Gerald Ford, he had served initially as deputy chief of staff and later as chief of staff; under George H. W. Bush, he was secretary of defense; and under Reagan, he had held the position of special envoy, with the mission of developing a secret, shadow government in case of an attack on Washington, D.C.

Cheney's legislative experience was equally deep. From 1979 to 1989, he had served in Congress as the sole member of the House of Representatives from Wyoming. By the time he joined George W. Bush's presidential campaign, he had already been White House chief of staff and secretary of defense, as well as serving five terms as a member of Congress. His resume was unmatched in the Bush campaign and the world of high-stakes Washington politics.

In contrast to the depth of Cheney's resume, George W. Bush's experience in public service was limited to five years as governor of Texas—a state with a strong legislature that gave its governor relatively little responsibility for policy making. His tenure as governor had been his only foray into public life, although he had had some previous exposure to national politics while working in his father's presidential campaigns and, to some extent, in his father's White House.

Once George W. Bush had captured the White House in turn, he selected his advisors and presidential staff primarily from his staff in Austin. He filled the White House with Texas loyalists—including Karl Rove, Karen Hughes, Margaret Spellings, and Dan Bartlett—whose resumes lacked substantive policy or Beltway experience. They were no match for Cheney, who easily captured Bush's ear as an expert on policy and legislation.

Although Cheney brought Beltway and policy experience to the ticket, his greatest appeal to Bush was considerably simpler: he posed no threat. It was understood that, because Cheney purportedly had no interest in seeking the Republican nomination in 2008, he would make policy recommendations that were in the best interests of the Bush administration, not a future Cheney administration. Bush saw him as a policy enforcer with no political reasons to champion his own agenda and redirect the Bush administration's priorities.

There was also another important point in Cheney's favor. He was not a young man. At nearly sixty, as he told all who would listen, he had no intention of staying in public life and fully planned to return to his home in Jackson Hole, Wyoming, at the end of the administration. Retirement, rather than another political office, would be Cheney's next challenge. He had run for president once, in 1994, and swore that he would never run again. His heart condition also guaranteed that his service as vice president would be his last engagement as a public official. Having suffered two massive heart attacks, Cheney would not endanger his health further.

Since Cheney had no future political aspirations, Bush was comfortable relying on his vice president for information and policy advice. And Cheney's advice always meshed with Bush's own broad goals for his administration. When Cheney wanted to develop a national energy strategy, Bush agreed. When Cheney wanted to restructure regulatory policy to reduce what he saw as burdensome regulations on business and industry, Bush consented. When Cheney made recommendations for departmental and agency personnel, Bush went along. When Cheney urged regime change in Iraq, or made recommendations for dealing with detainees and prisoners of war, Bush always agreed. Bush routinely endorsed the strategies that Cheney created and the policy recommendations that he offered, often with little or no discussion—he essentially rubber-stamped the recommendations his vice president made.

What is perhaps most interesting about Cheney's policy role was the lack of policy-making expertise or control by the White House staff. In recent administrations, particularly since that of John F. Kennedy, White House policy offices had played the dominant role in making policy recommendations to the president. This was true both in foreign policy, overseen by the National Security Council (NSC) staff, and in domestic policy, led by White House experts in domestic and economic policy. But the Bush administration was different. Led by Karl Rove and Karen Hughes, the White House staff under George W. Bush was a political, not a policy, apparatus, and, as the former White House staffer John DiIulio lamented, politics, not policy, was the focus of White House staff meetings. The vice president and his staff moved quickly to fill the policy vacuum.

Even the frequently disparaged signing statements—through which Bush told Congress that he would not enforce certain parts of a bill because he deemed them unconstitutional—were drafted in the vice president's office by Cheney's legal counsel, David Addington. Addington reviewed every bill Congress sent to the president to determine whether any parts overstepped what he perceived as legislative authority. The real power of the co-presidency can be seen in this seemingly small role Cheney's office played. It was Cheney and Addington who decided whether Congress had overstepped its legislative authority—not George W. Bush or the White House staff. In Cheney's view, Congress had eroded presidential power in the years after the Watergate scandal—and Cheney, as vice president, intended to reassert the power lost under previous administrations. Signing statements—managed by the vice president's office, not the president's office—were a key part of Cheney's drive to check what he saw as the burgeoning power of Congress.

While the term "co-presidency" was never discussed nor used by either Bush or Cheney, it aptly describes their shared power, and both men implicitly understood the concept. The co-presidency they operated allowed Bush more time to focus on the campaign issues that were important to him: standards and accountability in education; a tax package that reduced income and capital gains taxes and increased the threshold for inheritance taxes; allowing faith-based organizations to receive federal funding (which prior administrations had opposed on the basis that it violated the First Amendment protection of the separation of church and state); and reinforcing certain moral precepts. These issues were the focus of the president—leaving Dick Cheney to oversee the areas in which Bush had less interest and less experience.

Cheney was happy to oblige. In this division of labor, he pursued his own agenda: building a pro-business administration, protecting presidential power, and commanding the national security agenda. For Bush, this was a win-win situation, since it allowed him to focus on issues that he had mastered in his brief tenure in public life as governor of Texas. And it allowed Cheney to focus on issues that he had mastered in his nearly thirty years in public life, followed by five years as chief executive officer of the energy conglomerate Halliburton.

Dick Cheney planned the path to the co-presidency, but George W. Bush became a willing partner. And no aspect was more central to Cheney's plan than integrating the vice president's staff with the White House staff. Vice presidents had never before been significantly integrated into the White House or given wide-ranging policy-making authority. Cheney, with the full support of the president, created what he called a "single executive office." Cheney had domestic and national security policy staffs and a press secretary, legislative staff, legal counsel, and a chief of staff, as well as other extensive staff support—in essence, an organization that paralleled the president's. Cheney's staff was present at all meetings and included on the circulation list for all interoffice memoranda within the White House. As a result, Cheney and his staff became omnipresent in White House meetings, with the full encouragement of President Bush. No template existed for the role that Cheney wanted to play as a partner in presidential decision making. Cheney crafted his own.

In the eight years of the Bush presidency, Cheney's power permeated the administration. As transition director, he had chosen nearly all the cabinet members and their deputies. The only two cabinet members that Cheney did not bring into the administration were Secretary of State Colin Powell and Attorney General John Ashcroft. Not surprisingly, both men became thorns in Cheney's side, challenging his decisions—and often blocking their implementation—on weapons of mass destruction, regime change, torture, and wireless surveillance without court-approved warrants. The resignations of both Powell and Ashcroft at the end of George W. Bush's first term ended the early challenges Cheney faced in his control over national security policy.

The vice president's influence on personnel selection extended to the judicial branch, where he became the most important voice in recommending appointments to the U.S. Supreme Court and the federal judiciary, particularly the appeals court. The recommendations of John Roberts and Samuel Alito for the Supreme Court, for example, emerged from Cheney's office rather than from the White House counsel's office or the Department of Justice. The Senate confirmation hearings for Roberts and Alito were also managed from Cheney's office by his staffer Steve Schmidt, and White House counsel Harriet Miers took her orders from Cheney's office, through Schmidt, during the Senate hearings.[2]

Cheney insisted on controlling judicial nominations to ensure that nominees were ideologically committed to expanding presidential power, especially presidential war powers. Each of the two Supreme Court appointments—and nearly all appointments to the federal appeals court—were vetted on this issue by David Addington. They were chosen from the ranks of the Federalist Society, a conservative legal group that championed conservative constitutional interpretation and expansive presidential power. By controlling the federal judiciary, Cheney believed, he would have the support he needed whenever challenges arose to the administration's view of presidential power.

For the same reason, Cheney also controlled appointments to

key positions in the Justice Department, particularly the Office of Legal Counsel, whose opinions were legally binding on the executive branch. Addington, who was instrumental in these recommendations, ensured that Federalist Society members dominated all of these key positions. Within months of taking office, through his careful appointments across the administration, Cheney had built the framework for the most powerful imperial presidency—and vice presidency—in thirty years.

Cheney's power extended across the administration. He masterminded energy policy, economic policy, regulatory policy, environmental policy, and the drive to outsource federal jobs, while Bush managed his faith-based agenda and devoted ample time to the public presidency of hosting dignitaries and traveling the nation and the world. When their relatively clear division of labor was shattered by the terrorist attacks of September 11, 2001, and Bush suddenly became interested in national security policy, Cheney's role in the co-presidency gained further stature due to his experience on the House Intelligence Committee and as secretary of defense. Without Dick Cheney and his network of neoconservatives, whom he strategically placed throughout the defense establishment, the United States would most likely have limited its war on terrorism to crushing al-Qaʻida in Afghanistan. The justification for toppling Saddam Hussein in Iraq was championed by Cheney and his allies Donald Rumsfeld, Paul Wolfowitz, and Richard Perle—not by George Tenet, Condoleezza Rice, or Colin Powell.

The lines were drawn on national security policy early in the administration, and Cheney's network won by convincing George W. Bush of the necessity for regime change in Iraq. As the final days of the administration drew to a close in 2008, Cheney and his allies in the Pentagon took aim at Iran, choosing targets for military special operations teams.[3]

In spite of the significant power that the vice presidency accumulated during Cheney's tenure, however, it seems unlikely that future vice presidents will become co-presidents or even major players in policy making. The balance of power will shift back to the White House. Future presidents will ensure that their staffs have a wealth of policy talent, the ability to manage the full range of the president's agenda, and the capacity for crisis management. Responsibility for policy making will return to the Oval Office and White House, where it has resided since Franklin Delano Roosevelt built the first policy-making White House staff in U.S. history. Vice presidents will once again hold specific and limited job assignments. George W. Bush lost control of too many issues to Dick Cheney, from energy policy to national security policy, as well as too many management decisions, from signing statements to outsourcing.

Most regrettable are the destructive policy consequences of the Bush-Cheney co-presidency. By the end of the administration, the nation was spiraling into the worst recession since the stock market crash of 1929. Oil prices had escalated to record highs, the falling dollar led to record trade deficits, jobs were slashed in every sector, a war continued on two fronts, international distrust lowered America's standing, record numbers of home foreclosures mounted daily, and the financial system descended into crisis.

Cheney is largely to blame. Economic, energy, and national security policy had been his responsibilities. He asked for this portfolio, and Bush gave it to him, but Cheney failed in each and every area—perhaps because he operated in total secrecy. His policy recommendations were never refined through the electoral process nor subjected to the normal vetting process of the White House and federal bureaucracy. Cheney crafted his policy proposals in secret, with few participants. They were dictates to the agencies, not political compromises reached through the normal policy process of give-and-take. The result was failed policy after failed policy—all driven by Dick Cheney.

Not surprisingly, by the time that Bush and Cheney left office, talk of impeaching the president and vice president was common in the halls of Congress. Their co-presidency had been a disaster for the nation, ending with public approval ratings lower than those of Richard Nixon during Watergate or Harry Truman during the Korean War. Theirs was widely viewed as the worst administration of modern times, eclipsing even that of Herbert Hoover, who presided over the start of the Great Depression.

This book is an effort to explain how the Bush-Cheney administration was dominated by its vice president, Dick Cheney. It was essentially a co-presidency. There was no takeover by the second-in-command, no hijacking of the Oval Office, only an understanding, an accommodation, in which labor and responsibility were divided.

CHAPTER 2

The Bush-Cheney Ticket Emerges

The Melding of Compassionate and Conservative

A S A CONSTANT CHAMPION of smaller government, fiscal restraint, and regulatory cutbacks, Dick Cheney was the perfect political match for George W. Bush. Cheney's fiscal conservatism and Bush's compassionate conservatism together represented the heart and soul of America's conservative movement.

They shared the common goal of changing the way government does business. Both were focused on creating policies designed to cut taxes, reduce regulation, and reframe government priorities. Bush had consistently supported business interests as governor of Texas. Cheney had built nearly perfect scores from the American Conservative Union for his House voting record on government spending, taxes, and regulation. Bush, however, had the added goal of inserting religion into the business of government, through the faith-based agenda of "compassionate conservatism." Their records merged in a perfect presidential ticket that enabled Republicans to recapture the White House in 2000 and created a powerful political union that would last for eight years.

God and religion were central to George W. Bush's public life and guided his policy making. For Cheney, on the other hand, the principles that drove policy were always cutting government spending and shielding business from burdensome regulations. The compassionate conservative agenda in the 2000 presidential campaign was a comfortable accommodation that allowed Bush, with his religious zeal, and Cheney, with his pro-business focus, to advance their own priorities in the co-presidency they created after the election.

The journey that led to the governing philosophy known as "compassionate conservatism" began in 1994, during Bush's first foray into electoral politics.[1] That phrase, crafted by Karl Rove, became Bush's platform when he challenged Ann Richards, the Democratic incumbent, for the Texas governor's office. It was a platform that appealed to both Democrats and Republicans in the state, and it provided the same broad electoral appeal in the presidential election six years later.

Presidential campaigns had long shied away from integrating religion and faith into their political platforms. In 1960, when John F. Kennedy, a Roman Catholic, sought the highest office, he assured Americans that religion would have no place in his administration. In 1976, presidential candidate Jimmy Carter, a Baptist, made the same commitment. But George W. Bush never made such a promise. On the contrary, he aggressively asserted, during both his gubernatorial campaign in 1994 and the presidential campaign in 2000, that faith guided his life and would be an integral part of his governing philosophy.

Faith, however, had not always guided Bush's life. A midlife crisis led to his religiosity, and the path to his awakening was littered with personal failures. By the 1980s, his alcoholism had become a serious problem. The low point came in 1985, at his parents' summer home in Kennebunkport, Maine, when—according to various reports—Bush had clearly had too much to drink and became verbally abusive to a guest. Vice President and Mrs. Bush, who were hosting the party, were, as might be expected, furious at their son's misbehavior. Their solution was to ask the Reverend Billy Graham, a family friend, to talk with their errant son. After spending several days with Graham on long walks around Walker's Point, George W. Bush proclaimed himself a new, born-again man, no longer dependent on alcohol to handle life's pressures. He had finally found himself and a new strength in God.[2]

In the following two years, Bush tamed his excessive behavior, gave up alcohol, switched from Episcopal to evangelical Christianity, and became actively committed to his born-again faith. When Vice President George H. W. Bush ran in the 1988 presidential election, he was quick to build on his son's religious zeal and asked him to move to Washington, D.C., for the campaign. George W. Bush had lived in Texas throughout the 1980s, involved in a variety of oil companies, such as Harken Energy, Spectrum 7, Arbusto Energy, and Bush Exploration. In 1990, Bush sold 212,140 shares of Harken Energy, reaping nearly $850,000. He took his profits from the sale and moved his family to a townhouse near American University in Washington, D.C., at his father's request.[3]

Laura Bush—in an interview with Robert Draper for his book on the Bush presidency—explained the change she saw in her husband in those years:

George is pretty impulsive and does pretty much everything to excess. And we had little girls, and in fact that's what I remember most, having these two little babies, and drinking really didn't fit. . . . Another factor was that we were going to move to Washington. He knew he couldn't move there and work on his dad's presidential campaign and keep drinking like that. You just can't take that kind of risk.[4]

Although George W. Bush had a limited role in that first campaign, he courted religious conservatives and acted as liaison to the Christian Coalition, an organization founded by the Reverend Pat Robertson. His understanding of the political influence wielded by Christian conservatives became central to his own presidential campaign twelve years later. The 1988 campaign also exposed him to professional campaign staff and the broad range of policy issues addressed in a national campaign.

Once George H. W. Bush was elected president, he again called on his son to serve as a conduit to religious conservatives. George W. Bush returned to Texas for business reasons, but he remained an advisor and often visited the White House during his father's four years in office. In 1992, as his father's reelection campaign geared up, he assumed the role of point-person with religious conservatives, especially the Christian Coalition. His courtship of religious conservatives in 1992 shaped his future political battles, from the 1994 campaign for the Austin statehouse to the 2000 campaign for the White House.

The conversion of George W. Bush to his born-again faith in 1985 remained deeply embedded in his political life—from his work on his father's campaigns, and later in his father's White House, to his own political journey. Nothing would be more important to George W. Bush than his religion and desire to use the resources of government to create a moral and civil society. That goal would become the dominant focus of his gubernatorial and presidential campaigns.

In 1994—after working on two presidential races and advising his father in the White House—George W. Bush felt prepared to launch his own run for the governor's office in Texas. In order to capture the statehouse, he needed a short list of issues that would attract conservative Democrats while protecting his Republican base. Texas was, after all, a Democratic state, which had brought Lyndon Baines Johnson to the presidency and had an incumbent Democratic governor, Ann Richards.

But the state had become increasingly conservative and had supported Ronald Reagan in both his runs for the presidency. In his 1984 reelection bid, Reagan easily took Texas, with 63 percent of the state's popular vote. In 1992, George H. W. Bush and the third-party candidate and former Republican Ross Perot together garnered the same 63 percent of the state's popular vote. Clearly, Texas was now turning Republican.

The state, however, continued to elect Democratic governors, from John Connally to Ann Richards—although Richards had barely beaten the wealthy Republican oil and gas magnate Clayton W. Williams Jr. in 1990. Working with Karl Rove, his campaign consultant, Bush hoped to unseat Richards in the 1994 election. His strategy would be to focus on issues that appealed to voters in both political parties. Those issues became immigration, tax reform, crime, and Bush's ubiquitous faith-based references to compassionate government.

The issue of immigration reform—based on border control and work permits—became a central theme and drew voter support across the state. But Bush needed another issue to attract a broader segment of the state's electorate, particularly conservative Democrats. The issue he seized upon was an approach to government spending that he called "conservative." In a state where Democrats had controlled electoral politics for decades, it was unlikely that Bush could win by identifying himself as a Republican. Instead of using the word "Republican" to describe his political affiliation or governing philosophy, he used the term "conservative" to describe himself and his approach, hoping to attract both traditional Republicans and self-identified conservative Democrats.

Bill Clinton had used this same tactic in the 1992 presidential election to woo Republicans into the Democratic fold. Although Clinton had not referred to himself or his policies as conservative, he frequently used conservative clichés, referring to a smaller federal government and to reforming the federal welfare system. Building on the model of co-option that Clinton had created, George W. Bush called himself a conservative—a term that resonated with both Democrats and Republicans in Texas.

There was a second motivation for Bush to use the term "conservative" as he tried to attract Democrats. By 1994, Republicans had successfully accused the Clinton administration of liberal policies and big spending, primarily due to its push for a national health care system and the "don't ask, don't tell" policy for the military. Although Clinton had campaigned as a "New Democrat"—a term he coined and used to build Republican and conservative Democratic support in 1992—many conservative Democrats now viewed the Clinton presidency as one of continued big government and liberal policies. His pledge to be a new type of Democrat rang hollow for many Texans. George W. Bush was able to exploit this dissatisfaction in 1994 and attract Texas Democrats to the Republican ticket, under the political umbrella of compassionate conservatism. Once the votes were counted, Bush had defeated the Democratic incumbent, Ann Richards, with 53 percent of the votes cast.[5] The tide for Republicans in Texas had started to turn.

Karl Rove, Bush's professional campaign manager, was the architect of the strategy to capture dissatisfied Democrats and build a new electoral coalition.[6] Even though Richards had had a 70 percent approval rating at one time, Bush and Rove were able to cobble together a new coalition to win the election. Clearly, the nation was ripe for the conservative agenda, which George W. Bush and Newt Gingrich were both touting. Gingrich pulled off a similar political victory the same year when he and fellow conservative Republicans wrested the U.S. House of Representatives from the Democrats, who had been in control since the Eisenhower administration. Bush was unquestionably lucky. He was running for governor in a year of significant disaffection with the Clinton administration among both Republicans and conservative Democrats.

With victory in hand, Bush immediately began to act on his campaign pledge to deal with illegal immigration. On December 1, 1994, just three weeks after winning the election, he joined his father, former president George H. W. Bush, on a trip to Mexico, where they met with the newly inaugurated Mexican president, Ernesto Zedillo Ponce de Léon, who promised to improve relations with Texas and to address the complicated problem of illegal immigrants. "I am going to take him up on that pledge," George W. Bush stated at the time.[7] But the newly elected governor did not seek to punish Mexican workers and their families already settled in Texas—only to exercise greater control of the U.S. border. He urged the new Republican Congress to take the lead role in border management, which, Bush argued, should be a national, not a state, issue. To honor his promise of a "conservative" approach to state spending, Bush pressed for greater federal involvement, while at the same time seeking to strengthen ties with Mexico and to work with Mexican leaders to create viable options for dealing with illegal immigration.

Bush remained steadfastly committed to immigration reform, although he chose not to support a mandate in Texas that would have ended state aid to illegal immigrants, as California was attempting to do with Proposition 187, which state voters there had recently passed.[8] Instead, Bush supported a program—one he referred to as "compassionate"—that allowed illegal immigrants to continue to be part of the economy, since millions of dollars from legal Mexican shoppers flowed into shopping malls in San Antonio and other east Texas communities. "He says he does not share the resentment many Americans feel toward illegals," the *Christian Science Monitor* noted. "Having encountered them 'all my life,' Bush speaks admiringly of those who undergo hardships to come and earn more for their families. Once they are here, it's only 'good public policy' for Texas to educate their children, he says."[9]

Bush was now beginning to change his governing philosophy, moving away from the strictly "conservative" agenda of the 1994 campaign to a newly framed "compassionate conservatism." The term slowly emerged during his first term as governor and became central to his second term and, later, to his campaign for president.

Following his inauguration as governor in 1995, Bush sought to build a rapport with the Democratically controlled state legislature in order to move his signature proposals forward. Because Texans were generally conservative, regardless of political identity, Bush had little trouble building bridges to the state's Democratic leadership. As part of his effort to build a bipartisan governing coalition, he had breakfast every Wednesday with Lieutenant Governor Bob Bullock and House Speaker James "Pete" Laney, both Democrats. Bullock, a conservative, was one of his strongest supporters in the Texas legislature.

But the legislature refused to address the difficult issue of immigration reform, so Bush turned to another signature issue of his 1994 campaign, tax reform, which was the central issue for his affluent urban and suburban base. Property taxes had doubled in recent years due to the booming economy, causing homeowners to seek some tax relief from Austin. Bush had to address the issue or face losing his Republican base in a reelection bid.

His solution was to support a massive $5 billion property tax relief bill. Property tax revenue lost to the state coffers would be offset by a tax on certain corporations and businesses, called a "business activity levy." Although the tax affected only about 10 percent of the business community, it was perceived as a general tax on goods, since businesses would have had to increase their prices as a pass-through. The attempt to create the $5 billion tax relief failed, as did the tax on business, but a later attempt successfully provided for a smaller $1 billion property tax relief bill, without a concurrent tax increase. Tax relief was partly paid for by a $2.3 billion state tax surplus, mostly generated by previous administrations.

Having mustered some measure of success with property tax relief, Bush next needed to build bridges to less affluent Republican and conservative Democratic constituencies. Since he was unable to address immigration in any significant way, he needed to find another issue that embraced the same theme of compassionate government. He found it in prison reform, which had been an issue in Texas politics for many years. Prison overcrowding had become the center of federal litigation, but the state of Texas had been unable to significantly

reduce the number of prisoners, the number of prisons, or overcrowding. Prisons, however, were filled with people who Bush believed could
be redeemed, and his solution to the prison issues was to bring in a
faith-based group—Prison Fellowship Ministries, formed in 1975 by
the former Watergate conspirator Charles Colson—to help prisoners
find a moral compass.

The goal of Prison Fellowship Ministries was "for prisoners to
become born again and grow as fruitful disciples of Jesus Christ," as
well as to build character in prison inmates, "which they would carry
forward into society when they were released."[10] Its services—which
Governor Bush hoped would transform prisoners' lives—were paid for
with state funds. George W. Bush's born-again Christianity was now
intertwined with the job of governing through a "compassionate" approach that welcomed and supported faith-based groups.

After two years of working with the Democratically controlled
legislature—with little progress on his legislative goals—Bush saw
his fortunes improve in the 1996 elections, when Republicans gained
control of Texas government. Having a Republican-controlled legislature meant fewer policy, budgetary, and personal confrontations with
legislators. Bush was now able to work with his own party and move
his proposals forward. Unfortunately, he had relatively few proposals
and his immigration plan, his primary initiative from the 1994 race,
was only modestly successful. In spite of Bush's limited policy agenda,
he was now dealing with legislators who shared his broad goals and
didn't acrimoniously attack him for political gain.

Bush's political fortunes continued to improve in 1996, when President Clinton soundly defeated Senator Bob Dole in the presidential race.
Dole's defeat left the Republicans scrambling for new leadership in the
party. The Republican ticket of Bob Dole and Jack Kemp had failed
to ignite any voter enthusiasm, in spite of the Whitewater and Travel-
gate problems that the Clinton-Gore ticket had had to deal with. The
booming economy, particularly in the technology sector, left the Dole
team with few arguments that excited voters. The health care legislation
championed by Hillary Rodham Clinton in 1993, which had heavily
contributed to the Democrats' loss of the House of Representatives

in 1994, had been brushed under the table and replaced with welfare reform legislation, supported by both parties. Bill Clinton was able to co-opt welfare reform from the Republicans and claim it as a victory for his own administration. He won reelection in a landslide.

As a result, Republicans had no standard-bearer for the upcoming 2000 election. Dole and Kemp had been effectively taken out of contention by their lackluster showing in 1996. George W. Bush, as a result, suddenly became a dark horse contender for the Republican nomination as soon as the lights went out on the 1996 race. He was a Beltway outsider who had captured the governor's office from a Democratic incumbent in a predominantly Democratic state.

As he prepared for his gubernatorial reelection throughout 1997 and 1998, Bush began to seriously consider a run for the presidency. In the spring of 1998, he was buoyed by a new national poll indicating that he was favored among Republican contenders by Republican voters, and media speculation about his possible run for the 2000 nomination had already begun.[11] The *Houston Chronicle* reported in April 1998 that Bush was holding a series of fund-raising and speaking events in California but wanted to "dampen speculation" that he would seek the Republican presidential nomination in 2000.[12] When asked about the appropriateness of speaking to a group of conservative movie stars and film producers—known as the Wednesday Morning Club—Bush responded, "I'm not running for anything in California. I'm running for governor of Texas."[13] Bush told the Wednesday Morning Club that he had not decided to run for president in 2000—but, he admitted, "I think about it."[14] Bush was not only thinking about it, but laying the foundation for his presidential campaign.

He left California to attend fund-raisers in Phoenix, supposedly to support Senator John McCain. Publicly, Bush explained that he was traveling to California and Arizona to raise money for his November 1998 reelection campaign for governor. But his denials of any interest in the presidential race were ringing hollow. Not only was the national press taking note of his out-of-state fund-raisers, but the state Democratic Party was also beginning to issue press releases about them. "Governor Bush is traveling to California and Arizona this week on a political trip designed to raise money and raise his profile for the presidential race," a Democratic Party spokesman claimed.[15] Most Texas observers agreed with this assessment.

They were right. Bush started to gear up for his national campaign during the 1998 gubernatorial race, in which he raised and spent $25 million to his opponent's $3 million.[16] Karl Rove, who ran both the gubernatorial and presidential campaigns, realized that a landslide victory in Texas that year would catapult Bush into the contender's circle for the 2000 Republican nomination. Part of the $25 million had been raised by out-of-state Republicans, who were looking for a conservative GOP standard-bearer. Bush and Rove knew exactly what they were doing when they built their war chest.

Not surprisingly, one of the major points of Bush's stump speech on this trip was the need to deal with Mexico and the influx of illegal workers. "The most compassionate way to beef up the border is to keep people from wanting to come across the border. You've got to encourage free trade and open markets," Bush explained. The word "compassionate" had again moved into the campaign lexicon.

Bush proved to be an even better campaigner in 1998 than he had been in 1994, easily moving through crowds as he crisscrossed the state. On October 29, 1998, Candy Crowley of CNN posted a story that extolled his strength on the stump: "George [W.] Bush is a terrific campaigner, thriving on the limelight, diving into crowds. This George Bush is a retail politician, touching, hugging and autographing his way along the campaign trail."[17]

Days later, George W. Bush won reelection in Texas with 69 percent of the vote, making him a serious candidate for the 2000 presidential race. Although the Texas media had speculated about the possibility of a presidential run throughout the 1998 race, the Bush campaign remained focused on winning reelection in Texas and provided few clues about his interest in a national run. Not until the election appeared to be a landslide victory for Bush did the national media begin to speculate. Candy Crowley's glowing coverage of the gubernatorial race was an indication of their new interest in the Texas governor.

As he actively prepared to run for national office, Bush produced *A Charge to Keep*, a book published in 1999, in which he repeated his call for a "single, moral community."[18] It argued for a "new vision of the proper role for government" that would "welcome the active involvement of people who are following a religious imperative to love their neighbors through after-school programs, child care, drug treatment, maternity group homes, and a range of other services."[19] Bush called this expanded role for government-funded religious programs "compassionate conservatism."

The first real sign of a national campaign emerged when George W. Bush was inaugurated for his second term on January 20, 1999, on the promenade of the Texas capitol in Austin.[20] His inaugural address reached out to Christian conservatives, calling upon Texas to become "a moral and spiritual center" for the nation.[21] It focused on the *"values* of independence, hard work, strong families, duty to country, and *faith in God* [emphasis added]." He peppered his address with frequent references to the Almighty: "All of us have worth. We're all made in the image of God. We're all equal in God's eyes." He also reiterated his commitment to compassionate government, saying, "We must rally the armies of compassion that are in every community of this state. We must encourage them to love, to nurture, to mentor, to help, and thus to offer hope to those who have none."[22] Exactly one year later, he would be using many of the same phrases in his presidential inaugural address from the U.S. Capitol in Washington, D.C.

Only a month after Bush's second inauguration, public speculation intensified about who would be part of the presidential campaign. The *Austin American-Statesman* predicted—in a front-page article on February 28, 1999—that "when Gov. George W. Bush turns his attention to trying to become President George W. Bush, he will turn to aides, friends and advisors he has collected on his privileged path from prep school to the political big leagues."[23] Soon afterward, related stories on a Bush candidacy began appearing in major newspapers across the country.

As the press correctly guessed, the Bush presidential campaign was gearing up. At the center of the campaign's fund-raising organization was a Los Angeles businessman, Bradford Freeman—whose partner, Ron Spogli, had been a roommate of Bush's at Harvard Business School—along with Craig Stapleton, who was married to a Bush cousin, had raised money for George H. W. Bush, and had invested with George W. Bush in the Texas Rangers major-league baseball team in 1989.[24] Other members of the nascent presidential campaign were Joe Allbaugh, chief of staff to the governor; political consultant Karl Rove; communications director Karen Hughes; Midland businessman Donald Evans; appointments director Clay Johnson; and Harriet Miers, Bush's personal lawyer in Dallas. Not surprisingly, most of the inner circle later surfaced in key positions in the George W. Bush administration, from the cabinet to the White House staff.

On April 24, 1998, Freeman arranged the first major fund-raiser in California's Silicon Valley, ostensibly to raise money for Bush's gubernatorial reelection campaign. The visit gave wealthy California Republicans an opportunity to scrutinize the potential presidential candidate. Freeman, a Stanford University trustee, then arranged a small policy-oriented meeting on the Stanford campus, at the home of former secretary of state George P. Shultz.[25] Shultz had been on the faculty of Stanford's conservative Hoover Institution since 1989, after he left the Bechtel Corporation, based in San Francisco. The meeting included about ten Stanford University faculty, including the economists Michael Boskin and John Taylor; a domestic policy expert, Martin Anderson; a budget expert, Annelise Anderson; and Stanford's provost, Condoleezza Rice, a specialist in Soviet and Eastern European affairs.[26] All had worked in past Republican administrations at senior levels—Boskin, Taylor, and Rice in the George H. W. Bush administration and Shultz and both Andersons in the Reagan administration. Boskin had the closest ties to George W. Bush—as chairman of the Council of Economic Advisors for George H. W. Bush, Boskin had once shared a cottage in Kennebunkport with George W. Bush.[27] Except for Rice, all were part of Stanford's conservative Hoover Institution, and Rice worked closely with many Hoover Institution faculty.[28]

The Hoover Institution encouraged its faculty to become engaged in the national political scene, and the dinner party that Shultz hosted for

George W. Bush that evening was one of many meetings that Hoover faculty had with presidential hopefuls.[29] During the 1980 campaign, Ronald Reagan had met frequently with Hoover faculty. After a 1979 dinner party with candidate Reagan—also at the home of George Shultz—many of them joined the Reagan campaign and continued into the Reagan White House. Martin Anderson, for example, left Stanford to become the architect of Reagan's domestic and economic policies during the 1980 campaign and, after the election, became Reagan's White House domestic policy advisor.

Having made this initial contact with Hoover faculty, George W. Bush invited the group to Austin for the first of what became a two-year series of policy discussions. By the spring of 1999, the Stanford faculty and others were regularly visiting Austin to explain issues and offer policy positions. Another Reagan administration alumnus, Lawrence Lindsey, an American Enterprise Institute scholar who had served on the Council of Economic Advisors, also became a regular at the Austin policy meetings. Lindsey soon began inviting economic experts to the meetings and coordinating the agenda. Bush also added Indianapolis Mayor Stephen Goldsmith to coordinate domestic policy.[30] The meetings—which were convened in the formal dining room or in the conservatory of the governor's mansion—lasted about four hours, starting at 8:00 A.M. and ending at noon.

The level of policy discussion varied and was often more specific than Bush might have preferred. In one Austin policy meeting on February 18, 1999, Goldsmith presided over a health policy meeting consisting of thirty minutes of introductory remarks and a twenty-five-minute discussion of health care financing and delivery systems, patient care, acute to chronic conditions, diffusion of technology, and the rise of pharmaceutical therapy.[31] One participant bluntly commented that Bush still "had a lot to learn" about every policy issue. Another participant added, with the same degree of concern, that Bush had "a lot of growing to do."[32]

In the months that followed, as the campaign staff swelled and lost the informality of the Austin meetings, Hoover Institution faculty continued to play a senior role. Condoleezza Rice became the chief foreign policy advisor, and Edward Lazear, Michael Boskin, and John Cogan became senior economic advisors.[33] Hoover Institution faculty proved to be ideal tutors for the Texas governor.

Their expertise had the added practical advantage of immersing Bush in the policies of the Reagan Revolution. The Hoover advisors wore the mantle of the Reagan tradition, which Bush sought to preserve. Perhaps equally important, they added star power to the fledgling campaign's fund-raising efforts. What better way to bring national attention to a campaign than reaching out to intellectual talent from Stanford? It assured conservative Republicans familiar with Hoover faculty ties to the Reagan and Bush administrations that there would be continuity in policy direction. Bush was loudly signaling that he would be a conservative in the Reagan mold.[34]

In June 2000, national polls showed that Bush had strong support among independents and moderates. To solidify his ties to the Reagan-Bush years, he selected Dick Cheney, chairman and CEO of Halliburton, as vice president.[35] Cheney was promptly described as "a rock-solid conservative who poses little or no political risk"—unlike pro-choice Governor Tom Ridge of Pennsylvania, who might have upset the support Bush had with Christian evangelicals.[36] Fred Barnes, the executive editor of the *Weekly Standard*—the bible of many Republican conservatives—proclaimed that Cheney's "conservatism is not in doubt, though he's hardly a zealot."[37] For Barnes and other conservatives, it was important that both Bush and his running mate build on the Reagan goals and coalition and continue the policy efforts of the Reagan Revolution. Cheney met the test. Since he had been secretary of defense under George H. W. Bush, he had the necessary defense credentials, and he had logged a consistently conservative voting record as congressman from Wyoming in the 1980s.

Cheney's path to the vice presidency was unconventional, to say the least. While most vice presidents bring electoral, geographic, or other political benefits to the ticket, Dick Cheney, instead, brought more than three decades of Beltway experience, balancing George W. Bush's thin resume in public service. Cheney's career spanned both ends of Pennsylvania Avenue, from the White House to the Capitol and the shores of the Potomac at the Pentagon. He knew how the federal government worked. His five years in Houston with Halliburton—a company with which he had worked closely during his tenure as secretary of defense—added private-sector depth to his resume.

Still, the choice of Dick Cheney as vice president struck many as a poor one. He had little charisma and was not a campaigner; he was, as one writer put it, "a balding, overweight, middle-aged man who is not especially telegenic."[38] In his own brief bid for the presidency in 1994, Cheney had had to withdraw because of his uneasiness in the meet-and-greet side of campaigning.[39] He didn't like fund-raising, shaking hands at factories, and smiling at chicken-and-potato dinners, and he had difficulty asking supporters for money. Al Haig, Nixon's former chief of staff, said: "I'd go with him to a fund-raiser and he'd lean up against the fireplace and hold conversations about policy. He just didn't want to work the room."[40] In contrast, George W. Bush was quite good at that aspect of campaigning.

For George W. Bush, however, Cheney was the perfect addition to the ticket and strengthened the bridge he was building to Reagan conservatives. Cheney's record as a deficit hawk was an essential part of that appeal. As Gerald Ford's deputy chief of staff in 1974 and chief of staff in 1975, Cheney had been the administration's chief budget enforcer and had regularly battled Vice President Nelson Rockefeller over domestic spending.[41]

Rockefeller, a moderate Republican with a long list of domestic issues he hoped to address, was opposed at every turn by Cheney, who saw the list as too expensive and unnecessary. When New York City was on the brink of bankruptcy, Rockefeller, the former governor of New York, was particularly eager to ensure that the city did not default on its loans, and he pushed for federal guarantees. Despite Cheney's strong opposition, Rockefeller succeeded in winning Ford's support. New York City was protected from bankruptcy and soon rebuilt its financial strength in the bond market.

Rockefeller won that battle, but he lost the war with Cheney—who eventually pushed him off the 1976 ticket with Ford in favor of the more conservative Bob Dole. At every turn of the Ford administration,

Cheney argued for reduced domestic spending and greater attention to the deficit. He became the leading deficit hawk in the administration—more so than Ford, who only adopted Cheney's position as the economy sank during the energy crisis of the mid-1970s.

By the end of Ford's presidency in 1977, Cheney had gained a reputation as a fiscal conservative and deficit hawk. Addicted to political life by that time, Cheney uprooted his family and returned to Wyoming, where he successfully ran for the state's only House seat in 1978. Two years after leaving Washington as White House chief of staff, he returned as a freshman congressman. He went from being the second most powerful person in the executive branch to one of the least important members of the legislative branch. He was a first-term member of the House of Representatives.

Surprisingly, Cheney did not seek an appointment to the newly created Budget Committee or the Appropriations or Banking Committees of the House—perhaps, he thought, his constituency wouldn't understand the value of committees dealing with government finance. Cheney, instead, moved away from his fiscal focus into the arena of national security matters as a member of the Intelligence Committee. His meteoric rise in the executive branch—from mid-level manager in the Office of Wage and Price Controls in 1971 to White House chief of staff in 1975—was soon matched by his rapid rise in the House of Representatives. By 1982, he had been elected chairman of the Republican Policy Committee, defeating the well-regarded Marjorie S. Holt of Maryland. In 1986, he was elected minority whip and became a confidant of Bob Michel, the affable minority leader. He appeared to be on his way to becoming the next Speaker of the House before he resigned after George H. W. Bush named him secretary of defense.

Throughout his five terms in the House, Cheney had one of the most conservative voting records of any member. He voted against making Martin Luther King Jr.'s birthday a national holiday and against Head Start funding. His record, however, was built, not as a deficit hawk, although he certainly was one, but on his views of executive power. Cheney believed the power of the presidency had been eroded in the post-Watergate years.

Cheney's 1987 vote against the reauthorization of the Older Americans Act, for example, was a vote not only against increased federal funding but also against what he saw as an unconstitutional intrusion on presidential prerogatives. For Cheney, the Older Americans Act required the unconstitutional provision that the president send Congress material that detailed how the secretary of health and human services had reached certain decisions—a violation, Cheney believed, of the unitary executive. This would be the same argument, also in 1987, in the Minority Report on the Iran-Contra scandal. In a similar vein, Cheney viewed legislation such as the War Powers Act of 1973 and the Budget and Impoundment Control Act of 1974 as encroachments on the president's constitutional authority.

Without question, Cheney's view of presidential power had been framed in his short but intense tenure in the White House as deputy chief of staff and then chief of staff. The presidency had been severely damaged by Richard Nixon's administration. As a result of Nixon's imperial presidency, Congress sought to ensure greater transparency in the executive branch. Cheney, however, saw congressional demands for greater transparency and accountability by the president primarily as political tools of a Democratic Congress seeking to build its own institutional and political authority.

Those views crystallized in the mid-1980s as the Iran-Contra scandal erupted during Ronald Reagan's administration. By the time Congress began investigating the scandal, Cheney was not only the House minority leader but also ranking member of the House Intelligence Committee. That committee prepared a lengthy report to Congress that was highly critical of Reagan's refusal to follow the letter of the law in funding the Nicaraguan Contras against the socialist-leaning Sandinistas. The Boland Amendments, passed between 1982 and 1984, had barred Reagan from further funding the Contras' guerrilla force.

Cheney disagreed with the Intelligence Committee's final report and joined with other Republicans to issue their own report. Their Minority Report chastised Congress for intruding on the president's constitutional authority as commander in chief. Written by David Addington—who would later become Vice President Cheney's legal counsel—the report argued that "it is essential . . . to frame any discussion of what happened with a proper analysis of the constitutional allocation of legislative and executive power in foreign affairs."[42]

Cheney and Addington maintained in the Minority Report that notwithstanding the legislative prohibition in the Boland Amendments, Reagan had not overstepped his constitutional authority in delivering aid to the Nicaraguan Contras.[43] Cheney's penchant as vice president for protecting presidential power and his strong view of presidential authority in national security policy were largely driven by the views he carefully articulated in the Minority Report.

As George W. Bush built his presidential campaign in 1998 and 1999, Cheney stayed essentially in the wings. He at times joined the foreign policy advisors at meetings with Bush in Austin, but he was never a leader in those discussions. He let others talk, a trait that had become one of his hallmarks. In March 2000, after it was clear that the primaries would lead to his party's nomination in July, Bush invited Cheney to dinner at the governor's mansion and opened the door to a possible Bush-Cheney ticket; but Cheney declined. In April, Bush again sought to bring Cheney deeply into his inner circle by asking him to chair the vice-presidential search.

Cheney agreed and undertook a massive review of every candidate Bush considered. He prepared a detailed, 83-question form for each potential candidate, which was handed out to Senators Dan Coates of Indiana, John Danforth of Kansas, Frank Keating of Oklahoma, Fred Thompson and Bill Frist of Tennessee, and Chuck Hagel of Nebraska, as well as to Governors John Engler of Michigan, George Pataki of New York, James S. Gilmore of Virginia, and Tom Ridge of Pennsylvania, among others. One senator purposely excluded was John McCain of Arizona, apparently one of the few people actively seeking the job.[44] During the primaries, McCain had adamantly stated he would not take second place on the ticket, and Cheney chose to respect that declaration.

In May, Cheney had narrowed the list enough to start bringing candidates to Austin to meet with Bush. On May 24, 2000, Cheney called Lamar Alexander and told him that "Governor Bush would like to consider you as his running mate."[45] He also called Governor Tom Ridge on July 5 to arrange an interview with Bush, but Ridge withdrew from contention, citing family obligations and the need to be with his two teenagers. According to Cheney, about five people ended up on the short list for final consideration.

As the Republican convention grew closer, Cheney further narrowed the list of candidates for Bush. Several weeks before the event, the two men met at Bush's Crawford, Texas, ranch to discuss frontrunners. Over lunch, Laura Bush asked how the process was going and who was at the top of the list. Bush looked at Cheney and said to Laura, "the man I really want to be the vice president is here at the table."[46] That was the beginning of the end for all the other vice-presidential candidates.

Working with Cheney throughout the spring on the vetting process for vice president had convinced Bush that he wanted Dick Cheney for the job. Cheney didn't decline, but he suggested that his heart disease might be a problem. Karen Hughes, Karl Rove, and Joe Allbaugh then met with Cheney at the governor's mansion to discuss his health. He told them that he didn't think that the stress of being vice president was any greater than that of running an international business or being secretary of defense.[47] He thought he was up to the job.

And Bush wanted Cheney to be his vice president. Cheney was part of his comfort zone; he knew him, his father knew him, and both trusted him. One of the hallmarks of the Bush family was their loyalty—and, as one commentator noted, "it is no secret that the Bush clan values loyalty above nearly all else."[48] Bush and Cheney also shared core values, a love of the great outdoors, their business lives in the oil industry, and conservative political principles honed in the Reagan and Bush years.

Unlike many other contenders for vice president, Cheney also had relatively little baggage. Some of the candidates, like pro-choice Governor Tom Ridge, would alienate conservatives. Other candidates, like Frank Keating, had problems in their past that would be hard to explain away. But Cheney had a long marriage, no financial scandals, and deep experience in the federal government. As one Bush advisor put it, "the most basic rule of picking a vice president is 'First, do no harm.'"[49]

There was also the advantage of experience that Cheney brought to the table. Bush said when he made the offer to Cheney, "I don't know what's going to come on my desk, but I'm going to need somebody who's seen things before, who can give me advice to make good decisions."[50] Cheney appeared to be the least threatening of the choices brought to the table when Bush finally had to make the decision. Not surprisingly, Cheney himself brought the list to the table, and he was the one who vetted his own records. When a reporter asked Karen Hughes who was going over Cheney's financial information, she replied: "Just as with our other candidates, Secretary Cheney is the one who handled that."[51]

Once Cheney had agreed to join the ticket, he needed to change his voting registration. The Twelfth Amendment to the Constitution prohibits a president and vice president from residing in the same state, so Cheney had to move his primary residence out of Texas. That proved relatively easy, since Cheney owned a second home in Jackson Hole, Wyoming. He hastily flew to the resort community, where he had a condominium in a gated community, and completed his change of registration on Thursday, July 20. He was now in a position to accept a public invitation from George W. Bush to join the ticket. It would be Cheney's last chance to return to the political halls of power he had roamed for so many years and to which he so eagerly wanted to return. Five days later, on July 25—only a week before the Republican convention in Philadelphia—Bush formally made the offer to Cheney in a 6:30 A.M. phone call from the governor's mansion.[52]

Later that day, Bush made the public announcement to a crowd of supporters in Austin. The offer was by this time hardly a secret, since the campaign had leaked the decision the day before.[53] Responding to cheers, Cheney said, "I enthusiastically accept the challenge for this reason: I believe you have the vision and the courage to be a great president."[54]

To conservatives across the country, the primary campaign of 2000 and the selection of Dick Cheney delivered a clear message of a strong military, a reinvigorated strategic defense initiative, and less government regulation. That message had been crafted throughout 1998 and 1999 by the same advisors from Stanford who had crafted Reagan's platform in 1980. But a new message that focused on compassionate conservatism—framed by Karl Rove, not the Stanford faculty—also went out. Rove's message brought together Reagan-Bush fiscal conservatives and Christian conservatives and allowed George W. Bush to use his own experience with religion as a political tool. As he prepared to run for the presidency, the call for compassionate conservatism became his campaign centerpiece.

The phrase was meant to generate support from the conservative base that supported George H. W. Bush and extolled his Thousand Points of Light campaign. George W. Bush, however, also built on the term to rally Christian conservatives who supported compassionate government programs, implying that government should partner with private—including private religious—organizations to provide social services with government subsidies.

By weaving together the Reagan philosophy of smaller government and fiscal responsibility with the faith-based philosophy of compassionate conservatism, Bush hoped to build a strong enough coalition to defeat Vice President Al Gore. Not only would the Republican base support him, but so might a coalition of Catholics and evangelicals who sought to use government resources to stop federal funding of abortions, stem cell research, and cloning. Compassionate conservatism became a catch-all phrase that signaled a pro-life position. It also signaled that Bush would support directing federal funds to religious groups for certain social programs.

As the general election grew closer, the influence of Bush's Stanford advisors waned. Bush's political advisors believed that he had captured the conservative vote with his Reaganesque positions, developed for him by the Stanford faculty, but they needed to ensure a strong voter turnout in an election that polls consistently called a fifty-fifty toss-up between Bush and Gore.

Karl Rove, the architect of the campaign strategy, began to move Bush away from the fiscal policies of the conservatives to a broader theme of morality and religion. As the campaign wore on through the nomination and the general election, Bush increased his references to morality, compassion, and God. He often wove religious phrases into his speeches, ending them with the phrase "God bless you," and he gave speech after speech with religious overtones. Rove also actively pushed evangelical pastors to encourage their flocks to get out the vote for George W. Bush. By November 2000, the difference between winning and losing in a close election was the degree to which evangelicals voted in swing states across the Mason-Dixon Line, in Ohio, and in Florida. God and morality had become the defining issues for this key block of voters.

But Cheney would not preach religion. In contrast to the zealous faith exhibited by George W. Bush, Dick Cheney wore his religion close to the vest. He rarely discussed his religion or brought the subject up in speeches or meetings. Few knew much about his religious views, except that he held certain moral principles tied to conservative religious views.

During the 2000 campaign, for example, Cheney accepted an invitation to talk to the Fellowship of Christian Athletes at the group's headquarters in Kansas City, Missouri. The organization supported the Bush-Cheney ticket and was delighted to have a visit from the vice-presidential candidate. The seventy people who attended the meeting expected more than a stump speech emphasizing the importance of education. This was, after all, the Fellowship of Christian Athletes.

They expected, but did not get, any mention of religion in Cheney's brief remarks.[55] He was there to explain to young athletes and their parents the importance of education, which the Bush-Cheney administration would prioritize. Although his presence at the meeting reinforced the Bush team's reputation for religiosity, Cheney would not extol religion in his speech.

As Bush built his army of support among Christian conservatives, Cheney was dispatched, instead, to assure the business community that a Bush administration would support supply-side economics and address overregulation. While Bush signaled to Christian conservatives that his administration would be pro-life, pro-prayer, pro-religion, and anti–same-sex marriage, Cheney was signaling to the business community that the burdensome regulations that government imposed on business would be addressed.

Cheney and George W. Bush shared Reaganesque goals of tax cuts and reining in costs of government. They were both fiscal conservatives. However, each had his own interests, direction, and agenda. George W. Bush wanted to use the resources of government to build a moral society, encourage government to use the resources of faith-based groups, and use the bully pulpit of the presidency to expound God's teachings on the sanctity of life. Cheney, by contrast, wanted to use the resources of his office to peel away obtrusive government regulations on business and industry; to protect individual rights for landowners and business owners; and, finally, to reverse the erosion of power of the presidency that had been under way, in his view, for more than two decades.

Cheney balanced the outgoing Bush with his introverted, quiet personality and political outlook. While they would work together on core conservative goals relating to tax cuts and defense spending, Bush would pursue his education and his faith-based agendas, while Cheney would pursue deregulation for business and industry and the expansion of executive power. Division of labor and shared power became the strength of the administration and the framework for the co-presidency. By sharing power, each would be free to pursue his own agenda.

CHAPTER 3

Transition Planning

Cheney Gains Control of the Administration

O N ELECTION NIGHT, November 7, 2000, George W. Bush watched from his suite at the luxurious Four Seasons Hotel in Austin, Texas, as the national networks posted the election results. The suite was filled only with family—including his wife, Laura, her mother, Jenna Welch, and their two daughters, Jenna and Barbara. His parents—the former president and first lady—were also there, but most of his campaign staff had gathered with Karl Rove to watch the returns. The mood in Bush's room was quiet and somber, since the returns seemed to be pointing toward a Gore victory.

Cheney, meanwhile, was in his own, separate suite at the Four Seasons with a much larger, more gregarious group. Cheney had seen Bush only briefly that day, after flying in earlier from Wyoming by private jet. He had spent Sunday campaigning in California with Colin Powell, then gone to Jackson, Wyoming, for a rally on Monday not far from their Teton Pines home six miles outside of town. The next morning, he and his wife, Lynne, voted at the nearby Wilson Firehouse, before flying to Austin to await the election results.

Unlike the family group gathered in George W. Bush's suite, Cheney's entourage included not just family and friends, but also many of the power brokers who would soon fill the new administration. Joining Lynne and their daughters, Mary and Liz, were former secretary of state James Baker, former commerce secretary Nicholas Brady, Cheney mentor Donald Rumsfeld, the former Wyoming senator Al Simpson, the future White House chief of staff Andy Card, campaign chairman Don Evans, and longtime Cheney staffers I. Lewis "Scooter" Libby and David Addington.[1] Bush and Cheney, operating in their separate but equal spheres, began a pattern that night that would be repeated frequently over the next eight years.

The networks were starting to predict results in the eastern states, where the polls closed three hours earlier than in western states. By 7:00 P.M., before the polls had closed in Florida's Panhandle (which is in the central time zone), the networks began to give Florida's popular vote to Gore. At 7:50 P.M., Dan Rather of CBS News announced that Florida would go to Gore. Two hours later, CBS and other news organizations reversed that call and put Florida back in the undecided column. The night was turning into a roller coaster, with highs and lows for each of the campaigns.

Not long after the polls closed in Florida, Bush called Karen Hughes, who was still in Rove's office, to join his family at the governor's mansion.[2] Without waiting for a final outcome, Bush had decided to return to the governor's mansion for the rest of the evening. Cheney and his crowd, however, remained at the Four Seasons. As the hour grew late that Tuesday night, Florida emerged as the pivotal state for Al Gore and George W. Bush. Then, not long after midnight, Fox News called the race—proclaiming that Bush, not Gore, had won the Sunshine State. The other major news outlets quickly followed Fox, and all declared the election over, with the vote count weighted in Bush's favor. With the election apparently over, Gore's campaign chairman, Bill Daley, called the Cheney suite to talk to Don Evans. Gore, Daley told Evans, would be calling Bush to concede. Those gathered in Cheney's suite quickly moved to the governor's mansion to join Bush in a victory celebration after Gore's phone call.

But the ecstasy of the moment soon evaporated. Later that night, Gore's advisors urged him to retract his concession, since questions had arisen about the accuracy of the vote count. Gore then phoned Bush a second time at the governor's mansion to indicate that he would be challenging the election results in Florida. Incredulous, Bush said to him, "You mean you are calling me to retract your concession? Well, you've got to do what you've got to do."[3] Although Florida's Republican secretary of state, Katherine Harris—who was chair of the Bush-Cheney campaign in Florida—had certified the election for Bush, Gore challenged the final tally and asked for a recount.

The result of the election was now uncertain and headed to state court for resolution. As Cheney said of the uncertainties of that evening:

"They got Florida. No, they didn't get Florida. And they call it for us. Then Gore calls and says, 'No I take it back. I'm not going to concede.' You know, it was one of those nights. How often does it happen?"[4] But it did happen, and the Bush-Cheney campaign was prepared.

The Bush campaign, led by Rove, had known for some time that Florida might be close and had prepared a legal team to deal with any potential election problems. Once Gore raised the possibility of a recount, Rove and campaign manager Joe Allbaugh sent lawyers to Florida to oversee the arduous process. Bush, however, also wanted a recount manager to oversee his lawyers. He called James Baker— who was driving back to Houston from his brief election-night stay in Austin—and asked him to go to Florida to supervise the legal team and serve as the voice of the Bush-Cheney campaign on the ground. Baker accepted without hesitation and headed to Florida to oversee what came to be known as the Recount Leadership Team. Private funds totaling $9 million for the newly formed Bush-Cheney Recount Fund were quickly raised following a hastily drawn-up fund-raising letter from campaign chair Don Evans.

Having set the legal process in motion in Florida, there was little Bush could do in Austin except work, by phone, with Baker, Cheney, and the recount team in order to counter the legal challenges emerging from the Gore camp. On Saturday morning, November 11—four long days after the election—Bush and his family left the governor's mansion for their ranch near rural Crawford, Texas, a town with a population of 631. Bush had purchased the sprawling 1,583-acre ranch in 1999 and built a 4,000-square-foot architect-designed home, which was completed during the presidential campaign.

Crawford was a somewhat random location—it had been chosen by Byron Cook, an Austin developer—and the location had little connection to Bush's family or friends. Bush had asked Cook in 1998 to find a large site for a home that he wanted to build for his retirement. Money was no problem, since Bush had built up a reserve of funds from selling his ownership stake in the Texas Rangers.[5] The Crawford ranch became a sanctuary of sorts for Bush during the tumultuous weeks after the election and in years to come. During his presidency, Bush would make the 1,295-mile trip from Washington, D.C., to Crawford nearly sixty times for working vacations.

He dealt with the Florida recount from his Crawford home, working from the living room, which he and Laura had designed. Bush's time was not entirely devoted to election matters. He also focused on the less taxing pursuits of jogging, reading a biography of Joe DiMaggio, and working on chores around the ranch—and even had enough time to clear a new bicycle path.[6] Cheney, however, remained at the Four Seasons for several days, using his suite as a command center. Ensuring that all information about the recount was routed through him, Cheney spoke with Bush every morning at 8:00, giving him an update on the recount and surrounding legal issues. Confident that Cheney, Baker, and Rove were handling the election problems, Bush soon returned to Austin to manage the daily business of the governor's office.

Cheney, meanwhile, was already turning his attention to the transition, staffing the administration, and crafting how his own vice president's office would operate. Still at work in his suite at the Four Seasons, he met with his key aides, Libby and Addington, determining what roles they would play on his vice-presidential staff. Both were longtime Cheney loyalists, having worked for him during his four years as secretary of defense. Addington had an even longer relationship with Cheney, going back to his days in the House of Representatives. As the Intelligence Committee's lawyer, Addington had worked hand in hand with Cheney on the Iran-Contra Minority Report. Several years later, when Cheney was testing the waters in 1994 for the Republican presidential nomination, he had turned to Addington to head his political action committee.

Addington had no particular job in mind, but Cheney asked him to take the position of the vice president's legal counsel. Libby, a protégé of Paul Wolfowitz's, asked for and received the dual role of vice president's chief of staff and national security advisor.[7] In addition to Libby and Addington, Paul Wolfowitz and Steven Hadley—Cheney's deputies in the Department of Defense—remained with Cheney in Austin to work on the transition. Their jobs, too, were soon determined—

Wolfowitz would become deputy secretary of defense, and Hadley would serve as Bush's deputy national security advisor.

The co-presidency of Bush and Cheney was well under way, for it was during this harried period that Cheney began to control the appointment process and decision structures for the administration. He began to build not only his own powerful staff but an entire administration as the transition's chief architect.

Days after the election, Libby, Addington, and Cheney flew from Austin to Washington, D.C., to secure a location for the informal transition headquarters. Cheney strategically decided to take the offensive and act as if the Bush-Cheney campaign had won the election—in spite of their inability to use a government-funded transition office. Neither Al Gore nor his vice-presidential running mate, Senator Joseph Lieberman, pursued a Washington, D.C.–based transition office. Gore stayed at his Nashville, Tennessee, campaign headquarters, overseeing the Florida recount. Eventually, Gore followed Cheney's example, asking his former chief of staff, Roy Neel, to begin a transition process. But the move proved to have little substance, and it bore no resemblance to Cheney's detailed transition planning.

By the end of November, Cheney's transition team was operating at full speed in 20,000 square feet of rented office space in McLean, Virginia, conveniently located only minutes away from Cheney's home. The legal maneuvering was still under way in Florida, and neither Bush nor Gore had captured the needed 270 electoral votes, but Cheney was operating as if the election had already been decided. Official Washington did not share his view that transition planning was necessary and blocked his access to government-funded office space.

Federal law barred the General Services Administration from providing transition funds to either campaign until the election was officially decided—forcing Cheney to rent private space rather than use government offices.[8] Federal law also barred both of the campaigns from using election money for transition costs. The Bush campaign thus had access neither to its own campaign funds nor to the $5.27 million in federal transition money until the election was decided.

Without hesitation, Cheney appealed to private donors to pay for the informal transition work. A nonprofit corporation—the Bush-Cheney Presidential Transition Foundation, Inc.—was established and incorporated under Texas law.[9] In a November 28 press release, Cheney said: "We will file as a Texas nonprofit corporation and seek 501(c)(4) status from the Internal Revenue Service. . . . We will accept individual contributions within the limits specified by the statute [Presidential Transition Act of 1963] of $5,000."[10] Within weeks, private donations provided over $6 million to support the transition process that Cheney had set up in McLean. When the election was finally resolved, the Bush-Cheney campaign successfully sought reimbursement from the General Services Administration for their "transition-related" expenses from November 7 through December 13—without jeopardizing the $6 million that it had raised privately.

With a transition office fully operational, Cheney moved quickly to hire the ranks of political appointees needed for the administration. Over six thousand political jobs needed to be filled—from cabinet officers and deputy and undersecretaries to press secretaries across fourteen cabinet-level offices and various offices within the executive branch, including the White House itself.

Reporting to Cheney, as the senior member of the transition team, was Clay Johnson.[11] Johnson had known Bush from their years together at Phillips Andover Academy and Yale University, where they had been roommates. Johnson had built a successful business career in Dallas as head of Neiman Marcus's Horchow direct-mail division before signing on as Bush's appointments secretary and then chief of staff in the governor's office. Soon after Bush formed his presidential campaign in 1999, he asked Johnson to explore what needed to be accomplished during a transition.

Johnson talked to Stanford University faculty who were involved in the Bush campaign and had worked in the Reagan and George H. W. Bush administrations. He also visited with former George H. W. Bush secretary of state James Baker and former Reagan attorney general Edwin Meese, as well as with Condoleezza Rice, who was overseeing the foreign policy advisory team in the campaign.[12] After these discussions, Johnson generally knew what needed to be done, although he never created a detailed transition plan. By election day, Johnson had been quietly working on the transition for over a year, but Bush never knew how much he had done and never probed to find out. He was remarkably uninterested in details, as he would be later in the Oval Office. According to Johnson, "Occasionally he'd come in and say, 'How are you doing on your project?' Kind of randomly he and I would chat."[13] In August, soon after the Republican convention, Cheney was given formal responsibility for the transition, with Johnson now reporting directly to him. But Cheney did little on the transition during the final weeks of the campaign, allowing Johnson to continue his planning. As it turned out, Johnson did relatively little of substance.

His bare-bones timeline and broad goals included selecting the senior White House staff and building a White House organizational structure by mid-December 2000; selecting cabinet secretaries by Christmas and having them ready for confirmation hearings by January 8; developing a twenty-day, hundred-day, and hundred-eighty-day schedule for the president after the inauguration; and having a budget ready by mid-February. The plan also addressed the need to examine all executive orders and regulations that could be reversed, if necessary, when the Bush administration took office.

For Cheney—a former White House chief of staff who had already taken over a White House, created a legislative agenda, overseen the budget, and, as a former secretary of defense, supervised the largest department in the federal government—Johnson's broad transition outline was not particularly helpful. Cheney knew he had to staff the new administration, have that staff ready to work at 12:01 P.M. on January 20, 2001—while the newly inaugurated president was still sitting in the reviewing stands on Pennsylvania Avenue—and have programs in place to run with that very afternoon. In McLean, Cheney took full control of the transition, assembling a small group to secure space, furniture, and computers. "Within a week, with the invaluable assistance of miracle workers who set up the office," Johnson recounted, "we were effectively pursuing our outreach, press, department policy and personnel goals."[14] The miracle workers that Johnson referred to were Cheney loyalists—this was a Cheney operation now, with Johnson reporting to Cheney and with Libby and Addington playing key roles. The transition was laying the foundation for a co-presidency.

The key to controlling government decision structures, Cheney knew, was to put people in place who could be trusted. Loyalty had always been a hallmark of the Bush family, and both father and son had placed friends in positions of trust and power. Now it was Cheney's task to fill administration jobs for George W. Bush, and he was determined to appoint only select loyalists to key positions. Bush loyalists would manage the White House, but it would be Cheney loyalists who would manage the larger government.

But his definition of loyalists did not extend to former Reagan staff. Cheney's antipathy toward Reagan staff was deeply held, stemming from the political wars during the 1976 election, when Reagan was chasing Gerald Ford for the Republican nomination. Ford barely won on the first ballot, garnering 1,187 delegate votes to Reagan's 1,070. Later that evening, after Ford had accepted the nomination, Reagan spoke to the convention. He spoke without notes in his brief six-minute speech to the delegates. As Martin Anderson describes the point at which Reagan took the stage, "The shouting and applause thundered as he [Reagan] placed both hands on the wooden stand and leaned slightly toward them."[15] Although Ford had won the nomination, Reagan had clearly become a serious force within the party.

The Ford-Reagan animosity from the 1976 campaign lingered for years. In the years that followed, Ford and his staff—including Cheney, who served not only as Ford's White House chief of staff but also de facto campaign manager—remained angry at Reagan for mounting the challenge against Ford, which they believed had contributed to Ford's subsequent loss to Jimmy Carter. According to Ford, "I thought [Reagan's] challenge had been divisive, and that it would probably hurt the party in the fall campaign; additionally, I resented some of the things that he said about me and about my Administration's policies."[16]

The Ford-Reagan relationship would surface again in Republican politics in 1980, after Reagan had finally captured the party's nomination. On the eve of the Republican convention that year, Reagan had not yet decided upon a running mate. Sitting in his suite on the sixty-ninth floor of Detroit's Renaissance Center Plaza Hotel, Reagan was surrounded by a small group of advisors, including Richard Wirthlin, Martin Anderson, Dick Allen, and William Casey.[17] They had spent the winter and summer of 1980 campaigning for the presidency and only now were dealing with the problem of choosing a vice president. Ford was the leading contender in their view.

Their own polling had shown that Ford would be the strongest addition to the ticket, adding two or three percentage points to their margin over Jimmy Carter. Although Reagan was leery of adding Ford, he was a pragmatist. Ford remained popular among both Republicans and Democrats in spite of losing to Carter in 1976.

After Reagan made the decision to offer Ford the vice presidency, he asked Alan Greenspan and Henry Kissinger, who were both attending the convention and were close to Ford, to "feel out the former president" about accepting the offer.[18] Ford and his advisors were sitting in another suite, one floor above Reagan's, in the Renaissance Center Plaza Hotel. As Greenspan relates the story,

Henry and I called and asked [Ford] if we could stop by. We met with him and talked briefly that night. The following afternoon we came back so Henry could present the set of talking points about the vice presidency written by Reagan's counselor Ed Meese and others in the Reagan camp. Because a former president had never served as vice president, [Ford's advisors] were envisioning an expanded role that would make the job attractive and appropriate for Ford. In their proposal, Ford would be the head of the president's executive office, with power over national security, the federal budget, and more. In effect, while Reagan would be America's chief executive officer, Ford would be its chief operating officer.[19]

These were policy areas in which Ford believed he had strong experience from both his House of Representatives and White House years, and in which, conversely, Reagan had little experience. A Reagan-Ford ticket would be a division of policy responsibility.

As the night wore on, there was widespread speculation on the convention floor and in the press that Reagan would offer Ford the vice presidency, and that Ford would accept. Nothing, however, had been confirmed by either Reagan or Ford spokesmen. Finally, word leaked out of an offer. Walter Cronkite, the anchor for CBS News, announced to a national television audience at 10:10 P.M., "Gerald Ford will be his selection as his vice-presidential running mate. . . . They are going to come to this convention hall tonight to appear together on the platform . . . to announce that Ford will run with him." Ford's supporters were buoyed by headlines in the *Chicago Tribune*, as well as in Cleveland, Ohio; Charlotte, North Carolina; and Shreveport, Louisiana, declaring: "It's Reagan and Ford." Wire stories from the Associated Press and United Press International confirmed that Reagan would include Ford on the ticket, leading to 11:00 P.M. newscasts across the country relating the developments at the Detroit convention.

But it was far from a done deal on Reagan's side. When Ford and his team responded with their vision for a co-presidency, Reagan reconsidered his offer. A little after 10:00 P.M., Ford went downstairs to Reagan's suite and he and Reagan went alone to the back of the room. After a five- or ten-minute discussion, the two men shook hands, and Ford left. Reagan had completely rejected the idea of Ford serving as co-president. A few minutes later, he called George H. W. Bush and made him the offer of the vice presidency, which Bush immediately accepted. Next to a Reagan-Ford ticket, internal polls showed a Reagan-Bush team had the best chance of winning in November. The Ford-Reagan relationship never recovered.

In 1988, when George H. W. Bush gained the presidency, he too shared some of Ford's resentment of Reagan and his staff. The Reagan-Bush relationship had been rocky at best, stemming from Bush's criticism of Reagan's economic plan, which he referred to as "voodoo economics" during the 1980 primary. During the 1988 transition, George W. Bush had chaired a group, which included Margaret Tutweiler, Chase Untermeyer, and Lee Atwater, that "scrubbed" applicants for political jobs to ensure that they were Bush, not Reagan, loyalists.[20] Now, twelve years later, another Bush was preparing to move into the Oval Office, and a similar political scrubbing was taking place by Cheney and his transition team. Those with a connection to Reagan were scrubbed off the list of potential Bush jobs, even though many had worked in the Bush-Cheney campaign.

As Cheney's transition team looked through piles of resumes to fill the thousands of administration jobs, those most likely to be awarded jobs came from the presidential campaign. But Cheney's transition team ignored one key constituency: Stanford University faculty tied to Reagan. During his campaign, George W. Bush had assiduously courted the intellectual talent at Stanford who had worked in the Reagan administration, particularly those in domestic and economic policy. But few would be offered jobs in the George W. Bush administration, and only Taylor would accept one, as Treasury undersecretary. (Edward Lazear would be named chairman of the Council of Economic Advisers in 2006, as Cheney's influence in appointments was waning.) As a result of their Reagan ties, Cheney never considered the Stanford faculty his allies, and he controlled the appointment process.

Throughout his long tenure in government, Cheney had seen how important it was to control appointments and watched how former presidents had used that power to craft their administrations. Richard Nixon, for whom he had worked in the early 1970s, had put Harry Flemming in charge of political appointments, and instead of continuing the long tradition of having cabinet officers make their own hires, Flemming had pulled the appointment process into the White House personnel office. Gerald Ford had continued Nixon's practice. Cheney, as his chief of staff, managed appointments for Ford and mastered the art of using the White House to dictate staffing to cabinet officers.

The Reagan administration took control of the appointment process to yet another level when it started screening candidates with long, detailed questionnaires. When Reagan moved into the Oval Office, he had Lyn Nofziger create a questionnaire that asked job seekers whether they were Republican and whether they had worked for the Reagan campaign. White House Personnel Director E. Pendleton James then used that questionnaire in making recommendations to fill jobs during the Reagan administration.[21] For the first time, candidates for political jobs had to have strong ties to the president, the president's party, and the campaign. Policy expertise ran a distant fourth to political credentials.

In spite of Cheney's dislike for Reagan, he followed the same practice when he set up the Bush White House, carefully vetting candidates for their political and ideological symmetry with the administration. Cheney knew the people, the issues, and the relationships that made government work, and his allies dominated administration positions. Although some Reagan national security staffers moved into the Bush administration, most—including Paul Wolfowitz, Richard Perle, and Douglas Feith—had also reported to Cheney in the Department of Defense. They had, in Cheney's view, become Cheney loyalists.

As the informal transition inched forward during November, Cheney's time became increasingly focused on developing a short list of names for the cabinet and initiating an open dialogue with Republican members of Congress. Although the election results remained in limbo, Cheney was running the transition as if Bush had won. He still had a relatively small staff at this point and relied heavily on his daughter, Liz, as well as on Libby and Addington. Two other senior staff, David Gribben and Juleanna Glover Weiss, moved from the campaign to the transition team. Both had been part of Cheney's staff, not part of the larger Bush campaign staff.

Gribben had been a friend of Cheney's since high school in Casper, Wyoming, and had served as his assistant in the House of Representatives, his director of legislative affairs in the Department of Defense, and his congressional liaison at Halliburton. Gribben was named congressional liaison for the transition. Weiss, formerly Cheney's campaign spokesperson, became transition spokesperson.

To this close-knit group, Cheney added a general counsel, Michael Toner—one of many members of Cheney's team who had more Beltway connections than the president's own staff. Toner was a former counsel at the Republican National Committee and an associate of Fred Fielding's in the law firm Wiley, Rein & Fielding. Fielding had been involved in Republican politics for years, serving first as a deputy to White House counsel John Dean during the early years of the Nixon administration, as counsel to President Ronald Reagan for three years, and as a confidant to Republican insiders. He was well known to Washington's power elite, on both sides of the aisle, who regularly dined at the Palm Restaurant on Nineteenth Street. Cheney's transition team and the White House would later hire Fielding to oversee the credential checks of cabinet nominees and shepherd them through the confirmation process.[22]

Toner and Cheney worked feverishly in the weeks after the election to find key people to staff the administration. At times, Cheney would be juggling calls on three cell phones from his McLean townhouse, where he did much of his work.[23] The strain proved too much. On November 22, 2000—after countless eighteen-hour days—Cheney experienced chest pains at home early in the morning.[24] His wife, Lynne, and his Secret Service agents rushed him to the emergency room at George Washington University Hospital, without alerting Bush or anyone else. Shortly after Cheney arrived, doctors discovered a 90-percent blockage in one of his coronary arteries. He had had a mild heart attack that morning and needed surgery to insert a wire-mesh stent inside the artery. After the procedure, Cheney remained in the hospital for two days, but he seemed to recover quickly and was well enough the next day to do a telephone interview on CNN's *Larry King Live.*

Cheney's health had been a major concern for many years. He had a history of heart problems, including three previous heart attacks and quadruple bypass surgery. He had suffered his first heart attack at age thirty-seven in 1978, when he was seeking Wyoming's single congressional seat, and he'd had subsequent heart attacks again in 1984 and 1988. After his last heart attack, he had been proactive in managing his health and promised to lose weight and exercise, which had been difficult for him during his years in Congress.

As the door to the vice presidency opened, Cheney had sought to quell lingering questions about his health. His personal physician, Dr. Gary Malakoff, released a letter in July 2000 stating that the fifty-nine-year-old was "up to the task of the most sensitive public office."[25] His doctors assured Bush that he was healthy enough to campaign and serve as vice president. Yet four months later, following his fourth heart attack, Cheney's health was at issue again. Bush chose to stay out of the discussions and let Cheney's staff deal with the press, which became common practice. Karen Hughes said nothing about Cheney's heart attack, even though she was the official spokesperson for the campaign.

The uncertainty about the election had clearly taken its toll on Cheney. While he was juggling the transition, he was deeply engaged in the recount strategy with Baker. It would take nearly another month before the legal maneuvering was over.

On November 16, six days before his hospitalization, the Florida Supreme Court had denied Florida Secretary of State Katherine Harris's request to halt the Florida recount. Bush's legal team had immediately taken the issue to the federal appeals court in Atlanta, arguing that the recount was unconstitutional. On November 18, the federal appeals court had ruled against Bush, and on November 21, in a third legal defeat for the Bush team, the Florida Supreme Court ruled that the recount should continue. By this time, Gore was confident that a recount would hand him the presidency. Bush, however, was equally confident of a legal victory.

As Baker and his lawyers pushed their case—arguing to the U.S. Supreme Court in early December that the Florida Supreme Court had overstepped its authority in approving the recount—Cheney told reporters that he and Bush "were ready to get on with the business of dealing with the nation's problems."[26] Americans waited for the court to render its decision. Few comments came from either campaign, until December 12, 2000, when the waiting ended. The U.S. Supreme Court ruled in a five-to-four decision for the Bush campaign, denying Al Gore a recount. For all practical purposes, the election was over; George W. Bush was the president-elect. Gore conceded the race the following day.

Cheney could now begin the formal transition process, having run an informal one for over a month. Government funding for the transition could begin, and on December 14, 2000, General Services Administrator David Barram authorized the use of federal transition monies, including office space at 1800 G Street, NW. The Cheney team could leave its cramped McLean offices on Anderson Road for 90,000 square feet of office space in downtown Washington, D.C., which had been leased at a cost of $700,000 for the two-and-a-half-month transition. In a formal ceremony at the transition's new headquarters, the General Services Administration staff finally handed Cheney an electronic smart-card to the new offices. Some transition staff, however, remained in the McLean office, where volumes of material had already been assembled and from where they could more easily be dealt with.

Cheney's job over the next five weeks was to fill more than 6,400 jobs in the new administration, including 1,125 that would require Senate confirmation. As the transition formally began, it was also time for Bush to begin to hand over the governor's office to Rick Perry, his lieutenant governor. Texas elected its governor and lieutenant governors on different slates. Luckily for Bush, Perry was a Republican, so the gubernatorial transition was fairly easy. The president-elect soon began work in Austin with a speechwriter, Michael Gerson, on his January 20th inaugural address, mapping out the legislative agenda for his first one hundred days in office.

Cheney's relationship with Bush had been cordial throughout the election, the recount, and the transition, but they had not built a strong personal bond. They shared certain conservative goals for governance but had little else in common except their western roots and conservative values. While these bonds were adequate for forging a political relationship, they were not adequate for forming a personal bond. Not surprisingly, Cheney was hard-pressed in one interview only days before the inauguration to expand on Bush's strengths as the future president. When the *New York Times* reporter James Bennet asked him what quality had made Bush the president, Cheney didn't name Bush's strong knowledge of domestic policy issues, his strong understanding of international affairs, or the talented people around him. Instead, Cheney paused and said, "He's the guy who went out and put his name on the ballot."[27] Cheney's answer exposed his deepest feelings about Bush—and pointed to the policy vacuum that the vice president-elect would soon fill in the White House.

While Bush remained in Austin, Cheney was making the rounds on Capitol Hill. On Wednesday afternoon, December 13—the day Al Gore conceded—Cheney left his McLean headquarters to travel to the Senate to discuss Bush's legislative agenda.[28] He spent most of the day with five moderate senators—including Lincoln Chafee of Rhode Island, Olympia Snowe and Susan Collins of Maine, Arlen Specter of Pennsylvania, and James Jeffords of Vermont. Because the Senate would be evenly divided, with fifty Democrats and fifty Republicans, Cheney emphasized to the assembled group the importance of maintaining party-line votes. Since the vice president could break ties in the Senate, his vote would ensure a Republican victory as long as Republicans did not break rank.

Cheney later met with the head of the Senate Republican Policy Committee, Larry Craig of Idaho. He then turned his attentions to the House of Representatives, meeting with the head of the House Republican Policy Committee, Christopher Cox of California. Before leaving Capitol Hill, Cheney also met with Senator Charles Grassley of Iowa, who was to become chair of the Senate Finance Committee in January, and with Speaker of the House Dennis Hastert of Illinois.

That same day, George W. Bush made his first address to the nation as the president-elect from Austin, but it was Cheney who drew the most press attention. The networks had his picture on the evening news—smiling and relaxed, making the rounds on Capitol Hill, leaving the intended image of a vice president who was an equal partner with the president in the new administration. George W. Bush could have handled these meetings when he arrived in Washington, D.C., days later—there was no need for the vice president to do so. But Cheney wanted to signal to members of Congress that he would be a central player in the administration—a co-president.

The notion of a co-presidency had first crossed Cheney's mind twenty years earlier when Ford aides had raised the possibility of a Ford-Reagan co-presidency on the eve of the Republican Convention 1980. The scenario was much the same in 2000 as it had been in 1980, with an untested governor who had never held national office at the top of the ticket. As discussions moved forward on his own vice presidency,

Cheney recalled those conversations in Detroit exactly twenty years earlier. He also remembered Reagan's unconditional dismissal of the idea of a co-presidency, even though Ford brought unparalleled experience to the ticket.

Although Cheney thought the idea of a co-presidency could work in the George W. Bush administration, he realized that any private or public conversation about it would doom the plan—as it had for Ford. Instead, Cheney began executing a well-thought-out strategy to build his vice presidency into a policy-making apparatus, using the transition to build an administration stacked with his own loyalists and others who shared his pro-business agenda. He would later ensure that key legal offices were filled by lawyers who supported his expansive view of presidential powers.

Bush was comfortable with Cheney's appointments as long as all of the Texas contingent, and his own loyalists, were guaranteed key positions in the administration. Bush relied on Andy Card, his newly appointed White House chief of staff, for this aspect of the transition. Card, a former secretary of transportation and White House deputy chief of staff, filled the White House with Bush loyalists, mostly from the campaign. Karl Rove would oversee the newly created Office of Strategic Initiatives. Karen Hughes, who had managed the campaign's communications office, would handle the same job in the White House. Ari Fleischer, the campaign press secretary, would become White House press secretary. Dr. John DiIulio of the University of Pennsylvania, an expert on faith-based programs, who had been advising Bush on the subject for over a year, was given the newly created title of director of faith-based and community initiatives. Condoleezza Rice would become staff director of the National Security Council, a position that also made her the president's national security advisor. Other senior campaign staff, such as Michael Gerson, Joshua Bolten, Joe Hagin, Margaret LaMontagne (later Spellings), and John Bridgeland, also moved into the White House in senior staff positions.

Card chose only a handful of White House staff from outside the campaign. Reaching into his own political networks, he hired Jack

Howard and Nicholas Calio, a lawyer with a degree from Case Western Law School, to run the legislative affairs division. Calio and Howard had deep experience dealing with Congress. Both had worked in legislative affairs for George H. W. Bush, and Card knew and trusted them. After leaving the first Bush administration, Calio had formed a lobbying firm, O'Brien and Calio, which was considered a powerhouse in political circles. Howard had been the senior staff person for both Newt Gingrich and Trent Lott in the House and had then followed Lott into the Senate, where he was currently working. Both were viewed as consummate professionals, masters at moving legislation through both friendly and unfriendly territory.

While Card was building a White House staff, Cheney handled the larger job of staffing the agencies. Working with Clay Johnson, who would become White House personnel director, Cheney divided the work of staffing the fourteen cabinet departments between them.[29] Johnson took responsibility for most of the subcabinet political positions, while Cheney focused on recruiting the cabinet and key subcabinet political positions. Their task was simplified by the work that Cheney had done during the campaign vetting vice-presidential candidates. He had already developed a detailed list of questions on candidates' financial and personal backgrounds that could easily be reused for cabinet positions.

Although Cheney controlled the appointment process, others from the campaign also had roles in the transition. Joshua Bolten, the campaign's domestic policy director, took responsibility for creating the policy transition teams that would guide incoming cabinet officers. Bolten brought in Dr. John Cogan, an economist from Stanford University and the architect of Bush's proposal for individual Social Security accounts, to work on specific economic issues, along with John Bridgeland and Gary Edson from the campaign, to manage broader economic and domestic policy.[30] Bridgeland and Edson assembled small task forces of three or four policy experts to oversee each department's transition. The task forces—formally known as policy coordinating groups—interfaced with Clinton cabinet officers and staff, reviewed existing budgets and legislative mandates, met the political staff, and determined how Bush campaign goals would be interwoven into departmental priorities. These official transition teams—more formally known as the policy coordinating groups—involved a staff of eighty-five.

Cheney was unwilling, however, to relinquish his influence over the departments to the Bolten task forces. At about the same time that Bolten announced the creation of his policy coordinating groups, Cheney established what he called advisory teams for each of the twelve domestic departments. Two departments, State and Defense, did not have transition advisory teams, since lobbyists would ostensibly have no influence in or input into their decision making. Most of the individuals Cheney named to the advisory teams were lobbyists or corporate executives who had a vested interest in the actions of the departments for which they were recommending personnel and policies.

Cheney's advisory teams consisted of 474 individuals, who in total had given $5.6 million in contributions to the Bush-Cheney campaign in the 2000 election. In essence, the membership on an advisory team was a reward for a large campaign contribution. His energy advisory team had the largest number of participants, and they had given the most in contributions of any of the advisory teams—$800,000. It included future members of the Energy Task Force created by the vice president's office, among them Enron's chief executive, Kenneth Lay.

Cheney's advisory teams were encouraged to believe that they had a voice in the halls of the Bush-Cheney administration. The teams, with anywhere from ten to thirty members, were charged with providing advice and policy suggestions to incoming cabinet officers. But their advice proved to be one-sided, representing only the views of the businesses and industries that were being regulated. The Health and Human Services advisory team, for example, was dominated by the pharmaceutical and health insurance industries, including representatives from Eli Lilly, Merck, Pharmaceutical Research and Manufacturers of America (PhRMA), the American Hospital Association, the Federation of American Hospitals, and the Blue Cross and Blue Shield Association. The Labor Department advisory team included executives from the Chamber of Commerce and Union Pacific Corporation, but not a single representative from a union or labor organization. The Interior Department advisory team was dominated by coal and oil company executives, who were seeking opportunities for drilling on federal land. Some members of the advisory teams ended up with jobs in the administration, such as Eli Lilly's Randall Tobias, who was later named global AIDS coordinator.

One large lobbying group—the National Association for Convenience and Petroleum Retailing—placed an extensive discussion on its web site touting the fact that its staff were on advisory teams for the Departments of Energy, Labor, and Interior, as well as for the Environmental Protection Agency. The group noted in a memo to its membership that its representatives would "provide knowledge and perspective from our industry in shaping the new administration's vision for the country."[31] In other words, they looked forward to recommending new policies that would benefit the petroleum industry.

There were no formal meetings of the advisory teams, since their only function was to present ideas on what the administration could do for their particular business and their industry in general. Letters from advisory team members were duly assembled by Cheney's staff and given to incoming cabinet officers—not as part of the formal transition material prepared by Bolten's policy-related transition teams, but as separate material for their consideration. Bolten knew exactly what he was doing, in fact, when he called his transition task forces "policy coordinating groups"—separating the substance of Bridgeland and Edson's work from the fluff of Dick Cheney's advisory teams.

By creating these teams, Cheney intended to signal to corporate contributors that their views were welcome in the administration's decision making. The *Washington Post* quoted a description of them as "a way for the Bush team to do a favor for people, to show who their friends are. You want your clients to read about all the access you have."[32] The intensity of the energy advisory team sent another signal. Cheney was making clear to his business constituency that this was going to be a business-oriented administration, with an energy focus.

Cheney kept the Department of Defense out of Bolten's area of control. Cheney placed Zalmay Khalilzad, his deputy undersecretary for policy planning in the Department of Defense under George H. W. Bush, in charge of the transition team for the department. After leaving office in 1993, Khalilzad, born and raised in Afghanistan, had followed Cheney's path into the oil industry—working for UNOCAL, a large international energy conglomerate that eventually merged with Chevron, on developing oil pipelines in the Middle East. Cheney's choice of an expert on Middle East oil fields and pipelines was hardly a coincidence, given his particular focus on energy issues.

While Cheney's advisory teams and Bolten's policy coordinating groups were doing their work, Cheney was also narrowing the list of names for cabinet positions. Some were obvious choices. During the campaign, Colin Powell had indicated his interest in serving as secretary of state. Donald Evans, the campaign chair, was a logical choice for Commerce. At the top of the list for the Treasury Department was Alcoa chairman Paul O'Neill, Cheney's colleague from the Ford administration, who had been a senior staffer at OMB and worked closely with Cheney.

The rest of the cabinet had solid business credentials, Cheney's core requirement. For secretary of energy, Cheney recommended Spencer Abraham, the defeated senator from Michigan, whose automobile industry relied heavily on cheap oil. Abraham had been extremely supportive of the oil industry's quest for drilling off the continental shelf and in designated wilderness areas, particularly Alaska. He was also a member of the Federalist Society, which would become a key credential for many of Cheney's recommended appointments to the cabinet and federal judiciary.

To head the Interior Department, Cheney recommended Gale Norton, who had worked for a lobbying organization to reduce controls over federal park land. For the Labor Department, he recommended Linda Chavez, who was immediately opposed by labor unions because of her anti-union positions. Chavez eventually pulled out of the confirmation hearings and was replaced by Elaine Chao. She had few credentials in labor issues but was married to the politically important Kentucky senator Mitch McConnell and brought ethnic and gender diversity to the cabinet.

There was even a token Democrat as the nominee for Transportation, Norman Mineta—the Japanese American former congressman who had been tapped by Bill Clinton to run the Commerce Department. Mineta added broader ethnic diversity to the cabinet and a much-needed sense of bipartisanship after the bruising election. Bush had promised, after the contested election, to build a spirit of cooperation and change the partisan tone of Washington, D.C. Presumably, the appointment of Mineta was a first step in improving relations with congressional Democrats.

The selection of Cheney's old friend and mentor Donald Rumsfeld as secretary of defense demonstrated Cheney's nearly complete control over cabinet appointments. Colin Powell's choice for the Defense post was Pennsylvania governor Tom Ridge, a close friend of George W. Bush's from their days together as Republican governors. Cheney, however, easily convinced Bush that Ridge had too little experience in foreign or military affairs and, more important, that his pro-choice positions would alienate the administration's conservative base. Bush would still need the political power of their base to pressure Congress over the next four years and to vote in the midterm elections of 2002, as well as the presidential election of 2004. The rejection of Ridge was an early win for Dick Cheney—one of many—over Colin Powell.

One of the few cabinet posts over which Cheney had little influence was that of attorney general. For George W. Bush and his legions of Christian conservative followers, the Department of Justice had to be a stalwart ally. Bush favored Montana governor Marc Racicot, a fellow governor and a fellow runner, who had been a strong supporter in the presidential election—and at one point was even considered as a vice presidential running mate. Cheney dispatched a private jet from Sinclair Oil to bring Racicot to Austin to discuss the offer. Racicot declined to serve as attorney general, however, arguing that he had a minimal record on issues of importance to religious conservatives.[33] Bush then moved to his second choice—another former fellow governor, Missouri senator John Ashcroft. Karl Rove had worked for Ashcroft for decades as his political consultant and strongly promoted him for the Justice job.

Ashcroft, moreover, had the support of the elder Bush, who in 1991 had considered naming him attorney general to pull Christian conservatives into the reelection campaign. Tapping John Ashcroft as attorney general would also serve as political payback. In late 1998, Ashcroft had launched his own brief campaign for the White House, winning the support of Pat Robertson's Christian Coalition and other conservative religious groups. But Ashcroft withdrew in January 1999, before entering a single primary, and he later endorsed George W. Bush for president.

Moving Ashcroft into the Justice Department signaled the Bush administration's commitment to the pro-family, pro-life agenda long supported by Christian conservatives. Ashcroft, a Pentecostal, wore his religion on his sleeve, and Bible sessions and prayer groups were common in his Senate office. Ashcroft's father and grandfather were both ministers in the Assembly of God Church, where dancing and drinking were strictly forbidden. He even brought his own Bible to swear in his staff.[34]

But Ashcroft was not a Cheney loyalist. As one of the few cabinet members not indebted to Cheney for his job, he remained independent of the vice president. Several years later—in the aftermath of the September 11, 2001, terrorist attacks, when the vice president was overseeing policy decisions on the war on terror—Ashcroft would resist Cheney's proposals. And after the Abu Ghraib prison scandal erupted, battles over interrogation law raged between the vice president, Addington, and Ashcroft.[35] Both Ashcroft and Powell—the two cabinet appointments that Cheney did not control during the transition—proved to be thorns in the vice president's side when he pushed controversial policies, including wireless surveillance, the invasion of Iraq, and rejecting the Geneva Conventions' ban on torture. When Ashcroft left after Bush's first term, Cheney made sure he had an ally at the helm of the Department of Justice. He backed the nomination of Bush's White House legal counsel, Alberto Gonzales, who would continue to support Cheney's anti-terrorism policies, as he had in the White House.

Cheney's role in the transition focused on building the cabinet and subcabinet, but he left building the White House staff to others. As the White House staff emerged, largely built from the campaign staff tied directly to Bush, their policy focus appeared to be quite different from the pro-business orientation of Cheney and his team. The White House staff appeared to have two working groups: the political pragmatists, devoted to protecting Bush's political capital, and the social moderates, devoted to education reform, volunteerism, and faith-based initiatives. Rove and Hughes led the political pragmatists; Bolten, Bridgeland, and Edson led the social moderates. Throughout the transition, their work managing the policy coordinating groups was widely viewed as professional, even-handed, and thoughtful.

Bolten, Bridgeland, and Edson—and later John DiIulio—were the moderates in the White House who sought to build policy responses to campaign issues. They did not try to use the power of the presidency to build a new governing coalition, as Karl Rove did, or to tilt policy making toward business, as Dick Cheney did, or to create a moral and civil society, as George W. Bush did. Instead, they saw government as a bridge to use in building stronger communities, a repeating theme of compassionate conservatism.

This small group of policy experts sought to use the resources of the federal government to increase volunteerism and create new partnerships between communities and citizens. Each member of the group had been drawn to the campaign's theme of compassionate conservatism—implying, to them, a new role for government as the twenty-first century emerged—rather than the Reagan philosophy and tradition of limited government.

They were young moderates, with few ties to old governing coalitions. Bolten, a former Goldman Sachs executive and Princeton graduate, with a law degree from Stanford, became a neutral broker in the chief of staff's office. Bridgeland, a Harvard graduate, with a law degree from the University of Virginia, had served as chief of staff for the moderate Cincinnati congressman Rob Portman. While in Portman's office, he had authored the Citizen Service Act, which later framed the USA Freedom Corps, a program Bridgeland eventually directed. Gary Edson, another Stanford graduate, would lead the effort to create the Millennium Challenge Account for developing nations. John DiIulio, a Democrat and Harvard Ph.D. in political science, also drawn to the call of compassionate conservatism, oversaw the creation of the White House Office of Faith-Based and Community Initiatives. They formed the core of centrist policy making in the senior levels of the White House.

By the first weeks and months of the administration, there were three clear policy groups: Bush and the Christian conservatives, Cheney and the business interests, and the White House moderates. The Cheney organization in the vice president's office focused on regulatory issues, national security, and energy policy, while the Bush organization in the president's office focused on education policy and a broad definition of compassionate conservatism; in most cases, those two spheres never overlapped. In the middle were the Bridgeland-Edson-DiIulio policy units in the White House, which attempted to build a domestic policy agenda that didn't intrude on either the Cheney or Bush organizations.

The dominant agenda, however, was the vice president's. Cheney had used the transition to create an administration populated with business-oriented political appointees whose primary mission was to carry out policies benefiting their own business interests. With the exception of the education agenda, few domestic initiatives would move forward; Peter Baker of the *Washington Post* described the White House domestic agenda as "shipwrecked."[36] The ship sank, to put it more accurately, before it sailed.

Cheney would continue to gain the advantage in managing the administration's policy agenda throughout the administration, building his co-presidency and personally overseeing the business of government.[37]

CHAPTER 4

Full Transparencies

Merging the Vice President's Staff into the White House Staff

O N DECEMBER 13, 2000, George W. Bush appeared on national
television to accept Al Gore's concession and outline his agenda
as president-elect. After thanking his wife, Laura, and their daughters,
Barbara and Jenna, for their love, Bush thanked his vice president–
elect, stressing how important it was to have Dick Cheney by his side.
From that day forward, George W. Bush and Dick Cheney oversaw an
administration that virtually had dual controls. Bush and Cheney were
jointly running the government, making decisions and setting goals.

Cheney's emergence as co-president was hardly scripted or antici-
pated by the campaign staff or by George W. Bush when he brought
Cheney onto the presidential ticket in July. Bush and Cheney, unlike
Reagan and Ford twenty years earlier, never discussed sharing power
in a co-presidency. Cheney's unprecedented role in the administration
resulted, instead, from a confluence of factors that restructured the
traditional relationship between president and vice president.

It began with Bush's early decision to broaden the vice president's
responsibilities. Not wanting Cheney to suffer the indignities of the
vice presidency that his father, George H. W. Bush, had under Ronald
Reagan, Bush promised Cheney that he would have a substantive role
in his administration. Reagan had always been uncomfortable with
his vice president and former rival, George H. W. Bush, who had referred to his economic plan as "voodoo economics" during the 1980
primary. As a result of their primary battles, Reagan had given him
little involvement in policy making. Bush, of course, had not even been
Reagan's first choice for vice president. He was the second choice after
Gerald Ford declined Reagan's offer for the job.

The proposal for an expanded role for the vice president for Cheney
beyond that of president-in-waiting appears to have been more a generous
act on the part of a son who had seen his father badly treated than a

well-thought-out plan for a co-presidency. Little had been said during the campaign about specific responsibilities that Cheney might handle in the administration, other than the task of overseeing the transition process, and there is no record of discussions about the policy areas he would handle in office.

It appears that Cheney designed his own role—which Bush accepted, with few, if any, conversations with Andy Card, Karl Rove, Karen Hughes, or other advisors. According to Cheney, Bush said in a one-on-one conversation that "I'd have the opportunity to be a major participant in the process, to get involved in whatever issues I wanted to get involved in."[1] The co-presidency that emerged was cleverly pieced together by Cheney, building on Bush's determination that his vice president was to have more of a role within his administration than his father had had under Reagan.

Throughout the campaign, Cheney had largely been the silent partner, accepting the direction of the Austin political team. He had been a foreign policy advisor in the early months of the campaign, but played a relatively minor role. His role didn't take on significant proportions until April 2000, when he was asked to manage the vice-presidential search. It was at that point that Bush became increasingly comfortable with Cheney. As he began to consider Cheney himself for the vice presidency, Bush saw Cheney as a loyal soldier, without a personal agenda, and took him at his word that he had no political ambitions of his own. Cheney, it seemed to Bush, was neither building a power base nor making decisions to enhance his own political career during the campaign—points that Cheney repeatedly emphasized.

Cheney's verbal confirmation that his only role would be to serve Bush, not build his own base for a future presidential run, was critical for Bush. There was some speculation around Washington, D.C., that Cheney was building his staff to stay involved in a wide range of policy issues as he prepared to run for the presidency in 2008. The more issues that he was involved with, the higher his visibility. But Bush quashed this rumor. Soon after taking office, Bush told a meeting of congressional leaders being held at the White House that Cheney was not building a large specialized staff for political reasons. He said, "Dick's doing a good job because he's told me he doesn't want to be president."[2] As long as Cheney was not a potential presidential candidate with ambitions that could jeopardize the Bush agenda, Bush was comfortable with any internal staffing decisions that Cheney wanted to make.

The staffing decisions and organizational relationships in the White House ultimately paved the path to power for Cheney and enabled the co-presidency to flourish. Cheney created a new White House staff structure, with the full approval of Bush, in which staff from the vice president's office were regularly included in meetings and decisions on policy issues made by the White House staff. Libby was, in his own words, "invited to any meeting that Andy Card [White House chief of staff] goes to and he's invited to any meeting I go to." He went to the daily briefing of White House senior staff convened by Card and to any other meetings he chose to attend. Libby explained that having the staffs intertwined added depth to the decision-making process. "Two heads are better than one," he said, "and we've got two very good heads." Libby added that Bush "could throw the vice president [and his staff] into problems that they'd otherwise not think about."[3]

Within weeks after taking office, the two staffs were regularly working together and in constant communication. Routing slips within the White House never failed to include the vice president's staff. E-mails were copied to the vice president's staff. And even some internal e-mails, such as within the National Security Council, flowed to Cheney's office. This carefully constructed full transparency allowed Cheney to influence almost every policy discussion and decision made in the White House. And no one in the White House objected to the integration of the president's staff and the vice president's staff. Many in Bush's inner circle even welcomed Cheney's increased involvement in policy making. "Having a strong vice president is important," Hughes said, "for having a strong administration."[4]

Cheney's unprecedented influence in policy decisions was, at the same time, fueled by internal divisions within the White House. Melding the Texas loyalists on the White House staff—many of whom were driven by their evangelical zeal—with policy moderates from the presidential campaign proved a difficult task. The inexperience of White House staffers in managing the federal government further added to the influence of Cheney and his savvy team, drawn largely from Beltway think tanks and congressional offices.

In addition, Bush's very short list of legislative proposals left a window of opportunity for Cheney's agenda, centered on deregulation and pro-business policies. Bush was committed to education reform, tax cuts, and faith-based programs—issues he understood from his two terms as governor of Texas, and on which he had predicated his campaign. Further down the list were privately funded Social Security accounts, immigration reform, and, to a limited extent, emerging issues in the Middle East and Russia.[5] International affairs, however, were generally outside Bush's comfort zone. His work in the oil business and as part-owner of a professional baseball team had given him little exposure to diplomatic and military decisions, and his mastery of foreign policy details during the campaign was so minimal that he didn't even know the names of key world leaders. Bush's lack of interest and experience in international affairs left a gaping hole in his policy expertise, which Cheney and his staff would fill over the next eight years.

Bush's main priorities were faith-based issues and constructing what he called a moral and civil society. Once in office, he set in motion a broad array of programs enabling faith-based groups to receive federal funding. He also encouraged conversations on intelligent design and prayer in public school, rejected gay marriage as incompatible with moral teaching, and used the authority of the presidency to require that public schools teach abstinence before marriage or risk losing much of their funding. The narrow vision that Bush brought to his presidency allowed Cheney wide latitude to implement his own policy agenda.

Bush's view of a moral and civil society extended to the near reverence with which he viewed the Oval Office. Anyone working for Bush had to be appropriately dressed in the White House at all times. Suits were expected of men, and women had to be similarly well dressed.

Even White House visitors had to abide by a strict dress code. A sign posted outside the White House informed them that

Those not appropriately dressed and wearing the following will not be allowed to tour the West Wing:

- Jeans
- Sneakers
- Shorts
- Miniskirts
- T-Shirts
- Tank Tops
- Flip-Flops

This decorum was mirrored by a rigidity in the daily operation of the West Wing. There was little flexibility in the way George W. Bush ran his office. Meetings started and ended precisely on time, regardless of the possibility of further discussion. Andy Card, the White House chief of staff, would halt senior staff meetings at exactly 7:58 A.M.— often stopping staff in mid-sentence—so that he could arrive in the Oval Office at 8:00 A.M. for the intelligence briefing. There were no late-night pizza deliveries, as there had been in the Clinton White House, and staff were encouraged to work limited hours so that they could be home with their families.

Bush knew little about the power of the presidency, or how to control the executive branch and implement an agenda without legislation to support it. Cheney did, however, and his goals were expansive. He knew the power and reach of the federal government and how to use it. Cheney knew that the White House staff controlled the appointment to all six thousand political jobs in the administration, the agenda that would be handed to each of the fourteen cabinet officers, and the budget that each cabinet officer would work with. He knew what regulations could be written and who would write them. He knew the power of executive orders and proclamations that mandated certain actions without the encumbrance of legislation. Finally, he knew the power of the signing statement, which—when appended to a bill signed by the president—would declare any part unenforceable if its constitutionality were in question. Cheney planned to use all of these tools to advance his own agenda.

But Cheney was not president, and, as a result, he needed to become part of the White House decision-making structure for economic, domestic, and foreign policy. Cheney accomplished this by melding his organization, as much as possible, with the White House staff. Cheney, with his own large and well-appointed suite of offices in the Old Executive Office Building, ensured his proximity to Bush by taking a second office in the West Wing. He took one of the largest offices in the West Wing, flanked by those of the chief of staff, Andrew Card, and National Security Advisor Condoleezza Rice. In addition, Cheney had a ceremonial office in the Senate and another, smaller office in the House of Representatives, provided by Republican Speaker of the House Dennis Hastert. In January 2007, however, Democrat Nancy Pelosi, the new Speaker, decided that Cheney did not require an office in the House, since his constitutional role, she noted, was to deal with the Senate and cast tie-breaking votes in that chamber.

Casting tie-breaking votes proved critical during Bush's first six months in office, when each party controlled fifty votes. The vice president was called to the Senate to break the tie and give the Republicans a marginal victory whenever there was a vote along strict party lines. This happened rarely, however, and only during the early months of the administration. Once Republican Senator James Jeffords of Vermont became an Independent in August 2001, the Democrats gained control of the Senate, and Cheney's tie-breaking role was less important.

Although the vice president continued to play a significant role by lobbying House and Senate members for their support, he spent most of his time in his offices in the White House and Old Executive Office Building dealing with policy issues and reviewing recommendations made by his staff. Cheney had started building his own staff immediately after the election when he asked Libby and Addington to work in the vice president's office. In meetings at the Four Seasons Hotel in Austin two days after the election, Libby and Addington were assigned jobs, both as senior staff.[6] The vice president's staff was quickly expanded to include domestic and economic policy, national security, press, and legal experts, and he and his staff provided input to the White House on almost every issue. No decision escaped Cheney, whose staffers thoroughly briefed him on every matter, leaving nothing to chance.

Cheney's staff and the president's staff became so interwoven that when job openings occurred in the White House, Cheney's aides filled them. For example, Cheney's legislative liaison, Candida Wolff, became White House legislative director, and Ron Christie, Cheney's deputy domestic policy advisor, became deputy director of White House domestic policy. After essentially merging his staff and the president's, Cheney, who controlled the budget process, formally created a single executive office in the federal budget by deleting the Office of the Vice President as a separate appropriation and consolidating it into the larger appropriation for the Executive Office of the President.[7]

In any organization, titles matter, and to integrate his aides into the White House staff in the single executive office, Cheney gave them titles similar to those held by White House staffers, reflecting their equal roles. The staffing ladder in the White House had been well established for several decades. At the top are those—an elite group of about twenty (although the number varies slightly from year to year)—bearing the most prized of all White House titles, assistant to the president. They are among the few who know the president's daily schedule, the issues the president is grappling with, and, most important, the information on which the president makes decisions. The title designates senior status, direct access to the president, and participation in daily morning briefings by the chief of staff.

Historically, those with the title assistant to the president include the president's chief of staff, national security advisor, domestic policy advisor, economic policy advisor, press secretary, personnel director, and a few select others. Two members of Cheney's staff received this coveted title—Mary Matalin, counselor to the vice president and assistant to the president, and Scooter Libby, chief of staff to the vice president and assistant to the president. Although Matalin and Libby remained part of the vice president's staff, their additional title of assistant to the president ensured that they were included in Andy Card's

7:30 A.M. senior staff meeting every morning, as well as in all senior White House staff discussions.

Matalin and Libby received the same information as the president's closest advisors; nothing was kept from them. This extraordinary access allowed Cheney's staff to be fully informed of all decisions about to reach the president's desk and the options presented to him. If they wanted to influence those options, they had every opportunity to do so. But their access to information was even more important, because it ensured that Cheney's agenda never interfered with or jeopardized the Bush agenda. When a reporter asked Matalin why Cheney was building his own policy staff, she replied that his only goal was to serve the interests of the president. "The vice president has no personal or political agenda," she declared, "other than advising President Bush."[8] Perhaps Matalin believed this.

Below the elite group of assistants to the president is a slightly larger group with the title deputy assistant to the president. Many of these staffers manage large units within the White House and have considerable power in their own right, but they do not have direct access to the president or participate in senior staff meetings. Several members of Cheney's staff, including his speechwriter, John McConnell, and his counselor, Steve Schmidt, were given the title, further reinforcing the integration of the two staffs within one executive office. McConnell was so fully integrated into the White House staff that Bush's chief speechwriter, Michael Gerson, considered McConnell a member of his staff.

The lowest and largest of the three rungs on the White House ladder were staff with the title special assistant to the president. Staff members in all three groups were commissioned officers; each received a personally signed commission from the president of the United States, bearing the great seal of the United States, affixed by the secretary of state. As commissioned officers, these three ranks were entitled to certain White House privileges, including meals in the Navy-run White House mess. Although none of the vice president's staff were commissioned officers—unless they had the additional title of assistant to the president or deputy assistant to the president—exclusion from the

White House mess was a very superficial distinction. For all practical purposes, the staffs were equal.

By the end of the administration's first full month, Cheney had expanded his staff to eighty-five, or more, since detailees from the departments weren't always counted. This number undoubtedly rose over the course of the next eight years, but Cheney stopped releasing the staffing information. For nearly every senior White House staff position, he created a similar post in the vice president's office. His aides had titles that exactly matched most of the titles of White House staffers—such as chief of staff, staff secretary, assistant for political affairs, legislative affairs, domestic policy, national security policy, scheduling, advance, and so on. There were eleven assistants to the vice president, including not one but two assistants for national security affairs—an indication that this would be the largest of the many staffs in Cheney's office.[9] All of these senior aides had their own deputy assistants, special assistants, and other support.

Cheney's staff included Libby as chief of staff and national security advisor; Dean McGrath as deputy chief of staff; David Addington as counsel; Dan Wilmot as head of the advance team; Elizabeth Kleppe and Martha Lang as schedulers; Debbie Heiden as executive assistant; John Gossel in operations; Mary Matalin as communications director; Juleanna Glover Weiss as press secretary; a small group of domestic policy aides; and a larger national security policy unit.[10] While Cheney did not have a political director to match Rove, nearly every other job in the White House was matched by one in the vice president's office in Cheney's parallel universe.

Policy expertise in the vice president's office often mirrored or exceeded that in the White House, particularly in the area of national security policy. Cheney's national security affairs staff, for example, had the same policy expertise and organizational structure as the president's National Security Council (NSC). NSC staff had policy assignments matching geographic desk assignments in the State Department, and the vice president's national security staff had similar geographic designations. Cheney had European, Middle East, Latin American, Far Eastern, Russian, African, and other specialists—drawn from the ranks of academia and think tanks, most of them holding advanced academic degrees.[11]

His national security team included John Hannah, on loan to Cheney's office from John Bolton at the State Department; Eric Edelman, a foreign service officer who had recently served as ambassador to Finland; and C. Dean McGrath Jr., who had been chief of staff to Representative Christopher Cox of California (and had known Cheney when both served on a bipartisan panel on stolen military hardware years earlier). Matched with these experts were military staff, most of them from defense agencies. In sharp contrast to this large, specialized staffing structure, Vice President Al Gore had had a comparatively small national security staff, led by Leon S. Fuerth. Fuerth's designation as a member of the Principals' Committee of the National Security Council (NSC) opened the door for Libby to have the same role. In a February 13, 2001, National Security Directive, Bush designated not only Libby but Cheney's chief of staff, David Addington, to serve on the Principals' Committee. One can assume that Cheney had asked for this directive rather than Bush suggesting that Cheney have two members of his staff included.

The designation of two members of his staff to the Principals' Committee is indicative of the unparalleled influence Cheney wielded in national security affairs, and in every staffing decision in the single executive office. Libby also regularly participated in the daily staff meetings of the NSC and was as deeply involved in NSC discussions as anyone in the White House. Part of his access to the NSC machinery was made possible by Stephen Hadley, deputy director of the NSC, with whom he had worked under Cheney at the Department of Defense. The collaborative relationship between the president's national security staff and the vice president's national security staff was clearly enhanced by the Libby-Hadley relationship in the full transparency of decision making. As a result of Libby's regular interactions with NSC staff, Cheney probably had more influence over NSC decisions than Secretary of State Colin Powell.

To fill jobs in his domestic policy and legislative affairs units, Cheney drew heavily from congressional staffers. These included Ethan

Hastert, son of Speaker of the House Dennis Hastert; Cesar Conda, former legislative director for Senator Spencer Abraham of Michigan; Ron Christie, who had worked for Representative John R. Kasich of Ohio and Senator George Allen of Virginia; and Andrew Lundquist, who was the former staff director of the Senate Energy and Natural Resources Committee and an expert on oil and domestic drilling. In legislative affairs, Cheney hired Candida Wolff, who had worked for Senator Larry Craig of Idaho; Nancy Dorn, Dennis Hastert's former foreign policy advisor; and Stephen Ruhlen, former chief of staff to Representative Henry Bonilla of Texas.[12] Cheney's education advisor, Nina Shokraii Rees—who had been an education expert at the Heritage Foundation—was one of the few domestic policy staffers who had not come from the halls of Capitol Hill.

Cheney's congressional hires were a nod to the close working relationship he intended to build with Hastert and the Republican-controlled House and with the Senate Republicans, and it reflected his distrust of the career staff in the executive branch. By the time Cheney returned to Washington, D.C., for the Bush transition, he had been out of Beltway politics for five years, having moved to Texas as CEO of Halliburton in 1995. But he still had ties to the military-industrial complex, which he could use to staff his national security team. While he had connections in the military and foreign policy agencies from which to draw staff for his national security team, he had few connections in the domestic agencies. To further complicate matters, Cheney saw the executive branch as captured by liberals in both the political and career ranks. As a result, he turned to members of Congress to help staff his domestic and economic staff. Cheney sought their input, and they eagerly responded with recommendations.

Organizationally, Cheney divided his team between domestic and economic policy in one office and national security in another. This was slightly different from the staffing arrangement in the White House, which divided domestic and economic policy into two offices, following the Clinton model of having staff for both domestic and economic policy.

Cheney's domestic policy office was run by Cesar Conda and staffers Ron Christie, Andrew Lundquist, and Nina Shokraii Rees. Cheney's primary goal in focusing his domestic policy staff on energy and the environment was to review all federal policies and regulations that negatively affected the business community. By limiting his senior domestic policy staff to four—three of whom were experts in energy issues—he made it clear that he would restrict his domestic role to energy and related environmental policies and not interfere with the White House focus on faith-based and related issues. Decisions on environmental issues, such as drilling in national parks or off the continental shelf, directly affected energy policies, which Cheney was seeking to control.

A White House staff fully integrated between the president's office and the vice president's office had never been attempted before, but it proved to have few problems. Karen Hughes, White House communications director, described it as a seamless staff that flowed between the president's and vice president's offices. No matter what the issue, Cheney's staffers participated in White House policy meetings. For example, Conda joined the White House economic policy advisor, Lawrence Lindsey, in meetings with cabinet officers on energy policy, and Rees was a constant participant in White House policy meetings on the No Child Left Behind bill, working hand in hand with Margaret Spellings and White House education specialists.[13]

While the president's and vice president's staffs operated under full transparency, however, they focused on different issues. There appear to have been few cases in which conflicts developed between the two staffs in domestic policy, since each had its own sphere of influence. Not until the Valerie Plame incident—which involved leaks to the press about Plame's covert work for the CIA—did the two organizations actually clash, pitting Libby against Rove.

While Cheney was building his staff and creating his integrated organizational structure, Andy Card was building the president's White House organization. Card enthusiastically supported the seamless executive office that Cheney wanted to create and told the president's and vice president's staffs soon after the inauguration that they would be working together to accomplish George W. Bush's goals.[14] But Card had a more difficult task than Cheney in building a staff. While Cheney had a unified team from the outset of the administration, Card did not. His challenge was to merge the political loyalists from Texas with the policy experts from the campaign.

But building a cohesive team wasn't Card's only concern. He also needed to find a balance in his own role as first among equals. Throughout the process of staffing the White House, Card was always sensitive to how Bush's father had run his own White House staff, and the internal problems caused by the elder Bush's aggressive chief of staff, John Sununu. Sununu had been George H. W. Bush's gatekeeper at all times. Card had worked as deputy chief of staff and had seen the infighting that occurred regularly when he denied senior staffers access to the president. When George W. Bush visited the White House, he, too, was often at odds with John Sununu, as were many in the administration. After Sununu had finally pushed the entire White House too far with his arrogance, George H. W. Bush fired him for personal use of an official car and aircraft—an ethics violation disclosed by the White House staff.

Card would not be an autocratic gatekeeper like John Sununu. His task was to create an organizational structure that George W. Bush would find comfortable, not one that kept people at bay. Card needed a staff structure that allowed senior staffers access to Bush, but one that limited the number with such access. To accomplish this, Card added two deputy chiefs of staff to his own office—Joshua Bolten, campaign policy director, and Joe Hagin, deputy campaign manager and a longtime member of the Bush inner circle, who had worked as a personal aide to Vice President George H. W. Bush and later as his legislative director during his presidency. Card gave both Bolten and Hagin the title assistant to the president to bolster their authority within the White House and as presidential spokesmen. Card next reduced the number of staff with the title assistant to the president, downgrading many to that of deputy assistant to the president.

Bush wanted his senior staff—including Karl Rove, Alberto Gonzales, Clay Johnson, Margaret Spellings, and Karen Hughes—to have the freedom to walk in and out of the Oval Office when they wanted to, within reason. These were the Texas loyalists who had been tested by fire. They had worked side by side with Bush through political campaigns in Texas and across the nation.

Card needed to find them the right jobs and to build a cohesive staff and policy-making structure with this essentially political group. Hughes, whose second-floor corner office was one of the largest in the West Wing, took charge of the speechwriting and communications offices. Rove took charge of political affairs, public liaison, and intergovernmental affairs in his newly created Office of Strategic Initiatives. Many key campaign personnel moved into these units. Tucker Eskew, Dan Bartlett, Mark McKinnon, and Michael Gerson joined Hughes's communications division, along with Press Secretary Ari Fleischer.

Hughes was the public face of the White House staff and, at the same time, had the most influence on decision making in the Oval Office. Mark McKinnon, who handled media for the Bush campaign and then the White House, said of Hughes, Bush "trusts her completely. He trusts her like no one" for advice.[15] Their bond was largely personal, based on a shared evangelical view of the world.

When Card suggested that Hughes take the title of counselor to the president rather than communications director, she eagerly agreed. In her memoir *Ten Minutes from Normal*, Hughes said she appreciated the biblical connotation of the word "counselor," for in the Bible, wise counselors are expected to speak truth to people in power. "I hoped it would remind me of two things," she explained, "my great responsibility to my boss, and my ultimate identity, which rests not in any title or position, but as a child of God."[16] The circle of trust that emerged in the White House was premised on these shared convictions. Hughes had the strongest ties with those on the White House staff who shared her fervor for blending religion and policy.

While Hughes and her staff crafted messages and wrote speeches, Rove and his political apparatus focused on building bridges to state and local elected officials and party organizations. His goal was to build the coalitions necessary for Republican gains in the midterm elections in 2002 and for the president's reelection in 2004. Rove also had a broader goal: to remake the Republican Party and create a permanent new governing coalition.[17] He used his influence in White House staff meetings to keep policy decisions from veering outside what he viewed as acceptable limits for the upcoming elections: tax cuts, education reform, and defense spending. These were the issues, he felt, that would keep the administration in a strong position. By contrast, Rove offered little support for legislative action on faith-based initiatives, for fear they would jeopardize political capital for Bush's tax cuts—one of many points of tension that emerged in the White House.[18]

In addition to these Texas loyalists, there were outsiders in the administration with policy, professional, or Beltway experience. Although Nicholas Calio and Jack Howard had not been involved in the campaign, Card knew them well as seasoned Washington professionals and tapped them to head legislative affairs. Card also named the economic policy advisor Larry Lindsey and the deputy domestic policy advisor John Bridgeland to senior positions, based on their policy expertise. Each had worked in varying degrees with the campaign, but neither had any prior relationship with Bush and they were not part of the Texas clique that moved from the governor's mansion into the White House. Card also brought in Joshua Bolten, the campaign's director of domestic policy, who had little policy experience and few ties to the Bush loyalists. Finally, there was John DiIulio, an expert in faith-based organizations, who was a newcomer to the campaign with no ties to the Texas group.

Card's challenge was to merge these somewhat disparate groups. On the one hand, there were the staffers with close ties to Bush from Austin. This group—dominated by Rove, Hughes, and Johnson—was primarily political rather than policy-oriented. On the other hand, there were staffers—such as DiIulio, Bridgeland, and Lindsey—who had policy expertise but were not closely aligned with the Texas loyalists. Then there were Alberto Gonzales, another Bush loyalist, and Condoleezza Rice. Gonzales, a Texas lawyer whom Bush had appointed to a number of positions in Austin—including counsel to the governor and state supreme court judge—was named counsel to the president and built his staff from the Beltway legal community. Rice, whom Laura and George Bush had come to view as a family member, was named national security advisor. Rice was single; her parents were deceased, she had been an only child, and she and the Bushes had become close personal friends during the campaign.

There were also the professionals, Calio and Howard, who had to balance the political and policy goals generated by the two sides of the senior staff and pursue what they saw as a workable legislative strategy. Bolten, the director of domestic policy for the campaign, had little policy experience and few ties to the Bush loyalists.

Publicly, the plan was for the political and policy sides of the White House staff to form a team—a word that was repeated frequently in internal meetings and to the press. What really emerged in the White House, however, was a dance between the political and policy organizations. On one side was the political and communications apparatus, managed by Rove and Hughes, whose goal was to cast George W. Bush in the best possible light. On the other side was the policy apparatus, with Spellings, Bridgeland, and DiIulio serving as domestic advisors and Lindsey as economic advisor. Their goal was to devise policies in line with campaign promises and expand into new policy areas. When the policy apparatus conflicted with the political apparatus, the political apparatus generally emerged the winner. As a result, Rove and Hughes, who had been the masterminds of Bush's past campaigns, controlled most of the decisions.

Transforming a campaign organization into a governing staff is always a struggle in a new administration. Conflicts were predictable—first, between Bush's long-standing Texas confidants and newer campaign staff, and later between the political and the policy sides of the White House. But it was these internal conflicts that gave Dick Cheney the opportunity to insert his own staff into White House policy making. Cheney never sought to place his staff under Rove or Hughes or in any of the units that they controlled.[19] And, in general, staff managed by Rove and Hughes did not interact with Cheney's team. Rove was not a Cheney fan, and he would not allow the vice president to influence any of his operations. He had, in fact, opposed Bush's decision to bring Cheney onto the ticket, calling him "old and bald and Beltway and ideologically retro, a political Jurassic Park." Cheney, moreover, was a poor political choice, Rove argued. "Wyoming's three electoral votes weren't in danger of falling into Democratic hands."[20]

Gonzales was an easy target for Cheney, however, since he had almost no idea how to manage his job as the president's counsel. Not surprisingly, David Addington regularly attended meetings in Gonzales's office, and he recommended several senior staff members for Gonzales to hire. Later in the administration, Addington's close working relationship with Gonzales's staff allowed him to influence decisions on appointments to the federal judiciary, warrantless surveillance of U.S. citizens, torture of terrorists held by the U.S. military, and the expansion of executive authority.

The staffing process that Card created allowed the Texas loyalists, who formed the core of the White House staff, to focus on issues of greatest concern to them: compassionate conservatism, lower taxes, and education reform. This narrow agenda allowed Cheney to work quietly to control energy, environmental, regulatory, and national security policy. His self-appointed jurisdictions rarely overlapped with that of Bush, the Texas loyalists, or even the social moderates.

Once in office, Cheney added the management of the federal budget to his portfolio, which he oversaw in tandem with Mitchell Daniels of the Office of Management and Budget (OMB). In order to take control of the budget, Cheney needed a budget director whom he could influence and work closely with. He had seen how independent Richard Darman had been as budget director for George H. W. Bush. Darman was the final arbiter of budget decisions for that administration and provided no access points for appealing his decisions. Cheney, however, wanted to control how budget decisions were made by inserting himself into the process.

As transition director, Cheney recommended Mitchell Daniels to head OMB. His name had surfaced in the transition through Al Hubbard, the campaign's economic advisor. Hubbard and Daniels were Indiana business executives who had worked together in the business and political arena and had made substantial contributions to Republican candidates. The conservative Hudson Institute in Indianapolis—known for its positions against government intervention in the economy and controlling the deficit—had hired Daniels, whose political credentials included a brief period as political director in Reagan's White House.

Whereas Daniels had little exposure to the complex world of federal budgets, Cheney had extensive experience, stemming from his work in the Ford White House, ten years in the House, and four years at the Defense Department. Putting Daniels in the top position at OMB directly served Cheney's purposes, increasing his influence in the budget process. Cheney then placed Sean O'Keefe, who had been his comptroller general at the Defense Department, in OMB as deputy director, to further solidify his input into budget decisions.

After installing Daniels and O'Keefe, Cheney gave himself direct input into budget decisions by creating the Budget Review Group— composed of himself, Daniels, Secretary of the Treasury Paul O'Neill, Andy Card, and the White House economic advisor, Larry Lindsey.[21] The Budget Review Group, which Cheney chaired, served as an appeals process for cabinet officers dissatisfied with OMB's budget recommendations for their departments. One is hard-pressed to imagine OMB directors David Stockman in the Reagan administration, Richard Darman in the George H. W. Bush administration, or Leon Panetta and Alice Rivlin in the Clinton administration allowing the vice president to create a check on their budget decisions. Yet Cheney created a check system on Daniels that essentially guaranteed himself final decisions on the budget.

By integrating his staff into the White House decision-making process, Cheney expanded his influence in the administration and with the president. The creation of a single executive office gave the vice president's staff full access to all internal memoranda and policy discussions. Access to information gave Cheney power. The narrow lens through which Bush saw his presidency allowed Cheney wide latitude to implement his own policy agenda. Since the Bush staff had a limited agenda, Cheney moved into the areas that were of little interest to them, such as energy, environmental policy, and regulatory issues. He had the information; he knew Bush's goals. Cheney stayed away from issues of greatest importance to Bush and his staff, such as faith-based policies and programs with a moral component. Cheney never interfered with the faith-based presidency. His strategy was to let the White House manage its priorities, while he managed his own, empowered by the full transparency of the executive office.

In January 2001, when George W. Bush took up residency at 1600 Pennsylvania Avenue, Dick Cheney had already captured the policy-making apparatus of government. The blueprint for the co-presidency, resurrected from the 1980 discussions between Gerald Ford and Ronald Reagan, was finally operational. Experience, strategy, and opportunity gave Cheney more power and influence than any vice president in the history of the country.

CHAPTER 5

God and George W. Bush
The Faith-Based Presidency

M ANY WHO KNEW George W. Bush were aware of the depth of his religious beliefs, but few in the electorate fully understood them in the early stages of the 2000 campaign. That changed in a dramatic moment in a debate before the Iowa caucuses, when religion came to the surface in a seemingly secular discussion.

In the large, almost cavernous Civic Center of Greater Des Moines, the Republican presidential candidates stood at platforms on the stage, answering questions posed by John Bachman of television station WHO and by Tom Brokaw of NBC News. Bachman and Brokaw took turns walking around the stage, directing questions at each candidate. The atmosphere was casual, intended to put the candidates at ease. No clock was ticking away for this debate, which gave the candidates the freedom to speak as long as they wanted.

Bachman asked each of the six candidates onstage which philosopher had the most influence on their lives. The magazine publisher Steve Forbes mentioned John Locke and Thomas Jefferson. Former ambassador Alan Keyes talked about the founders who wrote the Constitution. Bush, however, responded, "Christ, because he changed my heart. When you turn your heart and your life over to Christ, when you accept Christ as the savior, it changes your heart. It changes your life."[1]

Bush's answer resonated with evangelicals in Iowa, who made up nearly 40 percent of Republican caucus-goers. It is unlikely, however, that his response was politically motivated; rather, it was a reflection of his deepest personal convictions. Whatever his intention in answering the question, Bush won the Iowa caucuses—a victory that began his march to capture the nomination in Philadelphia. Evangelicals rallied around him and delivered a strong message to the Republican Party that they could be counted on for votes if they had the right candidate. George W. Bush was not only the candidate of the Republican establishment; he was also now the candidate of Christian conservatives.

His staff in Austin, if not the electorate, knew the depth of his religious beliefs. When Bush resolved to enter the 2000 election, he brought the staff together at the governor's mansion to announce that he "had been called" by God to seek higher office.[2] He was a soldier in God's army with a higher charge, he said, and his job as president would be to do what God asked him to do. It was a conviction, according to one friend, that gave Bush moral clarity in his life.[3] Another friend, who had worked for both Ronald Reagan and George H. W. Bush, bluntly stated that the younger Bush "truly believes he's on a mission from God" in his presidency.[4]

Religious conservatives tipped the election in favor of George W. Bush. Never before had a group of voters turned out in such proportionately large numbers as Christian conservatives did in November 2000. In fire halls, elementary schools, and church meeting rooms in the South and Midwest, Christian conservatives voted as they never had before. Their numbers added up, enabling Bush to keep the Democratic nominee, Vice President Al Gore, from winning the White House. When Florida's twenty-five electoral votes were finally certified for Bush, they put him over the top, for a total of 271 electoral votes, in a competition that needed 270 for victory.

Bush delivered his first speech as president-elect in mid-December, only hours after Gore's concession. In a nationally televised address from the Texas statehouse in Austin, Bush used phrases laced with religious symbolism and themes. "I have faith," he said, "that *with God's help* we as a nation will move forward together as one nation, indivisible."[5] These words framed the basic tenets of his administration. "With God's help," he pledged, he would deliver a set of policies to help build a moral and civil society.

His religious fervor was constantly in evidence in the Oval Office, reinforced by a large oil painting he had brought with him from Texas. In front of the *Resolute* desk—made from timbers of the HMS *Resolute* over a century earlier—hung an oil painting by W.H.D. Koerner, entitled *A Charge to Keep*. Most of the paintings presidents typically choose to adorn the office come from the White House archives, but this one was on loan from friends of the Bushes.

The painting depicts a cowboy on horseback galloping up a hill, which Bush told friends had been inspired by a Charles Wesley hymn of the same title. The hymn begins, "A charge to keep I have, / A God to glorify"—words that became such a part of Bush's life that he used them for the title of his pre-presidency memoir, *A Charge to Keep*. The hymn, Bush said, "has been an inspiration for me and for members of my staff. [It] calls us to our highest and best. It speaks of purpose and direction. In many hymnals, it is associated with the Bible verse 1 Corinthians 4:2: 'Now it is required that those who have been given a trust must prove fruitful.'"[6]

However, the painting was not inspired by Wesley's hymn and had no religious connotation. Bush inexplicably attached a religious meaning to the painting because of its title, believing that the cowboy was a missionary or circuit-rider spreading Methodism across the Alleghenies during the 1800s. In reality, the painting depicts a horse thief escaping a lynch mob in Nebraska; it was commissioned in 1916 to accompany a short story entitled "The Slippery Tongue," published in the *Saturday Evening Post*.

The message that Bush drew from the painting and the hymn, that "those who have been given a trust must prove fruitful," would, he said, "epitomize our mission." Bush would use the power of the presidency to keep that trust, making decisions based on moral precepts and the word of God. He believed his presidency was a divine mission—even confiding to an Amish farmer, on a visit to Pennsylvania, that "I trust God speaks through me."[7]

Bush's religion and relationship with God guided his faith-based presidency. When he spoke, he often included religious thoughts or references. Even a simple question posed by the author Robert Draper asking Bush how he dealt with stress led to an answer that involved faith. "Prayer helps," Bush said, adding, without hesitation, "I'm also sustained by the discipline of the faithful experience."[8] Solace in the faithful experience would take many roads for Bush, particularly through frequent meetings with religious leaders. Only weeks before the inauguration, for example, he met with three dozen clergy in a Baptist church in Austin, seeking their guidance on policies for the broad, undefined agenda of social justice. "How do I speak to the soul of the nation?" he asked them.[9] Meetings with religious leaders—and prayer meetings in general—would become a frequent pattern throughout his eight years in office.

Bush's mission to create a moral and civil society was reinforced in regular prayer meetings he often attended in the White House, where prayer was commonplace. Every cabinet meeting began with a prayer. Bush asked members of the cabinet or the vice president to begin by saying a prayer of their choosing, and all would bow their heads as the prayer was spoken. His most senior advisors in the White House included Michael Gerson and Karen Hughes, who shared his intense evangelical convictions, as well as Andy Card, whose wife was a Methodist minister. "To understand the Bush White House," explained the Bush speechwriter David Frum, "you must understand its predominant creed. It was a kindly faith, practical and unmystical . . . the evangelicals in the Bush White House were its gentlest souls, the most patient, the least argumentative. They were numerous enough to set the tone in the White House, and the result was an office in which I seldom heard a voice raised in anger."[10]

Bush's private commitment to faith was reflected in his own daily routine. Every morning, before arriving in the Oval Office promptly at 7:00 A.M., he read passages from the Bible or his devotionals. His morning reading was likely to include the Old Testament or a selection from *My Utmost for His Highest*, a book of devotions by Oswald Chambers that was widely read by evangelicals.[11] His routine, moreover, always included one to two hours of exercise, which his staff ensured was part of his daily schedule. No matter where Bush was located, in any city around the world, not a day went by that he didn't do some form of exercise. It was a constant in his life, along with prayer and Bible-reading.

His public commitment to faith was evidenced through his faith-friendly positions, policies, and rhetoric. Even if he could not directly affect a policy issue, Bush used the bully pulpit of the presidency to state his point of view. In a 2005 federal court case over a Pennsylvania public school curriculum, for example, Bush sided with those who supported intelligent design—the view that human beings were created by an intelligent being rather than by evolution or natural selection.

Bush favored adding intelligent design to the biology curriculum of the school district, and possibly all school districts. "Both sides ought to be properly taught," he stated in reference to the Pennsylvania case, ". . . so people can understand what the debate is about." U.S. District Court judge John Jones clearly disagreed with Bush when he denied the school board's efforts to include intelligent design. There is "overwhelming evidence," he wrote in his opinion, "that intelligent design is a religious view, a mere re-labeling of creationism, and not a scientific theory."[12] For Bush, a faith-friendly policy would have allowed the curriculum to include intelligent design.

George W. Bush's strong religious views had been just as evident during his tenure as governor of Texas, when he actively promoted faith-based organizations and made frequent references to God. After winning a second term as governor in 1998, he included in his inaugural address the statement that "we're all made in the image of God. We're all equal in God's eyes." In one powerful line, he declared that everyone has "a worth, a dignity and a free will given by God, not by government."[13] Religious phrases were peppered throughout the address.

Bush's inaugural address as president was similarly laden with religious phrases, as was nearly every speech that followed in his eight years in the Oval Office. Embedded deep within the 2003 State of the Union Address, for example, was the memorable sentence "There is power, wonder-working power in the goodness and idealism and faith of the American people." These words came from an evangelical hymn, "There Is Power in the Blood," which describes God's power as "power, power, wonder-working power/in the blood of the Lamb." Such language, drawn from evangelical hymns, became commonplace in Bush's speeches, regardless of the audience.

Whether he was speaking about logging in a national forest or about the Declaration of Independence in the rotunda of the National Archives,

Bush's secular speeches were always tinged with religion and reverence for God. For example, speaking in Oregon's Deschutes National Forest about his Healthy Forests Initiative, Bush wove religious phrases into his speech as he extolled the value of logging in national forests as a tool to minimize forest fires. After he talked about the Biscuit blaze, which had destroyed 500,000 acres of forests the year before, destroying 75 percent of the vegetation and leaving thousands without homes or work, he said, "For those whose lives have been deeply affected we send our sympathies *and we wish God's blessings on their families.*" For whatever reason, he then turned suddenly to the subject of Iraq, suggesting that bringing freedom to Iraqis was part of God's plan—"that freedom is not America's gift to the world, *it is God's gift to every single human being on the face of the earth.*"[14] Perhaps Bush had drawn a connection as he was speaking between God's plan in the massive forest fire and God's plan in Iraq.

Even a speech celebrating the newly restored Declaration of Independence focused on faith. In the rotunda of the National Archives in Washington, D.C., Bush unveiled the Declaration of Independence, which had been reencased for preservation. Flanked by the Speaker of the House, the chief justice, and two other justices of the Supreme Court, as well as the majority and minority leaders of the Senate, Bush talked, not about the importance of the three branches of government working together, but instead about a government in which *"principles stand above every earthly power—the equality of each person before God."*[15]

No speech was as direct about his religious beliefs as the one he gave in the Old Executive Office Building to African American ministers, when he applauded administration-funded programs run through predominantly African American churches. *"We ought not to fear faith,"* Bush said, adding that we "ought not to discriminate against faith-based programs" with federal dollars. In his administration, he explained, decision making was based on values framed around principles of God and evangelical Christianity. "We base our . . . decision-making, our future," he said, "on solid values. The first value is, we're all God's children."[16]

For George W. Bush, restoring God and God's values to the public discourse was essential to reestablishing moral values in a civil society. This became the framework of everything that Bush did as president. According to Peter Wehner, White House director of the Office of Strategic Initiatives and a senior member of the White House staff, "the issues that animated the president the most were those that included a moral dimension."[17] Wehner's characterization of Bush was underscored by White House speechwriter Michael Gerson, who observed that for Bush, "the cultural confusion of elites was undermining the moral values that allowed normal people to live successful lives."[18] Bush's sense of morality was his compass for guiding the federal government.

Bush saw the value of government institutions promoting "hopeful change for society," as he called it, in his first run for public office, when he defeated incumbent governor Ann Richards of Texas. "George Bush believes," Gerson added, "that social reform and moral improvement is possible, because he believes that individual reformation is possible. And while government cannot directly create this reformation, it can promote institutions that do."[19] The faith-based presidency and the faith-based policies that it drove relied on government institutions to move forward programs for, as Gerson noted, "individual reformation."

The 2001 terrorist attacks on the World Trade Center and Pentagon only deepened the faith-based presidency and Bush's determination to use the tools of government to protect good from evil. Only hours before a speech to a joint session of Congress after the attacks, Bush met with a group of religious leaders in the Roosevelt Room of the White House, joining them in a prayer circle, after which they sang "God Bless America."[20] As he did so many times during his presidency, he sought solace in prayer and comfort from religious leaders.

Three days after the attacks, Bush used his presidential authority to give the nation the same comfort of prayer that he so valued. He declared September 14, 2001, a National Day of Prayer of Remembrance, leading a nationally televised prayer service in Washington's elegant

National Cathedral. Speaking from the pulpit, Bush, as the nation's chief executive officer, used religious, not secular, language:

On this national day of prayer and remembrance, we ask almighty God to watch over our nation and grant us patience and resolve in all that is to come. We pray that He will comfort and console those who now walk in sorrow. We thank Him for each life we now must mourn, and the promise of a life to come.[21]

These were not the words of the cathedral's dean, Episcopal bishop Nathan Baxter, who was leading the service, but the words of the president of the United States. A year later, George W. Bush again declared a National Day of Prayer and Remembrance in honor of the victims of 9/11, stating, "in the aftermath of the attacks, the words of the Psalms brought comfort to many. *We trust God always to be our refuge and our strength, an ever-present help.*"[22]

Biblical references were commonplace in speeches Gerson wrote for Bush, but none was more evident than in the five-minute address that Bush delivered on the evening of September 11, 2001, as the nation began to cope with the magnitude of the terrorist attacks. Ending his 8:30 P.M. address, he said: "Tonight, I ask for your prayers for all who grieve. . . . And I pray they will be comforted by a power greater than any of us, spoken through the ages in Psalm 23: 'Even though I walk through the valley of the shadow of death, I fear no evil, for You are with me.'"[23]

The war on terror quickly became the embodiment of good versus evil. Terrorists were evil. Osama bin Laden was evil. But Bush frequently used the biblical term "evildoer," from the Book of Psalms, and invoked the word "crusade" to define America's mission to root out terrorism—linking it to the medieval religious wars in which Christians fought Muslims.[24] While this rhetoric was effective in mobilizing support among Christian conservatives, it had the opposite effect in the Islamic world, where the word "crusade" reminds Muslims of historical Christian atrocities. For George W. Bush, God was on his side as he fought terrorists and protected America's freedom—which, he fervently believed, the terrorists were seeking to destroy. "This is civilization's fight," Bush declared. "God is not neutral . . . we'll meet violence with patient justice, assured of the rightness of our patient cause. . . . In all that lies before us, may God grant us wisdom and may He watch over the United States of America."[25]

Bush continued to justify military action in Iraq as part of God's plan for his administration in various speeches across the country. Speaking to a group in Wheeling, West Virginia, Bush linked God and freedom in unscripted remarks, suggesting that liberty is part of God's plan for humanity. "One of the greatest gifts of that Almighty God," he said, "is the desire for people to be free. . . . And therefore, this country and the world ought to say, 'How can we help you remain free? What can we do to help you realize *the blessings of liberty?*'"[26] The use of the phrase "blessings of liberty" reinforced the concept that freedom and liberty were part of God's plan. When Wehner was interviewed by *Christianity Today*, he described the frequent references to the phrase as reflecting "the President's belief that there's a moral imperative to treat human beings with dignity and decency, and that liberty is the design of nature. This explains why liberty leads to human flourishing."[27]

In addition, Bush often referred to "the transformational power of liberty." He believed that unless the United States brought freedom and liberty to the Middle East, the region would remain burdened by poverty, which fostered terrorism. Bringing democracy to Iraq, in particular, would lead that nation from poverty to prosperity, providing no footholds for terrorists. Bush frequently used that argument during the 2004 reelection campaign to invigorate Christian conservatives, who had supported him so fervently in 2000.

The biblical references to good and evil, and to transformational power, became a theme throughout numerous speeches, not only with reference to terrorists but with reference to broader international issues. When Frum was preparing a speech on the threat of Iran's nuclear arsenal, for example, he included a statement that Iraq and Iran were part of an "axis of hatred." Matt Scully, another speechwriter who reviewed the speech, then substituted the word "evil" for "hatred," since, he said, "we were already confronting *evildoers* [in the speech], *wickedness,* and the like."[28]

Frum says of this change that incorporated the word "evil": "Bush read the speech closely. He edited it in his own bold hand. He understood all its implications."[29] By changing "hatred" to "evil," the speechwriting staff had intentionally created a theological framework for a speech on Iran's nuclear arsenal.

Theology, not surprisingly, played a role in Bush's justification for the war in Iraq and would be incorporated into speeches that explained the intertwining of American foreign policy and religion. In a speech delivered in 2003, Bush called for a free Iraq that "honors religion" and "believes in the freedom of religion."[30] For Bush, the war in Iraq was about more than changing the geopolitical map of the Middle East; it was about building a society where freedom of religion was integral to the governmental structure.

It was, in other words, a just war. Howard Fineman, writing in *Newsweek*, argued that Bush saw the war in Iraq as one that unquestionably met the standards of a "just war" within the framework of Christianity, as "laid out by Augustine in the fourth century and amplified by Aquinas, Luther and others"—one that would liberate Iraqis and allow religious freedom to prosper.[31] Iraq's leadership under Saddam Hussein, Bush believed, had repressed not only Christians but also various Muslim sects, particularly Shi'ites. The Iraq War was one of protecting good from evil, protecting liberty, and protecting freedom of religion. Going to war was a moral issue, because it "was the right thing to do," as he told his staff.

Bush's Christian conservative theology also influenced the conduct of U.S. military forces in Iraq. Soon after the toppling of Saddam Hussein, American troops took over the dictator's palace in Baghdad. Above one of the three entrances, the troops painted a mural of the World Trade Center, with its twin towers framed by the wings of a bald eagle and words boldly declaring, "Thank God for the Coalition Forces & Freedom Fighters at Home and Abroad." On another entrance, a sign announced, "Bible Study—Wednesdays at 7:00 P.M."[32] Officers who ran the palace allowed and encouraged Bible study, transforming a secular military into a faith-based military in line with the Bush presidency.

In domestic policy, as well as foreign and military policy, Bush wielded all of the tools of his office to promote his religious views of good and evil. In domestic policy, those views were framed around building a moral and civil society. "Each of us," he said, "are responsible for loving our neighbor just like we'd like to be loved ourselves."[33] For George W. Bush, "love thy neighbor" was a biblical command, and he rallied the armies of compassion to help him do what God called him to do. He asked Congress to increase tax breaks for charitable organizations and to fund faith-based groups delivering social services. He used the power of his office to support adoption over abortion and to end federal funding for stem cell research, which destroyed embryos. Since the traditional family was the center of a moral society, he supported marriage counseling and backed a constitutional amendment banning same-sex marriage.[34]

Evangelical Christians such as Bush view good and evil as part of the lessons of the New Testament, where Jesus teaches that sinners need to work against evil to find redemption. One scholar of the evangelical movement explained, "Within American Christianity there is a long tradition of finding good and evil. . . . This goes back to the New England Puritans and runs through various strands of both revivalism and social reform, including, for example, abolitionism and the temperance movements. Today, evangelicals are the inheritors of this tradition."[35] For Bush, the world was seen through a lens of good and evil, right and wrong, found within evangelical theology. His world was built around his faith. As he said in the Iowa debate, "When you turn your heart and your life over to Christ, when you accept Christ as the savior, it changes your heart. It changes your life."

In one of his first acts as president, Bush gave faith-based agencies a direct line to the White House by creating the new Office of Faith-Based and Community Initiatives.[36] The sole focus of this new, free-standing office, according to Bush's executive order, was to establish "policies, priorities and objectives for efforts to expand faith-based and community organizations to provide social and community services."[37] He deeply believed that God had saved his life in 1985, when salvation replaced his alcoholism and despair. Bush now believed that he had the chance to repay that debt to God, using the tools of government to protect religious organizations from what he called federal discrimination in funding decisions.

By 2006, the Bush administration was funneling $2.1 billion per year to faith-based organizations and another $25 million per year directly to federal agencies administering the money. An audit prepared that year by the Government Accountability Office (GAO), found that the overwhelming majority of faith-based organizations receiving funding were evangelical Christian. In a small random sample in the audit, most were found to be Protestant, two were Catholic, and none were Jewish. Whether intentional or not, the evidence pointed to a process that disproportionately funded evangelical Christian social service programs.[38]

One of the largest categories of faith-based organizations to receive federal funding were federal and state prison programs, many of which were overtly Christian groups, such as Charles Colson's Prison Fellowship Ministries. The prison ministries had, with an infusion of federal funds from the faith-based initiatives program, begun to operate in numerous prisons across the country, providing counseling to inmates that encouraged them "to accept Christ as savior." However, after several years of expanding services during the Bush administration, a number of communities began to file lawsuits against the prison programs on First Amendment grounds, arguing that, as government-operated institutions, they should not incorporate religion into prisoner activities.

In Newton, Iowa, for example, a 2006 community-led lawsuit against a state prison contended that the facility provided separate and distinctly better facilities for prisoners who participated in a "Christ-centered" program "anchored in biblical teaching." Run by Inner-Change, a program operated by Prison Fellowship Ministries, it tried "to cure prisoners by identifying sin as the root of their problems" and taught prisoners "how God can heal them permanently, if they turn away from their sinful past."[39] After the case went to trial, U.S. District Court judge Robert Pratt ruled that the prison had engaged in an unconstitutional use of taxpayers' money for religious indoctrination.

Similarly, a group of taxpayers sued a rural Pennsylvania county for funding a vocational training program focused on religious activities. As in Iowa, the federal judge in Pennsylvania ruled that the training program was an unconstitutional use of religion in a government program.[40] In spite of opposition across the country and in the courts, the White House continued to strongly support these faith-based programs, heralding them in a two-day Los Angeles conference called the White House National Summit on Prisoner Reentry. In his 2004 State of the Union Address, Bush celebrated the prisoner programs, as usual, with biblical language: "America is the land of second chance, and when the gates of the prison open," he said, "the path ahead should lead to a better life."[41]

In addition to prison programs, the administration funded overtly Christian programs that dealt with teenagers who had drug and alcohol problems. Two of the groups that received funding, Teen Challenge and Victory Fellowship, relied on religious experiences they provided to change teens' lives. According to the director of Victory Fellowship, the organization did not "use drugs or psychiatrists or any of that, only Bible study."[42] Its stated philosophy was that "if you treat an addict with a drug rehab program, all you have is a reformed junkie. But if he meets Christ, he is transformed. He's a whole new person."

In a similar vein, a Cheyenne, Wyoming, group called Biblical Concepts in Counseling received funding from the Department of Health and Human Services to provide Bible-based marriage counseling services. While overtly Christian, the group denied that it required participants to ascribe to its religious beliefs, admitting only that it used biblical tenets in the counseling process. But the denials seemed to contradict its actions. According to its director, Charlie Reed, and to its mission statement, its purpose was "to provide Biblically based counseling" and "to lead the counselee to a Biblical solution to each particular problem identified."[43]

Programs outsourced to religious groups proliferated across the Bush administration. Margaret Spellings, Bush's second secretary of education, for example, encouraged public schools to create partnerships with churches. Attending a conference in Texas, Spellings lauded the Oak

Cliff Bible Fellowship, which had partnered with Carter High School in Dallas to provide a "core message to stay in school, abstain from sex, and avoid drugs and gangs."[44] Rather than investing in more teachers, updated facilities, and after-school programs, the Bush administration invested in religious organizations for educational programming.

Shifting the delivery of services from secular to faith-based organizations was not easy in a federal bureaucracy built on a wall of separation between church and state. To accomplish its goal, the Bush administration used the President's Management Agenda, in the Office of Management and Budget (OMB), as a tool to encourage career staff to support faith-based programs. Agencies were judged on their ability to meet certain standards. In the traffic-light grading system used by OMB, red lights meant poor performance and green lights meant excellence.

Senior agency executives were reviewed based on their success at outsourcing, financial management, and, among other areas, funding faith-based groups, and they received bonuses if they met those performance standards. Agencies with flourishing Offices of Faith-Based and Community Initiatives were awarded green lights, indicating that they had "met all standards for success" and boosting their overall scores for agency activities. Clay Johnson, who oversaw the President's Management Agenda, praised agencies on the OMB web site for achieving green lights and meeting the goals set for their faith-based offices.[45]

In general, however, once the administration funded a faith-based organization, no one questioned how the group spent its money. The GAO discovered, in a review of faith-based programming, that departments used much of their administrative funding to hold workshops for faith-based groups on the application process, but devoted little to overseeing the organizations. There were no penalties for violating regulations, such as overt religious activity, and few guidelines for audits. The lack of supervision may have been intentional and aimed at protecting religious organizations from government oversight of their activities. Kate O'Beirne, writing in the conservative *National Review*, argued that the "greatest risk of corrupting the mission of religious charitable groups would be posed by a grant program that permits bureaucrats too much discretion" over faith-based agencies.[46]

As a result of these faith-based policies, religion blossomed in programs across the administration, many headed by evangelicals who shared the president's religious fervor. Departments often based their hiring on political and ideological leanings and tended to favor candidates who were Christian conservatives. At the highest ranks of the Justice Department, for example, evangelical appointments included Attorney General John Ashcroft, a Pentecostal. Ashcroft approved the draping of a twelve-foot-tall statue of a woman, called the Spirit of Justice, in the Robert F. Kennedy Department of Justice Building in Washington, D.C., because her garment left one breast immodestly exposed; he also refused to allow his staff to participate in a Gay Pride parade during working hours, as had been the custom for several years.

Other evangelical appointments in the administration included Kay Cole James, dean of the Robertson School of Law at Regent University, an overtly Christian institution founded by the televangelist Pat Robertson.[47] James was named to head the all-important Office of Personnel Management, and her son, Chuck, a 1999 law school graduate, landed a position in Ashcroft's Justice Department. Another appointee, Monica Goodling—a senior counsel to the attorney general and 1999 graduate of Messiah College, later resigned after admitting that Christian conservatives were given priority hiring in the Justice Department. In a sharp rebuke by the department's inspector general in 2008, Goodling was charged with making hiring recommendations based on "political affiliation and religion."[48]

Ideology was also the defining feature of appointments in agencies where policies could be implemented around faith-based tenets. Many, like Jedd Medefind in the Department of Labor's faith-based office, had few management qualifications besides religion. The only qualification Medefind had for running the office was a book he had co-authored on Jesus titled *The Revolutionary Communicator*, which featured an endorsement by Chuck Colson on its back cover. Medefind demonstrated his religious zeal when he posted a prayer beginning

"Oh God Our Father" on the Department of Labor's official web site after the 2001 terrorist attacks.

It appears that there was a pro-life, pro-marriage, anti-gay litmus test, not only for some departmental jobs, but also for a wide range of appointees. One example of such a litmus test involved appointments to the National Institute on Drug Abuse advisory panel, whose members had previously been chosen purely based on their scientific and academic credentials. Before the Bush administration formally appointed one nominee to the panel, he was asked whether he held any views—such as pro-choice leanings—"that might be embarrassing to the President." The nominee was next asked whether he supported faith-based initiatives, whether he voted for President Bush, and whether he was pro-life.[49] He answered no to the last two questions and, subsequently, never heard back about the appointment. The administration denied there was a litmus test, but the same questions would be posed to other nominees for the drug abuse advisory panel.

Another case of a litmus test involved appointments to the Fogarty International Center, within the National Institutes of Health. Since the Fogarty Center develops international research and training programs in global health issues, staff had input into programs that involved discussions of abstinence, contraception, and abortion. During his three years at the Fogarty Center under the Bush administration, the director sent the names of twenty-six candidates to the White House for approval. Nineteen of the candidates were denied. In contrast, nearly all the nominations he had made during the Clinton administration had been routinely approved.[50]

Opportunities for career military officers and staff also depended on their ideological and political positions. Rajiv Chandrasekaran, covering the Iraq war for the *Washington Post*, interviewed Pentagon staff who were setting up the Coalition Provisional Authority (CPA) in Baghdad. "Two CPA staffers," he reported, "said that they were asked if they supported *Roe v. Wade* and if they had voted for George W. Bush." Another CPA staffer recounted that when he went to the Pentagon for his predeployment interview, "one of [James] O'Beirne's deputies launched into a ten-minute soliloquy about domestic politics that included statements opposing abortion . . . I felt pressured to agree," he said, "if I wanted to go to Baghdad."[51]

Evangelicals were especially numerous in the Department of Health and Human Services (HHS), which administered the bulk of the administration's social service programs. One of the department's most religiously conservative appointments was Wade Horn, former president of the National Fatherhood Initiative.[52] Horn, named assistant secretary for children and families, had promoted programs for fathers centering on discussions of how to "be relevant and show God's love in a practical way to fathers in the community" with the National Fatherhood Initiative. At HHS, Horn created a federal Fatherhood Initiative and promoted faith-based programs that encouraged not only committed fatherhood, but also the institution of marriage, parenting, and two-parent families. "I think," he said on PBS's *Frontline*, "that there certainly is a great role for faith-based organizations to play in helping couples form and sustain a healthy marriage."[53]

At one point, he suggested limiting Head Start to children of married parents, and his aggressive support for traditional marriage led HHS to create the Healthy Marriage Initiative, which the Republican-controlled Congress funded for five years, at a cost of $500 million. "Healthy" was the word the Bush administration used when it wanted to explain how its policies were better than the "unhealthy" old policies. The Healthy Marriage Initiative, which valued male-female marriage over other types of relationships, would reduce the number of people on welfare, Horn argued, because "research consistently finds that cohabitating relationships are far more unstable than marriage," and marital stability was key to economic stability.[54]

The Bush administration subscribed to the view that marriage was the fundamental relationship in society, and federal funding policy delivered this philosophy into the public schools. The HHS abstinence program, run by Wade Horn's Children and Families Administration, taught that "a mutually faithful monogamous relationship in the context of marriage is the expected standard of human sexual activity and that sexual activity outside of the context of marriage is likely to have harmful psychological and physical effects."[55] This was Horn's religious belief and did not represent long-held views within HHS. Like many Bush appointees, Horn defined social standards within the framework of his own evangelical convictions—convictions that George W. Bush shared. The abstinence program gave school districts substantial funding to focus on abstinence-only sex education—an approach that excluded information about contraception because, the administration argued, the use of condoms and other contraceptives undermined the abstinence message. The program was funded at $113 million in the 2007 federal budget, with a request for another $28 million.[56]

When a congressionally mandated evaluation showed that the abstinence program had no impact on teen pregnancy, states began to forgo federal funds and use a more comprehensive sex education curriculum that included previously forbidden information on contraception, pregnancy, and sexually transmitted diseases.[57] In 2005, the Senate Appropriations Committee became so frustrated with the abstinence-only curriculum that it sent a letter demanding that HHS expand it, charging that its material "was seriously flawed, providing erroneous and incomplete information about sexually transmitted diseases, the effectiveness of contraceptives, and sexual orientation."[58] As a result of the abstinence-only sex education program—according to a report published and submitted to HHS by Mathematica Policy Research, Inc.—teens had a "less clear understanding of STDs and their health consequences," and the program had "no statistically significant impact on eventual behavior."[59] Despite poor reviews by Mathematica and other policy analysts, however, the Bush administration continued to fund abstinence-only sex education in public schools.

The abstinence-only programs were also a mainstay of foreign aid programs that the administration ran in countries around the world. The State Department's Office of the U.S. Global AIDS Coordinator dedicated 33 percent of its budget on AIDS prevention to programs that advocated abstinence or monogamy within marriage. The State Department required field workers to focus on abstinence as the primary method of preventing AIDS, with less focus on prevention through the use of condoms and other contraceptive devices. Bush's sense of morality dominated foreign aid policy making. On a six-day trip to

Africa in early 2008, he explained that offering millions of dollars in foreign aid to many impoverished African nations was a moral issue "in the national interest and in the *moral interests* of the United States of America."[60]

The faith-based agenda related to issues of marriage extended to gay marriage, which the Bush administration strenuously opposed. In all cultures, Bush explained in a Saturday radio address, "marriage is the most enduring and important human institution, honored and encouraged in all cultures and *by every religious faith*. Ages of experience have taught us that the commitment of a husband and a wife to love and to serve one another promotes the welfare of children and the stability of society. Government, by recognizing and protecting marriage, serves the interests of all."[61] As a moral endeavor, marriage would promote a stable society and deserved government's support. Not surprisingly, Bush considered gay marriage immoral. He supported a constitutional amendment to ban same-sex unions—the Marriage Protection Amendment—and endorsed state referendums sanctioning marriage solely between a man and a woman.

To further reinforce the administration's opposition to same-sex marriage, Bush named Dr. James W. Holsinger Jr. as surgeon general in 2007, after Dr. Richard Cardona resigned, accusing the White House of political interference with his job. The surgeon general is a political appointee within HHS, and Holsinger, chancellor at the University of Kentucky Chandler Medical Center, had a well-known bias against the gay community. Earlier in his career he founded a recovery ministry, Hope Springs Community Church, aimed at helping addicts and homosexuals change their lifestyles. For Holsinger, homosexuals could be "cured" by turning to God.

His background included a degree in biblical studies and evangelization from Asbury Theological Seminary in Kentucky, which was committed to a "vital evangelical Christian faith." His view of homosexuality was well known from articles he had written asserting that homosexuality was neither natural nor healthy. When the Democratically controlled Senate failed to confirm Holsinger, Bush remained unwavering in his support and named him acting surgeon general.

Holsinger's appointment continued a trend in the Bush administration's social service–oriented departments, particularly HHS, where ideology and religion became key hiring credentials. David Gergen—an advisor to Presidents Nixon, Ford, Reagan, and Clinton, and himself a Republican—commented that "there has been a growing criticism [about] the administration favoring ideology over competence, and his [Holsinger's] nomination smacks of that."[62]

Of the many federal programs that fell within Christian conservative and evangelical ideology, however, none was more important than those that reinforced the pro-life agenda. According to Michael Gerson, Bush believed that "human life is an endowment, not an achievement," and he would do everything he could to protect it.[63] For many advocates, the pro-life movement had the fervor of a religious crusade, focused on the creation as well as the end of life.

In 2005, the Terri Schiavo controversy erupted over an end-of-life issue—whether a young Florida woman's husband could authorize removal of the feeding tube that was still keeping her alive. Although George W. Bush and his brother, Florida governor Jeb Bush, publicly opposed removing Schiavo's feeding tube, based on the view that all human life had to be protected, her husband legally removed it, and Schiavo died. George W. Bush then made the issue his first point in a national press briefing soon after: "I urge all those who honor Terri Schiavo to continue to work to build a culture of life, where all Americans are welcomed and valued and protected, especially those who live at the mercy of others."[64] His personal "charge to keep" included protecting both the unborn and those who were living only by medical intervention.

George W. Bush distanced the federal government from any policy that would support what he considered the destruction of human life. He annually proclaimed the National Sanctity of Life Day in January—on the same day that thousands of reproductive rights supporters were marching on the National Mall in Washington, D.C., to celebrate the anniversary of the Supreme Court's ruling in *Roe v. Wade*. Bush invited hundreds of pro-life supporters into the White House for coffee and doughnuts, meeting with them in the East Room and later broadcasting his support to pro-life crowds over loudspeakers on the National Mall.

His presidential proclamation that day included the call to "reaffirm our commitment to respecting and defending the life and dignity of every human being."[65] For George W. Bush, life began at conception, and his administration would actively work against any policies, such as abortion and stem cell research, that destroyed life. Foreign aid money was also restricted through the Department of State and other agencies in family planning programs, which were forbidden to discuss abortion. International family planning groups—such as the International Planned Parenthood Federation—that either offered abortions or discussed abortions were prohibited from receiving funding.

In a similar vein, the Bush administration opposed funding international organizations that supported abortion, under what was officially known as the Mexico City policy and unofficially as the "global gag rule."[66] Only two days after taking office, Bush directed the U.S. Agency for International Development (USAID) to deny funds to any nongovernmental international organization that advocated abortion, saying in his directive, "It is my conviction that taxpayer funds should not be used to pay for abortions or advocate or actively promote abortion, either here or abroad."[67] Anti-abortion policies became a central theme in Bush's domestic and international programming.

His opposition to abortion led to federal funding for group maternity homes for pregnant teenagers, through Wade Horn's Administration for Children and Families in HHS. In his reelection campaign, Bush specifically stated that abortion was not the answer to teen pregnancies, but that maternity group homes and adoption were good alternatives.[68] He offered support for adoption, urging a $5,000 tax credit for families who adopted, and used the Administration for Children and Families to promote programs for adoption, parenting courses, and a Safe and Stable Families program. Bush used his executive authority to decree an annual National Adoption Month—linking adoption, as he had marriage, to the creation of a stable family.

While he supported marriage, committed fatherhood, and adoption, Bush vigorously opposed any policy that allowed for abortion or for embryonic destruction. He opposed the Supreme Court's decision in *Roe v. Wade* and often said that he wanted it overturned. In 2004, in Tempe, Arizona, at the third presidential debate, the moderator directly asked Bush if he would hold his Supreme Court appointments to a commitment against abortion:

MODERATOR: [Senator Kerry] claims that you never said whether you would like to overturn *Roe v. Wade*. Would you?

BUSH: What he's asking me is, will I have a litmus test for my judges? And the answer is I will not have a litmus test. I will pick judges who will interpret the Constitution, but I'll have no litmus test.[69]

His appointments to the Supreme Court—John Roberts and Samuel Alito—said in their confirmation hearings that they would be strict constructionists in interpreting the Constitution. This was an affirmation that they agreed with Bush. *Roe v. Wade*, they believed, had been decided outside the constructionist view of the Constitution and could be reevaluated by a new court. This was as clear a litmus test as possible for Supreme Court nominees.

Justices Roberts and Alito were the most visible of the pro-life appointments George W. Bush made, but their views were typical of an administration that had little tolerance for anyone who did not have pro-life views. Nearly every job within the administration was filled by a person who opposed abortion. Cheney, who shared Bush's pro-life ideology, ensured that appointments were ideologically in tune with the administration in filling positions during the transition.

All senior staff, from the White House to the cabinet—with the exception of Colin Powell and later Tom Ridge—as well as nearly the entire subcabinet adhered to the pro-life culture. At the helm of HHS was former governor Tommy Thompson, who had actively worked to limit abortions in Wisconsin. Appointments at HHS included Eric Keroack, heading the division in charge of family planning programs. Keroack had been medical director of a Christian pregnancy counseling service in Massachusetts that provided adoption, not abortion, counseling. As expected, Planned Parenthood strongly opposed the Keroack appointment, saying it was "striking proof that the Bush administration remains dramatically out of step with the nation's priorities."[70]

The Bush administration opposed abortion at any stage of pregnancy. When Congress passed a law in 2003 banning late-term, often referred to as "partial birth," abortion, Bush enthusiastically signed the bill in a very public ceremony in the Reagan Building. Surrounding him, against a backdrop of American flags, were a host of House and Senate members who had worked on the bill's behalf. In signing the law, Bush emphasized that he was "protecting innocent new life from this practice," stating that the law "reflects the compassion and humanity of America."[71] The theme of compassion, often absent in presidential rhetoric since the election campaign, was rekindled here.

Another aspect of the abortion debate was evident in administration opposition to the Food and Drug Administration's approval of Plan B®, the "morning after" contraceptive pill, widely used in thirty countries, including France and England. The administration took the position that Plan B® should be equated with abortion, because it would cause, as Bush said, "more people to have abortions."[72] When Barr Pharmaceuticals, the drug's manufacturer, asked the Food and Drug Administration (FDA) for approval to sell it in the United States, several administration officials in HHS voiced a related concern—that its availability would affect teens' sexual behavior. This argument followed the administration's general moral philosophy, which fostered an abstinence-only policy and limited materials on contraception made available for teenagers.

Career FDA scientists overwhelmingly supported the approval of Plan B® and urged the FDA director, a political appointee, to approve it. He did not. Two years later the drug was again considered for FDA approval. After significant pressure, it was finally approved, with the stipulation that it would be available without prescription only to women eighteen years of age and older.

The uproar over the approval of Plan B® led to the resignation of a career scientist—the director of the Office of Women's Health at the FDA—who accused the White House of applying political pressure on issues related to women's health. One group, the Center for

Reproductive Rights, sued the FDA to determine whether scientific evidence from staff scientists in favor of approving Plan B® had been overruled by political appointees. In a deposition, evidence emerged that the director, Dr. Steven Galson, believed that he had had no choice but to reject Plan B® if he wanted to retain his job.[73] Once again, religious views were interwoven with, and often controlled, policy making in the Bush administration.

Closely related to Bush's opposition to abortion was his opposition to embryonic stem cell research. For the president, this was a moral, not a scientific, issue "at the leading edge of a series of moral hazards." The immorality of the issue centered on the destruction of embryos, since, he explained, "human life is a sacred gift from our Creator."[74] All federally funded research using embryonic stem cells would end, Bush declared, and only privately funded research would be able to continue. The National Institutes of Health would be directed to end its research, as would all universities and medical centers receiving federal funding for this work.

To validate his position that stem cell research was unethical and immoral, Bush created the President's Council on Bioethics, naming as chair Dr. Leon Kass of the University of Chicago. The council was anything but objective. Kass had frequently written against cloning and stem cell research, and other appointees to the council were screened carefully to ensure their consistency with Bush's position. They included Ben Carson, a Johns Hopkins University physician known for supporting religious values in public life; Peter Lawler, who publicly praised Kass's work; and Diana Schaub, who described embryonic research as evil. When Kass first convened the council, he asked each member to read Nathaniel Hawthorne's short story "The Birthmark," in which a young girl with a birthmark on her face is viewed as imperfect. Kass suggested that society should not approach imperfection as a problem, muting arguments for stem cell research or altering human life in any way.[75]

Congress, however, after intense lobbying from the public, finally passed legislation to support federally funded stem cell research. Needless to say, Bush vowed to veto the legislation. He did so with the full fanfare normally reserved for the signing of major administration-supported legislation. In an elaborate East Room ceremony in the White House, parents were holding babies who had been born through in vitro fertilization, using "adopted embryos"—underscoring Bush's position that embryonic destruction was the destruction of human life.[76] This was a morality question for George W. Bush, and he would never waver on moral issues.

For Bush, being a conservative meant more than reducing the size of government and lowering taxes. It meant building a moral and civil society, with the help of the federal government and its programs. In the moral and civil society that Bush sought to create for America, religious organizations were not discriminated against and would have full access to government monies. His faith-based civil society involved a call to volunteerism, engaging citizens to help each other in their own communities. In Bush's vision of a moral and civil society, families had mothers and fathers, the sanctity of human life was protected, and sex was acceptable only within marriage.

Nothing facilitated Dick Cheney's dramatic rise to power in the Bush administration more than the private and public role that God and religion played in George W. Bush's life. Whatever was not directly part of Bush's mission from God—and that proved to be a significant part of administration policy making—could be handled by the vice president in the co-presidency's division of labor.

CHAPTER 6

Dick Cheney and the
Business-Friendly Presidency

W HILE GEORGE W. BUSH focused on the faith-based presidency,
Dick Cheney moved forward his business-friendly agenda, designing policies that protected business and industry from what he
believed was an intrusive regulatory environment. Cheney shared
many of Bush's moral tenets, and his compassionate conservatism
was equally personal, although less public. He supported prayer in
public schools and amending the Constitution to ban same-sex marriage, while saying little about his daughter Mary, who was involved
in a same-sex relationship.

But Cheney's eight-year experience in the private sector had rekindled his outrage at the control that the federal government exerted
over business. In his view, government was often a burden on free
enterprise. He had consistently taken this position as White House
chief of staff, congressman from Wyoming, and secretary of defense.
Cheney's priority as vice president would be to use the resources of
his vice presidency to reduce the burden of government on the private
sector.[1] Topping his agenda was a plan to control federal agencies
that oversaw energy-related and environmental regulations, which he
considered some of the most onerous for business. As the former chief
executive of Halliburton, who continued to receive deferred compensa-
tion even as vice president, Cheney was intimately aware of the costs
that environmental regulations imposed on the energy-related mining,
oil, and gas industries.

To move forward his business-friendly agenda for the administration, Cheney developed a multi-pronged strategy. First, he would use
the appointment process to control policy making and reverse many
of the Clinton-era regulations. Second, he would support increased
privatization of government programs to reduce the ranks of permanent government personnel. Third, he would encourage Bush to use

tools such as signing statements to block unfavorable and intrusive legislative actions.

Cheney was not alone in his drive to move forward a business-friendly administration. The millions of dollars that business executives contributed to the Bush-Cheney campaign—many through $100,000 donations to its Pioneer Club—were aimed at putting a pro-business administration into office. Pro-business policies were also supported during the election by conservative think tanks, such as the Heritage Foundation. Its 300-page blueprint for the Bush-Cheney campaign, *Priorities for the President*, contained detailed recommendations on how to rein in the federal government. Chief among its demands was controlling what it called the burden of government—oppressive regulation of business.[2]

Cheney's principal strategy to advance his business-friendly agenda was to control the appointment process. His appointees would, in turn, then control the regulatory process. Using his hiring power during the transition, Cheney peppered executive agencies with political appointees who were in tune with his pro-business orientation. When he needed someone to manage surface mines, he turned to the mining industry. When he needed someone to manage the national parks, he drew from the logging industry. When he needed someone to manage environmental policy, he looked to the energy industry. Nearly all who managed policy areas that involved energy and environmental regulation came from the industries subject to regulation.

The hiring process took several months. Nothing in government was accomplished quickly, and hiring was always a slow process. Administration appointees needed to be vetted through the normal political process and by the FBI, had to sell their homes, and then move with their families to the nation's capital. Once hired and at their desks, it again took several months for political appointees to begin revising regulations. In many programs, the process of revising regulations had only been under way for a few months by September 11, 2001, when the terrorist attacks changed the course of history.

From that moment on, the Bush administration had free rein to rewrite regulations, because no one was watching. The national press turned its attention away from monitoring the administration's decision making and focused on the newly declared war on terror. Any interest the press might have had in pro-business regulatory changes disappeared. With little press coverage, few people knew about the regulatory actions under way, except those who read the *Federal Register* and knew what they were looking for, such as paid lobbyists.

Not surprisingly, the administration made no attempt to call attention to the regulatory changes. There were no press releases by the agencies or the White House, and no press conferences were called by cabinet officers. Unless someone in the press discovered, or a public interest group protested, that a regulation was being changed, the issue essentially remained off the public radar. Whenever there was some scant media attention, the president's press secretary responded with statements touting the economic value of regulatory change. "The president's policies have put us on a path to greater prosperity," he declared. "We need to pursue pro-growth policies . . . that keep taxes low and that eliminate burdensome regulations."[3] The administration's message was clear—reducing burdensome regulations would allow the economy to thrive, despite attempts by terrorists to destroy the economy and nation.

On July 14, 2004, nearly three years after the terrorist attacks, the *New York Times* ran one of the few significant investigative analyses about the massive changes being made to the federal regulatory process. With the headline "Out of Spotlight, Bush Overhauls U.S. Regulations," the article detailed the wide range of regulations the Bush administration was changing in its pro-business tilt.[4]

During the course of working on the article, the reporter asked John D. Graham, in charge of regulatory affairs for the White House in the Office of Management and Budget (OMB), if it was indeed true that regulatory changes had a distinctly pro-business bias. Graham didn't argue the point or suggest that the changes would benefit any other constituencies. He was, in fact, confirming the pro-business tilt.

Graham was one of many pro-business Cheney appointees. Before being named the administrator for the Office of Information and Regulatory Affairs (OIRA) in OMB, Graham had been on the faculty of

Harvard University, whose Center for Risk Analysis he directed. His appointment was strongly opposed by a host of scientists, university faculty, and public interest groups who challenged a study that he authored on the health risks from industrial pollution. Among those opposed to Graham's appointment was the Center for Science in the Public Interest (CSPI), which sent Bush a letter detailing its concerns about the pro-business orientation of the nation's new chief regulator. Central to their argument was that "Graham's preoccupation with risk-benefit analysis" could reverse existing regulations:

Under Dr. Graham's direction the HCRA [Harvard Center for Risk Analysis] has received substantial funding from government and from such corporate entities as the American Petroleum Institute, Association of American Railroads, Boise Cascade Corporation, Ford Motor Company, Goodyear Tire & Rubber Company, Kraft Foods, Merck & Company, Monsanto Company, Dow Chemical Company, Frito-Lay, Novartis Corporation, Pfizer, and the Union Carbide Foundation. That funding suggests an allegiance to corporate interests that would be improper for the director of OIRA. More troubling, and as documented in the Public Citizen report, Dr. Graham's and HCRA's positions, studies, speeches, and testimonies all too regularly support the positions of their industry funders.

We are concerned that Dr. Graham's preoccupation with risk-benefit analyses will be invoked to prevent many vitally important regulations. Artfully chosen assumptions may be used by industry to create misleading estimates of risks and benefits that could then be used as an excuse to undermine needed regulations. Moreover, while risk-benefit analyses can be useful, too often they are inappropriate or impossible to conduct. The inability to conduct accurate analyses could be used to prevent the adoption of important federal regulations that could provide significant—but nonquantifiable—health and environmental benefits. For instance, protecting wilderness areas and improving the utility of food labels are perceived by the general public as beneficial, but may reflect values that do not lend themselves to computation on an economist's calculator.[5]

CSPI's view that the administration would make regulatory decisions based on pro-business risk-benefit data proved warranted only days after the administration took office. In January 2001, the Environmental Protection Agency (EPA) stopped a key regulatory change initiated, but not completed, by the Clinton administration, which would have reduced acceptable levels of arsenic in drinking water from 50 to 10 parts per billion. Arsenic was a by-product of mining, among other industries, and the regulatory change would have led to millions of dollars in new costs to reduce mining by-products that entered streams. The wood products industry also used arsenic to pressure-treat wood, and the change would, similarly, have added costs to scrub waste material before it entered the water supply.

As could be expected, the National Mining Association lobbied heavily against the new regulation. It issued a statement implying that the Clinton administration's decision to reduce acceptable levels of arsenic had no scientific data to support its position. "We felt all along," the mining association said, "that it was really a political decision unsupported by science."[6] Questions about the accuracy of the scientific data, as in the arsenic debate, became a continual flash point during the Bush administration. Industries joined the administration in contesting scientific data that supported existing or potential regulation.

The science on the arsenic issue, which the mining association had challenged, emerged from a major study conducted in 1999 by the National Academy of Sciences (NAS), which determined that the arsenic standard of fifty parts per billion would lead to a one-in-one-hundred risk of cancer. As a result, the Academy recommended the ten-parts-per-billion standard that the Environmental Protection Agency adopted during the Clinton administration—a standard that had already been adopted by the European Union and World Health Organization. The science indicated a clear health risk in elevated levels of arsenic in drinking water.

Rather than relying on the scientific data of the National Academy of Sciences showing a correlation between arsenic in drinking water and increased health risks, the Environmental Protection Agency based its decision on economic data provided by outside sources. One risk-benefit analysis cited by the EPA, which was co-authored by the American Enterprise Institute (AEI), stated that "in our estimate, net costs [of the rule change] are between $10 million and $200 million, and the cost-effectiveness is never less than $6.4 million per statistical life. In addition, the rule saves relatively few lives in all scenarios. With an affected population of about 10 million people, the risk reduction is about one in a million, which is so small as not to be worth addressing, given the uncertainties in the data and the EPA's limited resources to develop regulations."[7]

The most relevant part of the AEI analysis was the statement that "the rule saves relatively few lives," assessing the cost impact on mining and other industries as more relevant than the health risks *and potential deaths* that might result from higher arsenic levels. The EPA's political appointees chose to rely on these data, but the decision was strongly opposed by the agency's career staff, who had conducted their own studies supporting the ten-parts-per-billion standard. The issue reached the halls of Congress, leading Henry Waxman of California to admonish the Bush administration for its proposed arsenic rule change "revoking modern standards to protect the public from exposure to arsenic in drinking water."[8] After a public outcry, the EPA retreated from the proposal.

When Graham left OIRA, his replacement, Susan Dudley, faced the same stiff opposition from the public interest sector as had Graham. Dudley, director of regulatory affairs for the Mercatus Center at George Mason University, oversaw risk-analysis studies underwritten by corporate sponsors such as ExxonMobil and BP Amoco. Public Citizen and OMB Watch were among the public interest groups that opposed the nomination of Dudley in 2006, describing her as an "anti-regulatory zealot with close ties to corporate interests" who would "cripple critical safeguards that protect the public from such dangers as unsafe products and environmental toxins." In spite of their opposition, Dudley took the helm of OIRA.[9]

The EPA's actions on the arsenic rule were a powerful indicator of the influence that Cheney wielded in the administration as he moved forward his pro-business agenda. Central to this agenda was controlling the regulatory process, as the appointments of Graham and Dudley at OIRA proved. Although Cheney was interested in controlling the entire regulatory process as it affected the costs of doing business for the private sector, he was particularly focused on regulations that dealt with energy-related and environmental policy. Regulations affecting energy-related businesses, such as the mining, oil, and gas industries, topped his list of those that needed the administration's attention.

To tighten his grip on the environmental policy apparatus—particularly the EPA and Departments of the Interior and Agriculture—Cheney first needed to gain control of the White House Council on Environmental Quality (CEQ), which he could use to coordinate federal environmental policy. For the CEQ's senior staff, he chose lawyers, lobbyists, and energy executives who shared his passion for cutting regulation, especially for energy corporations. Some, such as CEQ chair James Connaughton, had spent much of their professional careers fighting environmental regulations. As a corporate lobbyist with the large Washington, D.C., law firm of Sidley, Austin, Brown and Wood, Connaughton had fought the environmental regulations that he now oversaw. Connaughton had repeatedly sued the Clinton administration over its stringent environmental rules.

Among his clients was General Electric (GE), which sued to overturn the EPA's Superfund requirements for the mounting clean-up costs of its eighty-six toxic waste sites. As one public interest group fighting GE said of the company's legal battle with the EPA, "unfortunately, many companies, including General Electric, the top Superfund polluter, have decided that it is better for business to spend money on lawyers and lobbyists and to avoid their responsibility to clean up these sites, while simultaneously they work to weaken the law designed to make them pay."[10] In addition to General Electric, Connaughton represented a host of other corporate clients such as the Chemical Manufacturers Association, which was lobbying to ease environmental regulations for its members. Cheney's decision to add Connaughton to the White House staff was a veiled admonition to the EPA to reconsider its Superfund policies.

To further ensure that the Council on Environmental Quality remained friendly to business and industry, Cheney approved Connaughton's choice for his chief of staff, Philip Cooney—a lobbyist from the

American Petroleum Institute (API) who had led the petroleum industry's opposition to legislative caps on greenhouse gases. Both Connaughton and Cooney would soon become key players in Cheney's war against burdensome government regulations. And they would work closely with Cheney as they pursued common goals.

Throughout his four years at CEQ, according to his own testimony at a congressional hearing in 2007, Cooney regularly worked with Cheney's office to edit documents from various agencies to lessen the severity of conclusions about greenhouse gases and global warming. Cooney noted in the hearing that he had had "numerous conversations with" and would often "consult with" Kevin O'Donovan in Cheney's office to "compare notes" on wording in global warming material prepared by agency scientists. The evidence of Cooney changing the wording in official documents was pervasive. According to Rick Piltz of the U.S. Climate Change Science Program, "he was passing a screen over the [climate change] report to introduce language into statements about global warming. The political motivation of it was obvious."[11] Cooney left the administration in 2005 for a senior position at ExxonMobil.

Cooney's ties to the API and his support for the energy industry proved critical for stopping legislation that the EPA set in motion soon after the 2001 terrorist attacks. The legislation would have expanded the EPA's authority to require chemical industries to create secure sites, hindering terrorists' access to hazardous chemicals. The president of the API, Red Cavaney, strongly opposed the legislation and successfully lobbied Connaughton and Cooney to rein in the EPA. The agency retreated, and another regulation that would have cost business more money was stopped in its tracks because Cheney had put the right people in the right jobs.

Bush's complete lack of interest in the bureaucratic agencies involved in environmental policy made it much easier for Cheney to control them. Cheney understood the role that the CEQ could play in managing environmental policy, for example, but Bush knew nothing about it—perhaps not surprisingly, since his father had virtually ignored it. When Christine Todd Whitman, the EPA administrator, asked Bush for assurances that the CEQ would not dictate policy to her or her agency, he replied, "What's CEQ?"[12] As Whitman feared, however, Cheney and the CEQ did gain control over the EPA. She resigned two years later, after repeatedly losing policy battles to Cheney and Connaughton. Whitman was regularly undercut by the White House, including both Connaughton and Cheney. Soon after she had been in Europe meeting with European leaders and promising that the new administration would address global warming, she was told by Cheney that he would oversee the issue, not EPA. One national magazine observed of the relationship between the EPA and the White House that "it has become conventional wisdom that Whitman was consistently undercut by White House officials."[13]

Cheney extended his control over environmental and energy policy by supporting the nomination of Michigan's Senator Spencer Abraham, defeated in his 2000 reelection bid for the Senate, as secretary of energy. Abraham, in turn, chose as his deputy, Francis S. Blake, the general counsel of General Electric, who had worked closely with Connaughton on the Superfund litigation. In the early months of the administration, Abraham became one of Cheney's key allies as they worked together to prepare the National Energy Plan.

Their Energy Task Force—the National Energy Plan Development Group (NEPDG)—was overseen by a six-member staff in the vice president's office, managed by Andrew D. Lundquist, the Bush campaign's energy expert and a former staffer for Republican senators Ted Stevens and Frank Murkowski of Alaska. Created by executive order, the Energy Task Force formally included the secretaries of energy, interior, treasury, commerce, and transportation, the administrator of the EPA, the director of the Federal Emergency Management Agency, and three members of the White House senior staff. Cheney chaired the task force and managed the staff in his ceremonial office in the Old Executive Office Building and began meeting with a host of energy executives.

Chevron provided its own detailed energy plan to the group, since it had long-standing connections with Cheney, through Halliburton's multi-million dollar contracts, and Condoleezza Rice, who sat on its board for ten years before joining the Bush administration. In an astounding act of hubris, API president Red Cavaney came to one of the meetings armed with his own suggestion for an executive order that would open new federal lands for oil drilling.[14] Other companies also had significant access to the task force. The chairman of Royal Dutch Shell Group, Sir Mark Moody-Stuart, and Shell chairman Steven Miller met with the NEPDG. John Brown, chief executive of BP America, met privately with Cheney, although the meeting was not included among the documents of task force meetings.[15]

The list of private advisors to Cheney and Lundquist on the Energy Task Force included James J. Rouse, vice president of ExxonMobil, and Enron's chief executive, Kenneth Lay. Representatives of the National Mining Association and the Interstate Natural Gas Association of America were among the dozens of energy trade groups that also met with the NEPDG. Participants invited to meet with Cheney came largely from contributors to the Bush-Cheney campaign and members of the Cheney-created energy advisory team during the transition. While a few environmental groups were consulted at the end of the process, their views carried little weight.

After deliberating for just over three months, the Energy Task Force issued its report to the president on May 17, 2001. The cover letter from Cheney explained that the energy plan was premised on "increasing our energy supplies," a straightforward reference to increased domestic oil and gas drilling.[16] The plan had few proposals for energy conservation or developing alternative energy sources and primarily focused on expanding domestic oil production. The energy plan that finally developed, after four months of meetings, included $33 billion in subsidies and tax credits for the nuclear, oil, and coal industries and a recommendation to open the Arctic National Wildlife Refuge to oil drilling.[17]

As Cheney asserted in April 2001, before the plan was completed, "whatever our hopes for developing alternative sources and for conserving energy, the reality is that fossil fuels supply virtually a hundred percent of our transportation needs, and an overwhelming share of our electricity requirements. For years down the road, this will continue to be true."[18] Despite their pretense of examining alternative sources of energy, Cheney and the task force members were committed to an energy plan dependent on fossil fuel, such as oil and natural gas, and on nuclear energy. And they were committed to reducing the regulatory constraints on the energy industry and to opening federal lands for new oil and gas drilling. Among the many regulations that the task force wanted to change were those that blocked drilling for natural gas in the 600,000 acres of the Jack Morrow Hills in Wyoming's Red Desert.[19]

Environmental groups complained that the Energy Task Force had listened primarily to energy executives in its closed-door hearings.[20] In April 2001, as word of the NEPDG proposals leaked, Congressmen Henry Waxman of California and John Dingell of Michigan asked the General Accounting Office (known since 2004 as the Government Accountability Office, GAO) to examine the list of task force participants to determine how influential energy companies had been as Cheney crafted his energy plan. Cheney's legal counsel, David Addington, refused to provide the GAO with any information on the deliberations of the Energy Task Force or the role played by its nongovernmental participants, asserting that the vice president was constitutionally protected from the requirement to divulge whom he met with or why.

After the energy plan had been completed, Waxman and Dingell continued their quest for information on the plan's development. In January 2002, Waxman asked Cheney for specific information on meetings between the Energy Task Force and Enron executives. Addington again responded for Cheney, stating in a letter that the vice president had had only one meeting with Kenneth Lay and that staff had had several meetings with Enron executives. As Addington's letter concluded curtly, "it is our hope that submission of the information will help you avoid the waste of time and taxpayer funds on unnecessary inquiries."[21]

Faced with Cheney's refusal to divulge the names of the Energy Task Force participants, or any other information, to members of Congress, the GAO's comptroller general, David Walker, sued Cheney for the information.[22] While it is common for environmental groups to file lawsuits against agencies in order to rescind regulatory actions, it is uncommon for lawsuits to be filed against the vice president for his role in the regulatory process. In what would turn out to be the first of many lawsuits brought against Cheney, Walker sued for information on the composition of the Energy Task Force, concerned that it had been dominated by corporate interests.

The decision took a year, but in December 2002, U.S. District Court judge John D. Bates—appointed to the bench by George W. Bush in 2001—dismissed the lawsuit, ruling that the GAO had no standing to sue, since neither house of Congress nor any committee had issued a subpoena for the material. Cheney, Bates determined, did not have to release the names of task force participants. The remedy, Bates suggested, was for House members to subpoena the information and, when that failed, to return to court.[23]

At about the same time that the GAO was pursuing its case, the Natural Resources Defense Council (NRDC) was seeking similar material on the Energy Task Force participants through a Freedom of Information Act lawsuit. Through that lawsuit, some of the names of task force participants were finally made public, although "scrubbed," as the NRDC called it. As Waxman, Dingell, and many environmentalists had long suspected, energy executives dominated the list. In a one-sided process of information-gathering, Cheney and Abraham had met with four hundred individuals from one hundred and fifty energy companies, trade organizations, and lobbyists, but few representatives of environmental organizations.[24] According to the task force's own description, the list of meeting participants included several "other groups"—a smattering of environmental organizations whose advice it quickly discounted.

To complete the transformation of the nation's energy agenda, Cheney and Abraham reframed the mission of the Department of Energy from energy research and development to, as they phrased it, energy security. When the department was created by Congress in 1977 at the instigation of the Carter administration after the oil crisis, its purpose was to bring the Federal Energy Administration, the Energy Research and Development Administration, and other energy-related agencies together in one federal department. Its mission was also to encourage energy conservation, reduce fossil-fuel dependency, make alternative sources of energy viable, and find new technologies to power automobiles, industry, and homes.

Once the Energy Task Force completed its recommendations for increasing domestic drilling on public lands, the White House issued an executive order that all federal agencies identify opportunities "to expedite projects that will increase the production of energy."[25] Drilling in Wyoming's Red Desert, for example, could move forward. Decisions on environmental policy were no longer based on protecting public lands from environmental harm or degradation; they were driven by Cheney's energy plan.

One of the recommendations to emerge from Cheney's Energy Task Force was for the Energy Department, rather than the Environmental Protection Agency, to take the lead role in exploring ways to amend the Clean Air Act. Meeting the strict regulations of the Clean Air Act had been a costly problem for energy-related companies, which now saw the possibility of amending the law to reduce their current and future costs. The amendment to the Clean Air Act that the Energy Department ultimately developed was created in consultation with, and with the blessing of, James Connaughton at the Council on Environmental Quality. It sought to overturn the required investment of millions of dollars in modernizing pollution systems when industries invested in broad facility modernization.[26]

Stemming from legislation passed by Congress in 1977, the existing regulations, known as the new source review, required power plants that upgraded their facilities to install the most modern pollution control technology available. Congress hoped that this would allow power plants to build the necessary capital for upgrading over a number of years, instead of requiring them to install expensive pollution-control technology in the short term. Coal-fired power plants—the mainstay of most electric companies—were especially hard hit by the new source review requirements. Power plants balked at the regulations, preferring to update their facilities without installing the expensive pollution technology. Edison Electric, one of the nation's largest producers of electricity, was a vociferous opponent of the regulations, decrying the new source review requirements as "one of the most burdensome programs of the federal Clean Air Act."[27]

In February 2002, the Energy Department proposed that the Clean Air Act be amended to allow power plants, refineries, steel mills, and other similar industries to upgrade their plants without modernizing their pollution systems. Connaughton named these proposed amendments the Clear Skies Initiative, implying that the amendments would lead to less pollution, a cleaner environment, and "clear skies." The changes, however, were bitterly opposed by environmental groups. Many, including the NRDC, accused the administration of endorsing a change in policy that "would roll back the current law's public health safeguards protecting local air quality, curbing pollution from upwind states, and restoring visibility to our national parks."[28]

The NRDC and many other environmental groups saw the Clear Skies Initiative as an assault on the Clean Air Act that benefited industries affected by its regulations. When the White House released a statement in February 2002 describing the Clear Skies Initiative—which provided for existing levels of power-plant pollutants to remain in effect until 2015 rather than 2007—it emphasized the importance of protecting the industry's economic security. "President Bush has often said that environmental protection and energy production are not competing priorities. We can meet our environmental goals while providing affordable electricity for American consumers and American businesses."[29] According to the White House, power plant costs would start to skyrocket without relief from the Clean Air Act amendments. As in the controversy over arsenic levels in drinking water, economic considerations trumped health risks in the administration's cost-benefit analyses.

When the tide of public opinion seemed to be turning against the Clear Skies Initiative, Bush began to make a series of speeches that reframed the discussion from industrywide economic security to the individual economic security of power plant workers. If power plants could not operate economically, he argued, jobs in that energy industry would have to be cut. In a visit to Detroit Edison's plant in Monroe,

Michigan—one of the three largest coal-burning power plants in the country—Bush suggested that plant closures and job losses would inevitably result from the Clean Air Act's environmental demands. The Clear Skies amendments were critical, he suggested, to keep the power plants operating. "It makes sense to change the regulations," Bush told the plant employees. "The rules put up too many hurdles. And that hurts the working people. We trust the people in this plant to make the right decision."[30] Regardless of whether the issue was framed around the economic health of employers or employees, economics trumped environmental health as the standard in the Bush administration.

When changes to the arsenic rule in 2001 had been blocked because economic health seemed to trump personal health, the administration learned to reframe its arguments for regulatory change around the economic health of workers, not industrywide economic health. In order to convince the public and Congress that the new source review should be modified through the Clear Skies amendments, Bush and Cheney needed to frame their argument around the economic health of the workers, which they did. As Bush said in Michigan, "The rules hurt . . . the working people."

Rule changes, however, had only been possible because of Cheney's careful attention to the appointment process, which created departments with a pro-business, pro-energy tilt. Although the energy plan laid the groundwork, the departments would need to manage the process. While the Energy Department was central to his plan, the Department of the Interior also held the keys to building a pro-business environment. Cheney selected Gale Norton as secretary of the interior. Norton, who at one time supported the abolition of the Interior Department because she believed it to be overregulated, had a long history of anti-environmental positions. As deputy solicitor for the Department of Agriculture under Reagan, she supported drilling in Alaska's Arctic National Wildlife Reserve (ANWR). She was well known for her positions on individual property rights, such as her opposition to environmental restrictions on private property. At one point in her career, she even supported selling fish and wildlife refuges and abolishing the Interior Department's Bureau of Land Management (BLM).

Cheney, as the member of Congress from Wyoming, had been well aware, if not fully supportive, of Norton's positions during her earlier career. After she took charge of the Interior Department, she continued to be vocal about controlling government's regulatory power. And she continued to criticize government's regulatory power. "My experience as a Westerner," she said in July 2005, "was that decisions were made too often in Washington without understanding that the effect is a lot different in the West. I think that government ought to be limited."[31] Norton focused on individual rights, while Cheney focused on corporate rights. But their views were complementary and a powerful roadblock to environmentalists seeking regulatory action.

Norton was never shy about her approach to managing the Interior Department, particularly in opening federal lands to private and commercial use. In her confirmation hearings before the Senate Energy and Natural Resources Committee, she said that it was essential to "forge partnerships with interested citizens" in the "conservation of America's natural resources." She wanted, she said, "to think outside the usual boxes," boxes that had been created by the department's career staff.[32] In other words, she intended to work with business interests to craft policies for the Interior Department that allowed greater private and commercial use of public lands.

During Norton's tenure at Interior, regulations were changed to benefit business and industry and rarely to support environmental protection. Only weeks after taking office, she focused on Bill Clinton's designation of five million acres of federal land as national monuments. Since there was little she could do to overturn the designations, she created policies to allow commercial activities within those areas. In April 2002, the Interior Department published regulations in the *Federal Register* asking for public comment on managing the land in the new national monuments. "Our door is open," announced BLM director Kathleen Clarke, whose office managed 700 million acres of subsurface mineral resources on federal lands and 250 million acres of natural resources in national parks. "If the planning and management process for the monuments is to be effective, we must make sure it is citizen centered."[33]

This meant, in effect, that the private sector would be granted leeway in deciding how national monuments were to accommodate commercial activities. Clarke, a former staffer for Utah's Governor Michael Leavitt, subsequently rewrote the rules to give business greater access to the five million acres. It was another success story for Cheney in his drive to use the regulatory process to help, rather than control, business.

The list of pro-business appointees in the Department of the Interior was extensive, starting at the top with Norton and her deputy, Steven Griles. Griles was the co-owner of a Washington, D.C., lobbying firm, National Environmental Strategies, whose largest client was the coal-mining industry. After environmental groups complained that Griles would be working closely with mining executives on policy issues, he signed a statement that he would recuse himself for a year in any department decisions involving former clients. When evidence later surfaced that he had, in fact, been meeting with a former client—Harold Quinn Jr., president of the National Mining Association—Friends of the Earth, an environmental activist group, sued under the Freedom of Information Act for Griles's daily schedule.[34] Not surprisingly, it provided ample evidence of meetings with former clients and lobbyists, including Jack Abramoff.

During the transition, Abramoff had cleverly found a way to be included as a member of the Interior Department's advisory task force, giving him access to senior staff such as Griles within the department.[35] Abramoff met frequently with Griles to seek help for clients, especially Indian tribes with casino operations, permitted under the 1988 Indian Gaming Regulatory Act. The law allowed tribes to build gambling casinos on their reservations, within rules established by the Department of the Interior.

The relationship between Griles and Abramoff ended badly for both. Griles was eventually sentenced to federal prison, convicted of lying to Congress and a federal grand jury about his relationship with Abramoff. The federal judge was so outraged by Griles's misuse of the public trust that he doubled the five-month sentence recommended by the prosecution and sent him to prison for ten months. Abramoff, as it turned out, had made $84 million from his dealings with the Indian casinos. He was convicted of influence peddling and bribery and sentenced to eleven years in federal prison.[36]

Although many of the same allegations against Griles had been made earlier, Norton refused to fire Griles. In 2004, Earl Devaney, the Department of the Interior's inspector general, referred twenty-five possible ethics violations by Griles to the Office of Government Ethics (OGE), an independent federal watchdog agency. Griles was cleared by OGE of twenty-three of the violations, and the remaining two were referred to Norton, who refused to take any action against Griles. When Griles was finally convicted by the federal court in 2007, Devaney released a statement that said: "Today's guilty plea clearly establishes that former deputy secretary J. Steven Griles was ready and willing to serve as Jack Abramoff's 'man inside Interior.' In retrospect, all the warning signs were there. In March of 2004, my Office publicly released the results of our two year investigation that detailed Griles' ethical lapses; a report that was virtually ignored."[37]

The pro-business staff that Cheney built in the Department of the Interior included a host of energy executives, including Jeffrey Jarrett, a Cravat Coal Company executive, who was named to head the department's Office of Surface Mining. To many observers, his appointment resembled putting a fox in charge of the hen house. With deliberate intent during the transition, Cheney had ensured that the top regulators for mining—Griles and Jarrett—were both representatives of the mining industry.

One of the earliest changes Jarrett made was to reduce the mining reclamation budget; cleaning up abandoned mines would no longer be a federal priority. The Clinton administration's final budget provided $309 million for mining reclamation, but the Bush administration's first budget reduced that amount by $40 million. Budget priorities were one predictor of the administration's policy orientation toward the mining companies; others were regulatory changes that enhanced mining companies' profits. Among the most important of the department's actions were regulations written by the Army Corps of Engineers, in association with the Office of Surface Mining, that allowed mountaintop dirt removed by mining to flow down mountainsides into streams instead of being hauled away.

Environmental groups sued in federal court to block enforcement of the new regulation on mountaintop dirt removal, and in May 2002, a federal judge ruled that the administration had violated the Clean Water Act of 1972. According to U.S. District judge Charles H. Haden II in Charleston, West Virginia, "this obviously absurd exception [for the mining industry] would turn the Clean Water Act on its head and use it to authorize polluting and destroying the nation's waters for no reason but waste disposal." He added: "The regulators' practice is illegal because it is contrary to the spirit and the letter of the Clean Water Act."[38] In spite of the administration's best efforts, mining companies would now be forced to incur greater costs to haul away the removal dirt and coal by-products.

The Department of the Interior pursued other regulatory changes, particularly within the National Park Service. Norton put in place regulations that allowed private companies to build new roads through national parks for mining, logging, and oil drilling.[39] Previous departmental regulations had allowed these operations only where roads already existed, in order to protect forests in national parks from further degradation. Needless to say, the new regulations were a boon for the mining and oil industries, which had lobbied the department to increase their access to federal lands.

Ironically, many career staff in the park service objected to the expansion of commercial development. However, jurisdiction for those decisions fell to the Bureau of Land Management, whose priorities had tilted toward business rather than environmental considerations. Those priorities were driven by a directive from Gale Norton to all of the divisions within the Interior Department, which stated that all regulatory actions should "expand energy supplies," as Cheney's energy plan required.[40]

One of the most controversial commercial developments in the national parks was oil and gas drilling, which the administration aggressively pursued as part of Cheney's energy plan. Everglades National Park added off-shore drilling leases to its available inventory; in Utah's

Canyonlands National Park, the sale of new oil and gas leases went forward; and in Montana's Upper Missouri River Breaks National Monument, leases for eight natural gas wells were approved. In one month alone during 2005, drilling leases were sold for 232,000 acres of Utah's national parks.[41]

Norton also reversed Clinton-era regulations that banned snowmobiles from national parks. Despite objections from environmental groups that the vehicles produced damaging emissions, the Interior Department opened Yellowstone and Grand Teton National Parks to snowmobiling. Again, the department's decision was met by a legal challenge. The Greater Yellowstone Coalition of Bozeman, Montana, argued in federal court that the Interior Department's internal investigation, headed by new political appointees, ignored its own data that snowmobiles were harmful to the environment, insisting instead that snowmobiles would have "no adverse impact on the air quality, wildlife and natural soundscapes" in the two national parks where they would be allowed.[42]

The conflict centered on the issue of whether snowmobiles used in national parks would feature new engine technology, reducing the level of pollutants in their emissions. In rejecting the regulatory change, U.S. District Court judge Emmit Sullivan agreed with environmental groups in 2003 that snowmobiling without the new technology was environmentally hazardous. A compromise later allowed commercial vendors to run snowmobiling trips in the parks with upgraded vehicles. When the issue was revisited in 2008, Judge Sullivan restated his decision to limit snowmobiling in the national parks.[43]

Cheney's influence in changing the regulatory landscape to support business and industry permeated every agency that dealt with energy and environmental policy, as the examples of the agencies within the Department of the Interior portray. But other agencies across the administration were equally impacted by the pro-business tilt in regulatory policy. The Forest Service, for example, reframed its regulations to benefit certain industries, especially timber and energy industries. Part of the Department of Agriculture, the Forest Service controlled over 193 million acres of national forests. Its director, Mark Rey, undersecretary for natural resources and environment, had been the chief lobbyist for the timber industry, working for the corporations that he was now regulating. Rey advocated logging on federal lands and opening the national forest system to oil and gas drilling. This was another case of putting a fox in charge of the hen house.

According to the agency's long-held official mission statement, the goal of the Forest Service was "to manage all of the various renewable surface resources of the National Forests so that they are utilized in the combination that will best meet the needs of the American people." During the Clinton administration and previous administrations, the phrase "will best meet" meant protecting the environment. Under the Bush administration, the phrase "will best meet" meant meeting energy needs. Like public land held by the National Park Service, public land held by the Forest Service was opened to gas and oil exploration and drilling under this new interpretation. Federal lands had become an energy resource.

The Bush administration, moreover, proposed changes in logging regulations. Since 1970, loggers, and other commercial interests, had to prepare environmental impact statements and gain federal approval before exploiting forest resources. As part of the National Park Service's Healthy Forests Initiative, a plan that allowed loggers to thin national forests for wildfire management, ten million acres were exempted from environmental impact statements.[44]

Clear-cutting and other types of logging were also exempted in numerous national forest lands. As a result, loggers were allowed to use whatever size trucks and equipment, with whatever sized wheels and as many loggers as they wanted, and without concern for wildlife, vegetation, or endangered species. With no environmental assessments and no rules to govern logging, costs could be contained. Ironically, under the Healthy Forests Initiative, in the absence of environmental impact statements, the health of the forests was at risk. Connaughton championed the logging plan and had been the one to coin the phrase "Healthy Forests Initiative."

Cheney's influence in changing the regulatory landscape had been most pronounced in controlling appointments to the environmental policy network in the Council on Environmental Quality, Environmental Protection Agency, and the Departments of Energy, Interior, and Agriculture. As was to be expected, policies from these agencies had a decidedly pro-business tilt. However, just as important to building his pro-business administration was controlling the Office of Management and Budget (OMB), since it had final review of all proposed regulatory changes. Cheney's insistence on controlling OMB resonated with approval through the business community. Bruce Josten, the executive vice president for government affairs of the U.S. Chamber of Commerce, said soon after the administration took office that "[i]f you fix [OMB], you rein in all the agencies."[45]

Although Cheney had little direct input into agency regulations, a pro-business OMB did and could support his overall agenda. If OMB determined that a regulation was too onerous for business, it could terminate the rule before it became final—power that made it critical to Dick Cheney's control. The choice of Graham and Dudley for OIRA within OMB was central to Cheney's plan for moving forward the business-friendly agenda.

To run OMB, Cheney recommended Mitchell Daniels, who was once referred to as "Dick Cheney's Dick Cheney." Daniels became, according to Nicholas Thompson in the *Washington Monthly*, "the most powerful man in the Bush administration that you have never heard of."[46] Daniels, he added, "bears an uncanny resemblance to Dick Cheney. Like Cheney, he's calm, unassuming, likable, self-deprecating, and very smart." The vice president of the Indianapolis-based pharmaceutical company Eli Lilly, Daniels had spent two uneasy years in the Reagan White House as political director after working on Richard Lugar's senatorial staff. But his introduction to the Bush administration came through Al Hubbard, another Indiana business executive, who had been a classmate of George W. Bush's at Harvard Law School. Hubbard (later named to the White House economic policy staff) recommended Daniels to Cheney, and he was quickly hired to oversee OMB. Cheney now had a conservative business executive, known for cutting costs, to help him control the business of government. With Cheney loyalist Sean O'Keefe as OMB's deputy director, the vice president was assured of support for his pro-business regulatory changes.

The extensive list of regulatory changes approved by OMB under Daniels included those issued by the Mine Safety and Health Administration that loosened protections for coal miners from black lung disease and new regulations by the Department of Transportation that increased the allowable time for truck drivers on the road from ten to eleven hours. The Office of Management and Budget also approved a rule change that dropped the requirement for hospitals to install facilities protecting workers against tuberculosis.[47]

Regulatory approvals were just one of the tools that OMB had for promoting a pro-business atmosphere. Controlling the budgets of enforcement agencies was equally effective. In 2001, for example, the EPA tried to issue a nationwide warning on a home insulation product that contained asbestos. The warning had been in the EPA's pipeline for some time and was finally ready to go public. But OMB, in its standard review of regulatory actions, terminated the EPA warning. Whether it was a coincidence or a punishment, OMB also cut the EPA's enforcement budget that year.[48] Other enforcement budgets also saw the budget axe. For example, in 2004, budget cuts removed seventy-seven enforcement jobs from the Occupational Safety and Health Administration (OSHA).

Cheney ensured his control over regulatory actions by keeping decisions on regulations out of the hands of career staff. In January 2007, when the administration was entering its last two years, President Bush amended Executive Order 12866, to further centralize regulatory power in OMB's Office of Information and Regulatory Affairs (OIRA). The amended executive order required OIRA to review all regulations to ensure that there was a "specific market failure" that "warrants a new agency action." Departments, in other words, could only write new regulations if the existing regulation was necessary because of a market failure, not for health reasons, for example, or environmental reasons. Another move to centralize regulatory control within the political network that Cheney had created came with Executive Order 13422, which instructed every agency to have a political appointee, not a career executive, in charge of regulatory decisions.[49] Both executive orders kept decisions on regulatory actions away from the career staff and in the hands of political appointees.

The timing of the two executive orders came as the administration was losing its original political appointees, many of whom Cheney had brought in. Many had already been replaced once or twice. Original agency agendas had lost their focus, and relationships were disappearing across the administration. The executive orders reminded the new appointees how to conduct business in the business-friendly administration. Their timing also coincided with the results of the November 2006 midterm elections. Since the administration was concerned that the new Democratically controlled House and Senate might try to block new appointments, leaving career staff as acting policy directors, Bush's executive orders ensured that career staff—who were perceived by Bush and Cheney as hostile to the administration—did not gain control of the regulatory process.

The Heritage Foundation's call to "reduce the burden of government" on business was the centerpiece of Cheney's agenda as vice president. Throughout his tenure, he worked not only to install allies in departments who shared his mission to reduce burdensome government regulations but also to place pro-business appointees inside regulatory agencies. His reach even extended to the Consumer Products Safety Commission (CPSC), which one might have thought to be immune from the vice president's anti-regulatory agenda. It proved not to be. The CPSC, created in 1973 with a staff of eight hundred, was cut to four hundred staff during the Bush administration.

The CPSC's chairman until 2006, Harold Stratton, a lawyer from Albuquerque, New Mexico, specialized in oil and gas law and had deep roots in the energy community. His replacement, Michael Baroody, a lobbyist for the National Association of Manufacturers, withdrew his name from consideration after members of Congress strongly objected to control of the agency by a chairman linked to a manufacturing trade organization. Opposition to Baroody's nomination included the junior senator from Illinois, Barack Obama, who sent a letter to the Senate Commerce Committee urging the committee to reject

Baroody's nomination. "Leading the nation's premier product safety commission is too important a responsibility to put in the hands of someone who owes his career to the same companies whose products he is supposed to judge," Obama said.[50] When Baroody withdrew, Nancy Nord, a lobbyist for Eastman Kodak, was nominated, and she too faced stiff opposition from Congress due to her industry connections.[51] Nord was never confirmed, but she remained the CPSC's acting director in spite of calls from the Speaker of the House, Nancy Pelosi, for her resignation.

Policy decisions under Stratton and later Nord proved to be focused around industry rather than consumer needs, as one would expect in Cheney's business-friendly administration. After toys from China that had lead-based paint were recalled in 2007, a number of investigative articles focused on the Consumer Products Safety Commission and suggested that the agency was cozy with business. "Under the Bush administration, which promised to ease what it viewed as costly rules that placed unnecessary burdens on businesses," one article noted, "industry friendly officials have been installed at agencies that oversee the nation's workplaces, food suppliers, environment and consumer goods."[52]

Having captured the appointment and regulatory process, Cheney turned his attention to creating programs across the administration that supported his pro-business orientation, particularly the President's Management Agenda within OMB, which provided guidelines to the departments for "reforming government"—a code phrase for favoring business and reducing the role of career employees in program management. Outsourcing would be the next focus of Cheney's business-friendly agenda.

OMB's goal, according to the guidelines of the President's Management Agenda, was to increase the number of "market-based" services that could be outsourced to the private sector. The guidelines also urged departments to reduce the number of programs under the control of career departmental staff, moving to what it called a "citizen-centered not bureaucracy-centered" government. To meet this objective, OMB tried to cut the federal government's career staff in half and to outsource jobs to private companies.

This vision for government reform was prominently placed on web sites of the OMB and federal agencies:

President's Management Agenda

The President's vision for government reform is guided by three principles. Government should be:

— Citizen-centered, not bureaucracy-centered;

— Results-oriented;

— Market-based, actively promoting rather than stifling innovation through competition.[53]

Creating a market-based government, one of the three principles of the President's Management Agenda, required agencies to outsource their services whenever possible. Daniels (and specifically Clay Johnson, who was placed in charge of the program at OMB) pushed the agencies to outsource all jobs considered commercial in nature in a process called "competitive sourcing." For example, the Department of Defense was encouraged to outsource management of military hospitals and military housing; the Department of the Interior was encouraged to outsource staff within the national park system; and the Department of Labor was encouraged to outsource its job-training facilities. At times, the process drew loud protests from federal employees, such as when OMB pushed the Federal Aviation Administration to have air controllers compete for their jobs against private contractors.[54]

In 2001, the administration hoped that 850,000 civil service jobs that were not "inherently governmental" would be opened to privatization through outsourcing—which meant that nearly 50 percent of available federal jobs would be affected.[55] During the first year, the administration pushed the agencies to immediately find 15 percent of jobs for which the private sector could compete. By 2004, the administration wanted 425,000 jobs to be opened to competition to private contractors.[56]

For the Bush administration, outsourcing had benefits beyond creating a citizen-centered government. The move to private contractors would reduce the amount of information available to the public, since private contractors were not subject to Freedom of Information Act

(FOIA) requirements as were federal agencies. In addition, and perhaps more important for Cheney, outsourcing protected those agencies from public scrutiny.

Cheney, with his penchant for secrecy, saw outsourcing as another way to control public access to policy making. Agency staff were informed by political appointees that outsourcing was essential to a strong organization, and successful outsourcing became a way for agencies to earn a "green light" in their performance evaluations. OMB created a traffic-light system for the agencies and for each of their divisions. Red lights indicated poor performance and green lights indicated excellent performance. Managers received higher performance evaluations when their divisions had been graded by OMB with a green light. Successfully outsourcing programs, for example, was a key indicator for moving to a green light.

The Pentagon, over which Cheney had significant influence in personnel appointments, became one of the boldest advocates in the administration for outsourcing. One Pentagon political appointee explained that "competition is the driving force in the American economy. It forces organizations to improve quality, reduce costs, and focus on customers' needs. [The Army] will benefit greatly by introducing the dynamic forces of competition into the procurement of support services."[57] The Army immediately began a plan to outsource as many support services as possible, requiring over 154,000 Army civilians to compete for their jobs in the first year of the program.[58]

In fall 2001, the military services began to classify their employees as "core" (soldiers) and "non-core" (soldiers in non-military roles). The goal was to move service members out of non-core jobs into core jobs, boosting the strength of the fighting military. Non-core jobs could then be outsourced. The Army referred to this strategy as the Third Wave, differentiating it from previous attempts to outsource military-related jobs.

Dick Cheney, who had actively advocated outsourcing during his tenure in the Department of Defense under George H. W. Bush, drove military outsourcing. Before leaving office in 1993, Cheney commissioned a Halliburton subsidiary, Brown and Root, to prepare a $3.9 million study to determine how military support services, such as housing, food, and laundry, could be privatized.[59]

By outsourcing support services, the size of the armed forces appeared to be smaller than it actually was to congressional committees, which often opposed increasing military spending. Although the work that civilians and non-core military personnel had previously performed was now being handled by private contractors, the administration appeared to be reducing the military's size. Halliburton, which later hired Cheney as its chief executive officer, became a major beneficiary of the Pentagon's outsourcing under the George W. Bush administration, reaping hundreds of millions of dollars in federal contracts.

Non-core jobs outsourced in this contracting explosion resulted in two very public failures: managed care at Walter Reed Medical Center and security for American diplomats in Iraq. Walter Reed Medical Center, located in suburban Maryland just outside of Washington, D.C., had long been the crown jewel of American military medicine. But its medical and support staff had been increasingly outsourced, as were many civilian jobs under Bush and Cheney. The facility itself fell into severe disrepair, and soldiers complained about being released from the hospital because of a bed shortage while still needing medical attention. After a series of reports in the *Washington Post* in early 2007, the commander of the facility was forced out. The surgeon general of the United States, responsible for oversight of Walter Reed, was also forced to resign. What received little attention, however, was that the problems at Walter Reed had been the product of failed outsourcing.[60]

Diplomatic security was another example of military outsourcing that gave the administration a black eye. The State Department awarded a private corporation, Blackwater USA, primary control for protecting its diplomats in Iraq, rather than relying on military security or its own security staff. Princeton University professor of economics and international affairs (and future Nobel laureate) Paul Krugman called the extensive privatization of security and other activities taken over by Blackwater the administration's "hired gun fetish."[61] The North Carolina–based security contractor had a one-thoudand-person security staff in Iraq working for the State Department. In addition, the department outsourced smaller security contracts to DynCorp International and Triple Canopy, Inc.

The controversy over Blackwater's security role erupted in September 2007, when Blackwater guards were accused of killing more than a dozen Iraqi civilians in downtown Baghdad.[62] Under pressure to investigate, the State Department determined that Blackwater security had been involved in at least fifty-six shootings while guarding diplomats. In 2008, five Blackwater guards were indicted for manslaughter for civilian deaths in Iraq. Apparently, Blackwater had been operating with little oversight from the State Department and established its own rules of engagement for its security staff. Not surprisingly, the Blackwater contract and other federal contracts approved by the Bush administration appeared to have a political connection. Erik Prince, the chief executive and founder of the privately held firm, had been a regular contributor to the Republican Party, donating over $200,000 in recent years. His reward was over $1 billion in contracts from the Bush administration.[63]

By keeping the number of private contractors, such as Blackwater, out of the official count of American military or State Department staff in Iraq, as Cheney wanted, the Bush administration underrepresented the actual number of Americans engaged in the war. The process of outsourcing allowed the administration to manipulate the number of American military and civilian staff in Iraq while giving private contractors a free rein. Oversight was minimal. While the number of contracts dramatically increased, there was no increase in auditing staff within the agencies. The Office of Management and Budget had cleverly designed a process that encouraged agencies to outsource their programs to private contractors, with almost no oversight of program management and performance.

One of the agencies with the greatest degree of privatization was the National Aeronautics and Space Administration (NASA). Under the direction of Sean O'Keefe, who left OMB and was named NASA administrator in late 2001, NASA outsourced 90 percent of its functions to private companies, with $9 out of every $10 in the space program designated for private contractors. The largest contractor, the United Space Alliance—a joint venture of Lockheed Martin

Corporation and the Boeing Corporation—managed the entire space shuttle program, with ten thousand employees at the Kennedy Space Center in Florida, the Johnson Space Center in Texas, and the Goddard Space Center in Alabama. In contrast, NASA had only eighteen hundred of its own employees.[64]

Not only did OMB aggressively push outsourcing, it also explored ways to cut entire divisions. Soon after Bush's second term began, OMB proposed that Congress endorse its proposal to give the president authority to reorganize federal agencies. The proposal, the "Government Reorganization Performance Improvement Act of 2005," allowed the president to create commissions to study the effectiveness of an agency and make recommendations to Congress to eliminate or maintain it.[65] Since the White House controlled appointments, however, the act would have made it possible for special interests to control recommendations. As a result, Congress never seriously considered the proposal.

By the end of the Bush administration, the drive for outsourcing was significantly slowed. Agencies began to resist OMB's efforts to force half the federal civilian workforce to compete for their jobs. And, finally, as the outcry over the long- and short-term problems that outsourcing created across the administration grew louder, Congress began to hold hearings. The general conclusion was that outsourcing caused morale problems among federal workers, consumed their time by making them bid for their own jobs, and failed to preserve long-term institutional memory, because thousands of federal workers left government's employ.[66] Eleanor Holmes Norton, the delegate representing the District of Columbia in the House of Representatives, warned that "we are going to be left behind with an inexperienced workforce" and a "human capital crisis."[67]

In the waning weeks of the administration, the Office of Management and Budget again took the national limelight as it issued last-minute regulations—more often called midnight regulations—before President-elect Barack Obama's administration took office. Susan Dudley, the OIRA administrator, who had been strongly opposed by public interest groups in 2006 when she took office, actively moved forward over 130 last-minute rule changes, most of which benefited business and industry. Among these rule changes were several from the Labor Department, including a proposal to change the assessment process for evaluating toxic chemicals that workers might be exposed to. This drew outrage from unions and public health officials and strong disapproval from the incoming Obama administration.[68]

Another rule change by the Labor Department proposed giving employers more discretion to allow workers to use their paid leave as part of leave taken under the Family and Medical Leave Act of 1993. Vacation and sick leave, for example, could not automatically be rolled into the unpaid leave that the law requires. Other last-minute rule changes included provisions that kept lawsuits out of state court—where damage awards are higher than in federal court—for cases involving negligence on the part of manufacturers. The National Association of Manufacturers, with its membership of fourteen thousand business owners, was a prime lobbyist for this rule change.

Business-friendly appointees, most of whom had been placed in office by Dick Cheney and his allies, sought to protect the business community even as the administration drew to a close. The fierce loyalty of these appointees to Cheney's pro-business agenda was evident. Some, such as Dudley, seemed to circumvent even the White House. Joshua Bolten, White House chief of staff, issued a directive in May 2008 stating that "except in extraordinary circumstances, regulations to be finalized in this administration should be proposed no later than June 1, 2008, and final regulations should be issued no later than November 1, 2008." When asked why OMB was allowing regulations to be issued past Bolten's deadline, Dudley responded that the Bolten memo "was not intended to be a moratorium" on final rule making, which would continue as long as necessary.

Working with the numerous departmental appointees he placed in office, Vice President Cheney built the most pro-business government in two decades and attempted to transform the federal government from a professional, nonpolitical civil service into a rich source of government jobs for commercial interests. The business-friendly presidency created by Cheney was as successful in its implementation as the faith-based presidency of George W. Bush.

CHAPTER 7

What Happened to the Domestic Agenda?

E XACTLY AT NOON, on January 20, 2001, George W. Bush prepared to be inaugurated as the forty-third president of the United
States. The nation's capital was filled with its quadrennial influx of
supporters and tourists, but this year was different. Nearly five hundred thousand supporters who flooded the streets were joined by tens
of thousands of protesters carrying placards—proclaiming "Hail to
the Thief" and "Selected Not Elected"—denouncing the election process. In order to help with crowd control, police called in an additional
sixteen hundred officers from neighboring Virginia and Maryland.
Not since Richard Nixon's second inauguration in 1973, when sixty
thousand marched against the Vietnam War, had the city faced such
an onslaught of inaugural protesters. This new generation was marching against the bitterly contested election that had brought Bush and
Cheney into the White House.

As the rain continued without a break on that blustery Saturday morning, George W. Bush and Dick Cheney stood on the Capitol's portico and
waited to take their oaths of office. After the Reverend Billy Graham's
invocation, Chief Justice William Rehnquist—in his flowing black robe,
with its four distinctive gold stripes across each arm—administered the
oath, first to the vice president and then to the president. Minutes later,
the new forty-third president of the United States gave his inaugural address outside the West Front of the Capitol. In keeping with a campaign
platform focused on domestic policy and compassionate conservatism,
Bush centered the brief address on the promise to use his presidency to
build a moral and civil society. "A civil society demands from each of us
good will and respect, fair dealing, and forgiveness. We must live up to the
calling we share. Civility," he stated, "is not a tactic or a sentiment."[1]

Reflecting that pledge, Bush's domestic agenda championed programs that he believed met the tests for building a moral and civil

society: education reform, volunteerism, and faith-based programs. These were policies that he had supported during his tenure as governor and sought to repeat at the federal level. They also satisfied the somewhat diverse political demands of the social and fiscal conservatives who had carried him to the presidency.

Faith-based programs, which allowed religious groups to receive federal funding, bridged the demands of social and fiscal conservatives by reducing government's role in service delivery and handing programs over to the private—albeit religious—sector. Although fiscal conservatives never particularly championed faith-based initiatives, they did not oppose them, content that they were part of the larger outsourcing of government services, which would shrink the size and role of the federal government. Compassionate conservatism reflected a merger of these two philosophies of governance, marrying the Bush philosophy of compassionate government, with its overarching religious and moral themes, with the fiscal reform philosophy of conservatives calling for smaller government and lower taxes.

Stephen Goldsmith, the former mayor of Indianapolis, who was serving as a domestic policy advisor to the Bush campaign, explained compassionate conservatism as bridging the needs of social and fiscal conservatives when explaining it on the campaign trail. He quoted a statement made during the campaign by Bush, who had said, "It is conservative to cut taxes and compassionate to give people more money to spend. Only by fully empowering people to select freely among various options do we treat Americans as proud, dignified self-governing citizens able to make disciplined and responsible decisions in their own lives."[2]

This interpretation allowed fiscal conservatives like Dick Cheney to work hand in hand with compassionate conservatives like George W. Bush.[3] And, once in office, Bush would focus on building a moral and civil society and Cheney would focus on fiscal issues, the environment, energy, and regulatory policy. As a result, the administration's domestic policy was essentially divided, with Bush addressing one set of polices within his office and Cheney addressing another set of policies within his office.

The domestic agenda that Bush framed involved education re-form, tax reform, funding for faith-based organizations, and new initiatives that would support his vision for a moral and civil society. Education reform was first. The legislation that the administration sought created standards in education and held schools accountable for meeting those standards—an education package that became the No Child Left Behind Act. A tax package that cut income taxes, re-duced capital gains taxes, and increased the threshold for inheritance taxes was second. Programs that allowed faith-based organizations to receive federal funding were third. Previous administrations had refused to fund faith-based organizations on the grounds that to do so would constitute a First Amendment violation of the separation of church and state. Finally, Bush wanted the federal government to reinforce certain moral precepts, and he wanted programs to address them. He planned to use the resources of the federal government to build a moral and civil society—a phrase he used repeatedly in his campaign, his inaugural address, and numerous speeches during his administration.

These domestic priorities were overseen by the White House staff and became the centerpieces of the Bush domestic agenda. Cheney had little to do with the domestic agenda established by Bush, and instead focused his attentions and that of his staff on the economic and envi-ronmental agenda. Although his staff participated in many of the policy discussions on these agenda items, they had relatively little input.

Since the domestic agenda had clear goals, such as education reform and creation of faith-based initiatives, the White House divided its staff into units that addressed these policy areas. One unit was led by Mar-garet Spellings, the education expert; another was led by John DiIulio, who handled faith-based initiatives; and a third was led by John Bridge-land, who oversaw an assortment of other domestic policy issues.[4] The tax package was handled outside of the domestic policy apparatus by Lawrence Lindsey in the National Economic Council and by Nicholas Calio in the legislative affairs office.[5] Spellings, DiIulio, Bridgeland, and the others each pursued their own policy areas in a somewhat com-partmentalized policy process. Throughout the first eight months, they each focused on their policy areas, with few other domestic initiatives emerging from the White House.

But in the days and weeks after the September 11 terrorist attacks, the domestic policy apparatus changed course and took a leadership role in dealing with the problems that New York City was facing. Joshua Bolten, the White House deputy chief of staff, created the interagency Domestic Consequences Principals' Committee, which included both senior departmental staff and domestic policy staff. He tasked them with addressing, first, the immediate needs of the victims and residents of New York City and, second, the longer-term needs of border security and the airline industry. Although its agenda was constantly in flux as the enormity of the crisis unfolded, Bolten's basic directive to the Domestic Consequences Principals' Committee was to

- provide public health advice on the air quality around the World Trade Center in New York City
- examine how the victims of the attacks could be compensated
- determine what kinds of federal assistance would be needed for New York City
- reopen civil air space
- reopen the financial markets
- examine how to return border security to normal operations, and
- evaluate legislative proposals to bail out the airline industry after losses incurred in air travel from the terrorist attacks.[6]

The energy of the domestic and economic policy apparatus in the White House was now focused on responding to issues raised by Bolten's committee. But Cheney soon became involved.

On September 14, 2001, three days after the attacks, Cheney suggested the creation of a new White House Homeland Security Office—including a Homeland Security advisor and a Homeland Security Council—to provide the same advisory structure for the president on domestic security as the National Security Council provided on national security. This was not a new idea; it had been floated in past administrations with mixed reviews, but Cheney resurrected it. Within weeks of his suggestion, Bush signed an executive order creating a

White House Office of Homeland Security and a separate Homeland Security Council.

The Homeland Security Council became the fourth policy-making council in the White House—after the Domestic Policy Council, the National Economic Council, and the National Security Council. Governor Tom Ridge of Pennsylvania, Bush's close friend, was placed at the helm of the new office, but Cheney cleverly inserted one of his own staff as deputy director, ensuring that he would be actively involved in its decision making. Cheney had made a similar move with the National Security Council when he inserted Stephen Hadley as deputy director.

The Office of Homeland Security soon overshadowed all other policy offices in the White House and became the center of George W. Bush's attention, to the point where he became detached from domestic issues. Days after the terrorist attacks, Bush called his cabinet members together and bluntly stated that he expected them to continue with their programs, but that his administration was now entirely focused on terrorism. "This is now the purpose of this administration," he said, in an unequivocal restatement of his priorities.[7] The limited agenda that the domestic policy staff had been focusing on before the terrorist attacks would not be expanded in the years to come, as Bush redirected his attention from domestic to national security policy.

Bush's domestic agenda was expanded to some small degree after the terrorist attacks, however, when volunteerism gained new importance. As part of the administration's war on terror, Bush created a new domestic volunteer program, the Citizen Corps, which trained retired medical professionals for national emergencies and recruited truckers, letter carriers, ship captains, and others to report "suspicious activity" to local, state, and federal authorities.[8] Until the terrorist attacks, volunteerism had always been connected with social service programs, not defense or intelligence, and it had never been fully integrated into the domestic policy apparatus. With the war on terror suddenly dominating domestic and national security policy, however, the Citizen Corps and the larger issue of volunteerism became a key part of Bush's domestic agenda by virtue of its connection to national security issues. Volunteerism was dramatically expanded under the new USA Freedom Corps—an umbrella agency that Bush created by executive order to house all volunteer programs, including the Citizen Corps, Peace Corps, Senior Corps, and AmeriCorps.

The refocusing of Bush's relatively slim domestic agenda to actively include volunteerism led to staffing changes in the White House and the creation of an entirely new office. Bridgeland moved from Spelling's office, where he had served as director of the Domestic Council, to head the new volunteerism office, where he had the title of assistant to the president and director of the USA Freedom Corps. Now volunteerism—like faith-based initiatives, another single-policy issue—had its own office, staff, and high-level director.

As the White House domestic policy offices turned much of their attention to the national security programs, such as the Citizen Corps, the task of building a moral and civil society was left to the agencies to implement administratively through programs created by political appointees such as Wade Horn at HHS. With the exception of the education bill, passed by Congress in December 2001 and signed in January 2002, Bush focused on national security issues—a decision that he believed was supported by the American people. When he signed the education bill in a public ceremony at a high school in Hamilton, Ohio, for example, the crowd was not only cheering the legislation, it was chanting, "USA! USA!"[9]

After the Citizen Corps was established in January 2002, the USA Freedom Corps became the most prominent of the domestic policy offices. By then the education legislation had been passed and Margaret Spellings was focusing her energies on implementing the law with the Department of Education staff. Faith-based programs were being carried out in the departments with minimal guidance from the White House. After DiIulio resigned in August 2001, his office never regained its early stature.[10]

Even the once vigorous USA Freedom Corps eventually lost prominence after the original staff of the domestic policy offices left. Although Bridgeland made significant strides in building the new volunteer organization, the office was downgraded after his departure. Bridgeland's replacement in 2003, Desiree Sayle, had previously run both the White House's and Laura Bush's Correspondence Units. Instead of choosing a policy expert to run the office—the centerpiece of his domestic agenda at that point—Bush installed an inexperienced member of the First Lady's staff. Sayle was given the title of deputy assistant to the president, while Bridgeland had held the title of assistant to the president.

Within two years of taking office, Bush had downgraded two of the three principal domestic policy offices in the White House—faith-based initiatives and volunteerism. In addition, the Domestic Policy Council had little work to do once the No Child Left Behind Act had been passed. Bush's lack of interest in domestic policy after the terrorist attacks was the principal reason that the offices were downgraded, but the problem was compounded by the narrow domestic agenda established in the campaign. It left little room for new initiatives.[11]

Although there were other factors, the downward slide of domestic policy in the White House was primarily due to the terrorist attacks. Bush simply lost interest. Throughout the remainder of Bush's first term, the wars in Afghanistan and in Iraq dominated all areas of domestic, economic, and national security policy. Funding for domestic programs dried up, as the administration shifted its limited resources to the wars. The combination of reduced revenues from Bush's tax cuts and increased expenditures for the military led to across-the-board cuts in domestic programs, including education and volunteer programs.

Bush's mission to build a moral and civil society persisted, but that goal was somewhat overshadowed by his new mission of protecting America's citizens from terrorism, for which he would use all the resources of the presidency and the U.S. government. For Bush, it was a mission from God, who, he said, had called upon him to "defend our nation and to lead the world to peace."[12]

While the president and vice president met regularly with the CIA and Defense staffs on possible action in Afghanistan and later Iraq, other domestic policy work came to a standstill. The White House domestic policy units became primarily reactive, rather than proactive, mainly dealing with departmental issues that needed resolution. For the next three years, most of the administration's domestic efforts would be overshadowed, if not subsumed, by the wars in Afghanistan and Iraq. Domestic policies that moved forward were those already in place before 9 / 11, which included establishment of faith-based centers within domestic departments and the creation of abstinence-based sex education and other morality-based programs in the Department of Health and Human Services.

As the administration approached the end of its first term, moreover, all of the energy of the White House focused on reelection. The domestic policy office pulled back even further from leadership roles for fear of alienating constituent groups. The election was shaping up to be a battle, as it had been in 2000, and Rove wanted to minimize any possibility that the conservative base would move away from the administration. Polls indicated that Bush and his Democratic opponent, Senator John Kerry of Massachusetts, were in a dead heat for capturing the White House.

The war in Iraq had, by this time, become a stone around the administration's neck. Instead of an easy victory as an incumbent in 2004, Bush faced a challenging campaign for a second term. He pulled out a victory, however, garnering 286 electoral votes and 52 percent of the popular vote. On January 20, 2005, he and Dick Cheney once again stood with Chief Justice William Rehnquist on the portico of the Capitol in Washington, D.C., taking their oaths of office. And once again, protesters carried signs protesting the Bush-Cheney campaign. This time, however, they were carrying placards that read "War Starts With W," "Out of Iraq," and "Impeach Bush." The war was taking its toll on the administration, but its focus continued to be terrorism and the war in Iraq.

The domestic policy offices in the White House had been on life support after the 9 / 11 terrorist attacks, but they died in the second term—due to the combination of Bush's very limited and quickly achieved agenda, changes in White House personnel, and the war on terror. In his first term, Bush had populated his domestic policy offices with campaign staff focused on the domestic agenda for which he had campaigned—education, faith-based initiatives, and volunteerism. In the second term, however, priorities had changed, as did the players.

The last member of the original domestic policy team, Marga-ret Spellings, left the White House in January 2005, to take over the Department of Education from Rodney Paige, who had returned to Texas. The education bill had passed, as had the bill expanding vol-unteer programs. Although charitable-choice legislation was blocked, faith-based offices were flourishing in the departments. Bush had few other programs that he wanted to move forward in the domestic policy arena, and his seasoned domestic policy staffers had departed. Spell-ings, DiIulio, Bridgeland, and Lindsey had all left the White House, and only Spellings remained with the administration.

As Bush's second term began, senior staff in the White House do-mestic policy units were replaced by social conservatives, whose pri-mary goal was to support and expand programs centered on the moral agenda. The most important domestic policies pursued were those that reengaged religious conservatives and reasserted Bush's commit-ment to the pro-life agenda—against abortion, euthanasia, stem cell research, and cloning.

Bush's first appointment to his domestic policy team in the second term was Claude Allen, a former aide to Senator Jesse Helms of North Carolina and a former Virginia commissioner of health and human services. Bush's choice of Allen to oversee the White House domestic policy office was an unmistakable signal to Christian conservatives that they would be represented in the halls of the West Wing and that moral tenets guided administration policy making. Bush had previ-ously nominated Allen, an African American born-again Christian who had been working as a deputy secretary of HHS, to the Fourth Circuit Court of Appeals in 2003. But Allen, whose credentials alien-ated even the Republican-controlled Senate, failed to be confirmed by the end of the legislative session in December 2004. In Virginia, Allen had built a reputation as a "social policy czar." He opposed, among other state programs, health insurance for children, because the leg-islation allowed for abortions for underage girls who were victims of rape, incest, or sexual abuse, and he strongly advocated abstinence education. His wife homeschooled their four children to ensure that they had a strict moral upbringing.

Although most senior White House appointments were announced with effusive press releases, generally days or weeks before their first day on the job, Allen's appointment was handled with little fanfare. In a terse six-sentence statement, titled "Personnel Announcement," his appointment was released by the White House Press Office on January 5, 2005—the very day he took office—with little mention of his background or White House role.[13]

His interest in domestic policy seemed to be limited to HHS social service programs, and little was known of him outside a small circle of the department's staff. The White House web site revealed few entries about Claude Allen, and not a single book written about the Bush administration, even those written by White House staff, included any mention of him. He was invisible. His low profile and apparent lack of broader policy involvement was reminiscent of his predecessor, Margaret Spellings, who had taken few proactive positions aside from the No Child Left Behind bill. According to the online magazine *Slate*, which was researching a story on Spellings in 2003, the White House web site yielded only four documents involving her. Spellings, the *Slate* story continued, was a "ridiculously low profile domestic policy adviser," who appeared to have produced few policy recommendations.[14] But, unlike Allen, Spellings was actively engaged in one policy issue: education. Allen did not have a single policy area that he managed.

The only significant policy that Allen dealt with in the White House involved federal assistance for the victims of Hurricane Katrina. After Katrina made landfall in August 2005 in New Orleans and along the Gulf Coast, Allen coordinated the White House Task Force for victims of the catastrophic storm. It appears, however, that he did little and his task force did less. The Department of Homeland Security, which included the Federal Emergency Management Agency (FEMA), had primary authority for providing aid to hurricane victims. Michael D. Brown, undersecretary of Homeland Security and FEMA director, had operational control.

There is no evidence that Allen used the resources of the White House in any way to support Katrina relief efforts or to help with crisis management during or after the hurricane. More important, when it became clear that Brown was failing as relief coordinator, Allen failed to fill the void in leadership. On September 12, 2005, Brown resigned under fire for failing to manage relief for the hurricane victims; only ten days earlier, Bush had praised the disgraced FEMA director, telling him, "Brownie, you're doing a heck of a job."[15]

Katrina was perhaps the greatest single domestic crisis of the Bush presidency, and its mismanagement of disaster relief remains the administration's greatest domestic failure. When the hurricane struck New Orleans, the president's primary response was to pledge that "America will pray" for its victims, while he met with John McCain at a country club in El Mirage, Arizona, to celebrate the senator's sixty-ninth birthday.

Hundreds of thousands of people were evacuated in New Orleans as the water rose. Nine thousand residents crowded into the Superdome, but air conditioning and restrooms failed, and food and water were nowhere to be found. At no point did the federal government mobilize to provide the minimal necessities for the nine thousand hot and hungry evacuees inside the Superdome—nor did it later provide adequate temporary housing as the waters subsided.

Claude Allen failed to harness the massive resources of the federal government to manage the Katrina crisis or to minimize FEMA's incompetence—a task that should have been his top priority as White House domestic policy director. Allen, however, had not been chosen for his management or policy expertise, but rather as a signal to Christian conservatives of the administration's loyalty to their goals.

The domestic agenda of the Bush administration was about compassionate conservatism, and FEMA had never been a priority of the domestic agenda. In Bush's first term, FEMA's budget and personnel were repeatedly slashed—partly in line with the Bush-Cheney philosophy that state and local governments should bear greater responsibility for disaster response. The reduction in FEMA's budget and staff, however, also reflected the new priority of the Bush administration—fighting terrorism. In 2002, FEMA was incorporated into the newly created Department of Homeland Security, where the federal response to natural disasters was eclipsed by the focus on government's response to possible biological and chemical terrorist attacks.

Allen was not going to insert himself into budget battles that had already been fought and won by the Cheney-dominated Department of Homeland Security. And he wasn't able to penetrate FEMA's political network, with its direct link to Karl Rove, Karen Hughes, and George W. Bush. Joe Allbaugh—Bush's chief of staff as governor and later his 2000 presidential campaign director—had been named director of FEMA in 2001. When Allbaugh left, he recommended as his replacement his college friend Michael Brown, who lacked experience in any type of emergency management. But experience in emergency management was not a necessary credential in an administration where, according to Brown, "individuals must take personal responsibility for being prepared" in a natural disaster.[16] From the earliest days of the administration, FEMA was a haven, if not a dumping ground, for political appointees.

Unfortunately for the citizens of New Orleans, it was a hiring process dominated by incompetence. It quickly became clear that neither the White House nor the designated response agencies could cope with the Katrina crisis. "The lethally inept response to Hurricane Katrina revealed to everyone that the Federal Emergency Management Agency, which earned universal praise during the Clinton years, is a shell of its former self. The hapless Michael Brown—who is no longer overseeing relief efforts but still heads the agency—has become a symbol of cronyism," Paul Krugman charged in the *New York Times*.[17]

Despite the debacle of the Katrina response and the barrage of criticism leveled against Michael Brown, Claude Allen and the Bush White House were soon refocused, months later, around the faith-based presidency. The problems of emergency management would be left to the Department of Homeland Security. As the midterm elections neared in 2006, Karl Rove and political strategists used Allen to reassure their base that the Republican-controlled Congress would be reelected. To help strengthen the support of the conservative base, Allen repeatedly infused religion into secular activities. For example, as coordinator for the White House Conference on Aging in December 2005, a secular event, Allen invited a minister to open the conference, who began with the following offering: "The first command given by the Creator to humanity was 'be fruitful.' As we grow older, we should bear the fruit of knowledge."[18] The domestic policy operation had returned to its primary role of building a moral and civil society.

In spite of his political value as an advocate for social and religious conservatives, Claude Allen had a short tenure in the White House. A year after he joined the domestic policy staff, he was arrested in suburban Washington, D.C., for shoplifting from a Target store. Allen claimed that it had simply been a misunderstanding with store managers, but surveillance cameras proved otherwise. He was charged with theft and quickly resigned his $161,000-a-year job.

After Allen left the White House in 2006, Karl Zinsmeister succeeded him as director of the Office of Domestic Policy. A social conservative like Claude Allen, Zinsmeister previously had worked as the editor of *American Enterprise*, a publication of the American Enterprise Institute (AEI). Zinsmeister ran the AEI magazine from his home in north-central New York state, near Syracuse, where he, like Allen, homeschooled his children to provide them with moral structure. In a PBS interview with Ben Wattenberg, which aired on June 15, 2006, Zinsmeister argued that "you have to have some sort of compass built into citizens if they're going to be good citizens and if our society's going to be healthy," adding that "religion is a very important tool" for building that inner compass. When asked by Wattenberg how he felt about abortion, Zinsmeister responded that he strongly supported laws outlawing abortions and would support jailing doctors who performed them.[19]

By Bush's second term, it was becoming clear that the White House domestic policy apparatus had been converted into a political arm for Christian conservatives. Rove worked closely with the domestic policy office to craft positions on abortion, cloning, stem cell research, abstinence education, and a host of issues supported by Christian conservatives and by George W. Bush. By the time that Zinsmeister took over domestic policy, the domestic policy office had been reorganized to include the AIDS policy office, the National Drug Control Policy Office, the USA Freedom Corps, the Council on Environmental Quality, and the Office of Faith Based and Community Initiatives.

During Zinsmeister's tenure, however, few policies emerged from any of these offices. Like his predecessor Claude Allen, he was more comfortable advising Bush on issues that social conservatives endorsed rather than those involving crime, drugs, and poverty. And, like Claude Allen, he kept a remarkably low profile at the White House. Zinsmeister provided little direction and offered few ideas on broader issues of domestic policy.

One of the rare issues in which he was directly involved, by default, was the substandard medical care and facilities for soldiers returning from the wars in Afghanistan and Iraq. After articles appeared in the *Washington Post* on the failings of Walter Reed Medical Center, which treated many of the most severely injured soldiers, Bush created the President's Commission on Care for America's Returning Warriors, chaired by former senator Robert Dole and former HHS secretary Donna Shalala. Zinsmeister was responsible for coordinating the commission's recommendations to improve soldiers' medical treatment and the support system. But he would be responding to the commission's recommendations, rather than taking a leadership role himself. As would so often be the case in the Bush administration, Zinsmeister was leading a White House domestic policy office that was reactive, rather than proactive.[20]

Critics of the Bush administration's domestic agenda suggested that there was a systemic failure in domestic policy during his administration, but the evidence does not support this. There was never a promise to provide housing for the poor, food for the hungry, or health care for the uninsured. Those were the promises of Lyndon Johnson's Great Society, not George W. Bush's compassionate conservatism. For Bush, the focus of the domestic agenda was to create a structure of empowerment, allowing individuals to control their own destiny without the "crutch" of the federal government. The administration pushed for programs that minimized economic support and encouraged individuals to take responsibility for their own lives. The administration also encouraged programs that created partnerships with private organizations to empower individuals and to build self-reliance.

While the White House domestic policy advisors encouraged a culture of self-help and self-empowerment and espoused principles of morality as tests of government policy, the most significant part of domestic policy was being managed by the vice president's office, which oversaw regulatory action and energy, environmental, and economic policy.

In one of the rare times that Cheney became invested in a domestic policy issue managed by the White House staff, he was able to sway the final outcome in a manner that addressed his own policy agenda of protecting business interests through less regulation. The issue was global warming, which drew Cheney's attention because of its implications for business and industry in regulating levels of pollutants. Bush was drawn into the debate when pressed by several members of the Senate for his position on global warming and his intentions to support the Kyoto Protocol.

In late February 2001, not long after Bush gave Cheney the assignment to prepare a National Energy Plan, four Republican senators—Chuck Hagel of Nebraska, Jesse Helms of North Carolina, Pat Roberts of Kansas, and Larry Craig of Idaho—sent a letter to Bush asking for his position on regulating industrial emissions of carbon dioxide. They also, according to their letter, sought a "clear understanding of your Administration's position on climate change, in particular the Kyoto Protocol."[21]

The inquiry by the senators was prompted by lawsuits that had been filed at the end of the Clinton administration against seven power plants for violating the Clean Air Act. Clinton's attorney general, Janet Reno, issued a statement announcing the lawsuits, asserting, "When children can't breathe because of pollution from a utility plant hundreds of miles away, something must be done."[22] The senators were concerned about the status of the lawsuits in the Bush administration and about the position that the new administration would take on regulating industrial pollution. The Clinton administration had aggressively sought to enforce the industrial requirements of the Clean Air Act, but the Bush administration was taking a different position on compliance. In addition, the Bush administration had a different position on the Kyoto Protocol, arguing that science did not support the assertion that global warming resulted from man-made causes.

The United States was one of the few countries in the world not to ratify the Kyoto Protocol—an international treaty that required the signatories to cap their levels of carbon dioxide emissions—and it faced significant pressure from the international community to change its position. Although the Clinton administration supported the treaty, the Senate failed to ratify the accord after an intense lobbying effort by industry. When the Bush administration came into office, it faced mounting pressure to support the treaty and push for Senate ratification. But it had no intention of doing so.

The ratification issue became even more complicated when, days before Bush took office, the Intergovernmental Panel on Climate Change (IPCC)—an international panel of scientists working through the United Nations—issued a report that the scientific community believed that global warming was largely induced by man-made pollutants. The report stated that it was "the IPCC's conclusion that most of the observed warming of the last fifty years is likely to have been due to the increase in greenhouse gas concentrations."[23] The panel added that that this was the "current thinking of the scientific community" studying global warming. In other words, scientists around the world shared the view that global warming was caused by increased auto emissions and industrialization. For Cheney and the Energy Task Force, those conclusions were a problem.

Cheney's response was to use the White House to challenge the IPCC's conclusion. He turned to the White House domestic policy apparatus, which was available to him through the carefully constructed integration of staffs he had engineered during the transition in the single executive office plan. Using these resources, Cheney encouraged the creation of a cabinet-level task force to study global warming. Chaired by Condoleezza Rice, it was managed on a daily basis by John Bridgeland and Cesar Conda, the vice president's domestic policy advisor.

After two months of deliberation, the task force decided to question the National Academy of Sciences (NAS) about the science that the IPPC had reported "as the current thinking of the scientific community." Bridgeland prepared a letter to the NAS seeking its review of the IPCC's data, co-signed by Gary Edson, deputy assistant to the president for international economic affairs. Edson had become involved because Bush would be attending his first G-8 summit in Genoa, Italy, in July 2001, and the administration's position on global warming and the Kyoto Protocol would be questioned and most likely challenged.[24] The White House hoped that the National Academy of Sciences would provide some cover for Bush's opposition to signing the Kyoto Protocol—cover that the IPCC data had failed to provide.

In a brief letter dated May 11, 2001, Bridgeland and Edson asked the National Academy of Sciences to summarize the finding of the scientific community on global warming. The letter asked the NAS to identify the most and least settled science on global warming:

The Administration is conducting a review of U.S. policy on climate change. We seek the Academy's assistance in identifying the areas in the science of climate change where there are the greatest certainties and uncertainties. We would also like your views on whether there are any substantive differences between the IPCC [Intergovernmental Panel on Climate Change] and the IPCC summaries. We would appreciate a response as soon as possible.[25]

The National Academy of Sciences, however, also failed to provide the cover that the administration wanted. In June 2001, the Academy responded to Bridgeland and Edson in a forceful statement that the IPCC data were accurate and that greenhouse gases were causing the earth's temperatures to rise, although it could not specify the exact impact of industrial and other pollution. There were not differing positions within the scientific community on the role that greenhouse gases played in global warming, much to the administration's dismay. The National Academy of Sciences stated:

We know that greenhouse gases are accumulating in Earth's atmosphere, causing surface temperatures to rise. We don't know precisely how much of this rise to date is from human activities, but based on physical principles and sophisticated computer models, we expect the warming to continue because of greenhouse gas emissions.[26]

Ralph Cicerone, National Academy of Sciences president and the former chancellor of the University of California at Irvine, spoke on PBS's *NewsHour with Jim Lehrer*, after releasing the Academy's findings, where he said, "We added our voice to the view that the observed warming, i.e., the fact that the planet is warming up and that it has been warming up for the past few decades, but with particularly rapid warming in the last twenty years, we agreed with the previous findings that the weight of the evidence, the weight of the scientific opinion is that most of that warming of the past twenty years is caused by human activities."[27] He was very clear—global warming was largely man-made.

Although the National Academy of Sciences agreed with the IPCC that global warming was significantly affected by man-made pollutants, Cheney and Bush went on the offensive to deny that scientific evidence confirmed the IPCC conclusions. When the findings of the cabinet-level task force on global warming were released on June 11, 2001, only six days after the National Academy of Sciences released its findings, Bush suggested that "we do not know" how pollution has affected global warming, in spite of the warnings from the scientific community.

The Academy's report tells us that we do not know how much effect natural fluctuations in climate may have had on warming. We do not know how much our climate could or will change in the future. We do not know how fast change will occur or even how some of our actions will impact it.[28]

The cabinet-level task force report argued that the science on global warming was constantly changing, and that little was known about the true impact of greenhouse gases. Its conclusion was that the administration's policy on global warming should be "measured, as we learn more from science" and "flexible to adjust to new information and take advantage of new technology."[29] Cheney himself asserted that the scientific community had "conflicting viewpoints about global warming."[30] The energy-related industries, the Bush administration signaled, did not need to take immediate action to regulate greenhouse gases.

Cheney had won. He had captured the White House task force responsible for evaluating scientific evidence on global warming. The vice president had also captured the environmental process across the administration by inserting industry-friendly policy makers—especially James Connaughton and Philip Cooney at the White House Council on Environmental Quality and senior staff in the Department of the Interior and the EPA. In June 2003, when EPA scientists prepared a report on climate change, political appointees went so far as to demand deletion of a sentence stating that "climate change has global consequences for human health and the environment."[31] Cheney's careful selection of industry-friendly appointments was paying off.

In 2004, the managerial and scientific staff at *Scientific American* were so disturbed by the Bush administration's failure to accept science as the basis for policy making that the magazine charged in an editorial, "it is increasingly impossible to ignore that this White House disdains research that inconveniences it."[32] Scientific data unquestionably inconvenienced the vice president, who was seeking to minimize regulatory demands on the energy industry, especially environmental controls. Failure to accept scientific data on global warming became a hallmark of the administration's efforts to minimize regulatory action on greenhouse gases and of Cheney's pro-business policy agenda.

The administration's record on global warming policy issues remained dismal, for it consistently and consciously disputed the scientific consensus on the impact of greenhouse gases. Scientists who worked for the federal government were routinely muzzled, and their work was censored. In response, the Union of Concerned Scientists released a statement by sixty-two scientists, including Nobel laureates, National Medal of Science recipients, and members of the National Academy of Sciences, entitled "Restoring Scientific Integrity in Policy Making," which accused the administration of widespread "manipulation of the process through which science enters into its decisions." They added that "there is a well established pattern of suppression and distortion of scientific findings by high-ranking Bush administration political appointees across numerous federal agencies."[33] By 2008, the number of signatures on the original document had risen to more than twelve thousand.

In 2005, panelists at a meeting of the American Association for the Advancement of Science complained that the Bush administration had pressured government scientists to deliver certain results that supported White House policies.[34] It was all part of a larger "war on science," as some called it, carried out in many quarters of the administration, in which political appointees manipulated scientific data to benefit corporate coffers or faith-based tenets.[35]

Efforts, especially by Cheney, to have scientific policy conform to the interests of business surfaced repeatedly, particularly with policies involving the Endangered Species Act. In southern Oregon, for example, federal scientists determined that the endangered shortnose sucker salmon could only survive if Upper Klamath Lake was permitted to maintain its water levels. When the Department of the Interior's U.S. Bureau of Reclamation subsequently stopped channeling irrigation water from the lake into the Klamath River basin to protect the salmon, farmers and business owners protested that their livelihood was being irreparably damaged. The only recourse for the business community was to challenge the data on which scientists had based their conclusion that this species of salmon was endangered. Their protests were soon joined across the country by other business interests that saw the demands of the Endangered Species Act as harmful to their own interests.

As so often happened during the Bush administration when environmental regulations threatened the economic interest of the business community, Cheney stepped in. The *Washington Post*, in an investigative study of Cheney's relationship with decision making on the Klamath River basin, reported that "because of Cheney's intervention, the government reversed itself and let the water flow in time to save the 2002 growing season, declaring that there was no threat to the fish. What followed was the largest fish kill the West had ever seen, with tens of thousands of salmon rotting on the banks of the Klamath River."[36] The science that supported the policy decision to protect the salmon had been summarily ignored.

Several years later, pro-energy appointees in the Department of the Interior also abandoned the Endangered Species Act when it conflicted with business interests. In 2008, with only months remaining in the administration, departmental regulations were revised so that environmental reviews would no longer be required for certain construction projects, such as dams or highways. The revised regulations barred assessments of whether emissions from these construction projects would contribute to global warming or have an effect on plants and animals. In his no-nonsense efforts to protect developers from costly environmental assessments, Secretary of the Interior Dirk Kempthorne stated in a press conference that the new regulations would prevent the Endangered Species Act from being used as a "back door" way to stop construction.[37]

The *New York Times* ran a scathing editorial about Kempthorne's revision of the Endangered Species Act. The newspaper pointedly and angrily charged that the Bush administration routinely developed regulatory proposals that benefited commercial interests and ignored environmental concerns:

The Endangered Species Act has, on the whole, been successful in arresting the decline of many species that might otherwise have gone extinct. . . . But many property owners and commercial interests, including developers and loggers, dislike the act because, in their view, it unreasonably inflates costs.

The Bush administration has tried hard to accommodate their interests. It has gone to great lengths to circumnavigate the clear language of the law by rigging the science (in many cases ignoring their own scientists), negotiating settlements favorable to industry and simply refusing to obey court orders. This time, however, the administration means to rewrite the law itself, albeit through regulatory means.[38]

The Bush administration's well-documented war on environmental regulations was part of the larger war on science, which routinely challenged scientific evidence that increased costs for business and industry. While Cheney used the war on science to advance his business-friendly agenda, Bush used it to advance his faith-based presidency. In his administration, it would be ideology rather than science that governed policy making. His base of compassionate conservatives, moreover—many of whom were evangelical Christians—often saw contemporary science as challenging their moral precepts. As a result, Bush advocated domestic policies that denied federal funding for embryonic stem cell research, arguing that such research was repugnant to the protection of human life. Similarly, he opposed any abortions or use of the morning-after pill, and he denied federal funds for cloning research.

When scientists and the public at large protested many of these policies, Bush created the President's Council on Bioethics to evaluate the science surrounding biotechnology, especially stem cell research. But the membership on the council was dominated by pro-life conservatives, led by Leon Kass, who concluded that stem cell research offered questionable scientific promise.

One scientist on the panel, Elizabeth H. Blackburn, an expert in cell biology, suggested that the decision making by the majority of the panel lacked scientific integrity. Her questions on the absence of scientific data were ignored, and she was soon asked to leave. Several years after her brief tenure on the President's Council on Bioethics, Blackburn was interviewed by Claudia Dreifus of the *New York Times*, who introduced her as a future contender for the Nobel Prize in Medicine. Dreifus asked her about the council's decision making regarding stem cell research. Blackburn replied:

Basically it was, "You don't need any of those pesky embryonic stem cells because everything is wonderful with adult stem cells." When one would ask, "What's the evidence?" you'd hear, "Somebody wrote a review article about adult stem cells." And I'd say, "That is not the same as primary data. Anyone with a word processor can write a review article." There was a lot of that, and I was always saying, "Let's look at the science." My persistence didn't endear me to Leon Kass, I felt. One day, I was asked to call the White House personnel office where an official said, "Thank you. Thank you for serving." I asked him, "Why are you thanking me?" "You will no longer be on the council." I was one of two members who hadn't been reappointed for a second two-year term.[39]

Blackburn had challenged the council's prevailing view by suggesting that science should play a significant role in discussions on stem cell research. Her views fell on deaf ears, and she was replaced. Her experience was repeated across the administration, which summarily ignored scientific data and based policy making, instead, on moral precepts. Although Dick Cheney did not share the deep religious views of George W. Bush and most of his White House staff—especially Karen Hughes, Peter Wehner, and Michael Gerson—he was able to manipulate their value structure and anti-science bias to advance his pro-business agenda. George W. Bush justified the war on science for moral reasons, and Dick Cheney waged it for economic and business reasons. The co-presidency had symbiotic advantages.

To some extent, domestic policy making was resurrected in the second term. With its original domestic agenda largely fulfilled, the administration turned to its economic agenda, especially issues that had failed to move forward during the first term, in the aftermath of September 11. Top priorities included restructuring some of the New Deal entitlement programs, especially Social Security. Peter Wehner wrote to Bush supporters after the 2004 election that "for the first time in six decades, the Social Security battle is one we can win—and in doing so, we can help transform the political and philosophical landscape of the country."[40]

In 2005, as the second term took shape, Karl Rove, the longtime political guru who had managed Bush's political career, was given the new job of overseeing the domestic agenda. Under his new title of deputy chief of staff for policy, Rove coordinated the Domestic Policy Council, National Economic Council, the National Security Council, and the Homeland Security Council. Having crafted two successful presidential election campaigns, he was now the president's chief advisor on policy. His primary objective was to narrow the domestic agenda and focus on shepherding the Social Security bill through Congress. Reforming Social Security would become a centerpiece of the programs demanded by fiscal conservatives for reducing costs incurred by the federal government. In what had become a frequent intertwining of the goals of compassionate and fiscal conservatives, Rove marketed Social Security reform as an essential part of both agendas. Social conservatives and fiscal conservatives rallied to the administration's cause.

Using the rubric of "an ownership society," Rove built the case, long advocated by social conservatives, that government should not serve as society's safety net. Fiscal conservatives such as the Stanford University economist John Cogan, chief architect of the plan, argued that individuals could achieve greater rates of return on their Social Security accounts than could the government.[41] A key element of the reforms was the creation of private Social Security accounts for younger workers. In spite of the support of a Republican-controlled Congress, the administration failed to pass its Social Security legislation. When Democrats gained control of Congress in 2007, after the devastating Republican losses of the 2006 midterm elections, the reforms were dead.

Throughout the second term, Rove dominated domestic policy and tasked Ed Gillespie with designing "kitchen table issues"—small, inexpensive programs that could be handled without legislation.[42] But the administration's low public approval ratings, stemming from the war in Iraq, left it with precious little political capital for moving even small kitchen-table issues forward.

As the Bush administration drew to a close, its domestic agenda was all but empty. The 2006 budget slashed funding for numerous domestic agencies, including the National Science Foundation, the Social Security Administration, and the Army Corps of Engineers, while the Department of Defense continued to receive substantial budget increases. The administration's record in domestic affairs had been irreparably damaged by its response to Hurricane Katrina in August 2005, which left the city of New Orleans under water for weeks, thousands of people all but abandoned, and hundreds of thousands fleeing to neighboring states, many never returning.

In reality, however, the administration's response to Hurricane Katrina was consistent with its view that the federal government should play only a limited role in people's lives. Under the Bush administration's theme of compassionate conservatism, neighbor should help neighbor, and faith-based organizations should be at the center of community empowerment. It was not an administration, moreover, that had empathy with minority populations. As soon as he took office, Bush removed the Office of Race Relations from a staffing role in the White House, and domestic policy lacked an office dedicated to problems of race and poverty. The administration actively opposed affirmative action, filing an amicus brief against the affirmative action policy of the University of Michigan Law School.

As the Obama administration prepared to take the helm of government in 2009, it was clear that the carefully tailored domestic agenda that had built a coalition of Christian conservatives and Reagan fiscal conservatives had been successful. The education and tax cut bills had passed, volunteer programs were in place, faith-based centers were operational in many of the departments, and social policies had been tailored to meet the administration's objectives. Many HHS pilot programs promoting abstinence and healthy marriage were fully funded through a combination of the administration's discretionary funds and congressional appropriations. Programs that suffered funding cuts after September 11 were generally not related to Bush's limited compassionate conservative agenda.

Most of the domestic policies championed by fiscal conservatives similarly thrived—including the three tax cuts, changes to the tax code for dividends and inheritance taxes, and Medicare prescription drug reform. The administration did fail, however, in some of its second-term policy goals, including legislation to allow individuals to have greater control over their Social Security accounts and to give illegal immigrants "guest worker" status. The failure to achieve these reforms may have been something of a blow to fiscal conservatives, but it did not, by any means, define Bush's domestic agenda, which focused successfully on building a moral and civil society.

Still, the shift in budgetary priorities—brought about by the escalating costs of the wars in Afghanistan and Iraq and the burgeoning Department of Homeland Security—limited Bush's domestic goals. The domestic side of the administration became cash-starved, and most federal agencies lost staff and program funding. Had more funds been available, the administration would probably have increased the budgets of programs associated with compassionate conservatism and built an institutional structure that might have lasted past the Bush administration. But war and homeland security dominated the budget after 9/11.

Both George W. Bush and Dick Cheney were comfortable with the lack of funding for domestic programs. Neither used the bully pulpit to argue for more money, and neither tried to interfere when OMB wielded its budget axe. Widely known as a deficit hawk, Cheney had aligned himself with fiscal conservatives throughout his public career. Once in office, that base strongly supported his business-friendly domestic agenda. By stripping away federal regulations and reducing staff and budgets for regulatory agencies, Cheney shrank the government and served the interests of fiscal conservatives. In a smart political move, however, his budget-cutting axe never touched the programs in Bush's faith-based, compassionate agenda.

The costs of war and changes in budget priorities had, in the end, little to do with the success of the administration's priorities. Domestic policy was not, as some alleged, a national train wreck.[43] Instead, it was moving, haltingly, in the direction the co-presidency set. George W. Bush was moving forward his faith-based presidency and Dick Cheney was moving forward his business-friendly presidency. How little Bush was engaged in the broader policy issues, and his complete focus on faith, was reflected by comments made by Michael Brown, the short-lived director of FEMA. "Very shortly after 9/11 I was leading a briefing in the Roosevelt room about smallpox. The president was there, the vice president. Condi was there. The president didn't ask a lot of questions. Don't get me wrong—he did ask some questions. But the majority of the questions came from either Condi or the vice president. As the president was leaving the room, he turned to everybody and said, God help us all. We should all say very strong prayers tonight for guidance. It really stuck in my head. You're the president of the United States basically saying, I'm going to pray tonight, and I hope all of you pray, too, because this is much bigger than all of us."[44]

CHAPTER 8

Cheney's Penchant for Secrecy

"WHERE'S DICK?" was the most frequently asked question across the country in the weeks after September 11, 2001. Cheney wasn't home behind the high wrought-iron fence of Number One Observatory Circle, the vice president's official residence in Washington, D.C. As it turns out, he was in a secret, undisclosed location where—according to his press secretary—he was receiving regular briefings with the president via secure communications. Cheney remained out of town and out of sight for weeks in his secret, protected location to ensure, as he said, a line of succession should the president be targeted by more terrorists.

If there is anything we know about Dick Cheney, it is his penchant for secrecy. He never wrote things down, never used e-mail, and tried never to leave a paper trail about what he said or whom he met with.[1] Although he had a press secretary, he never held press conferences, never released his daily schedule, and never willingly talked to the media. He was so secretive that to ensure their safety, all the papers in his office were stowed in a large Mosler safe at the end of each day. He wasn't a spy, but he carefully protected his office and all of the material in his office from any form of public scrutiny.

Cheney fundamentally believed that presidents, and vice presidents, had a constitutional right to privacy in their conversations, meetings, and deliberations. Neither the press nor Congress, he maintained, should have access to how presidents and vice presidents arrived at their decisions. This view reached absurd levels when Cheney kept the names of executives who met with the Energy Task Force secret; kept the names of his own staff from being listed in federal directories; refused to release Secret Service logs of visitors to the vice president's residence; asserted that the vice president's office was not subject to the Freedom of Information Act; and declared that the vice president's office was not part of the executive branch and, as a result, did not need to identify how it classified and declassified documents.

His determination to maintain the privacy of his decision making first emerged earlier in his career, when he served as Gerald Ford's deputy chief of staff. Not surprisingly, one of his goals at that point in his career was to protect Ford and the presidency from what he perceived as an overly aggressive Congress in the aftermath of the Nixon presidency. After Nixon resigned, the Democratically controlled Congress enacted a series of laws that tried to ensure open government by subjecting presidential decision making to increased scrutiny by the press and congressional committees. Cheney opposed most of these open-government laws.

One of the laws passed during this active period of congressional oversight of the executive branch came in 1974 when Congress amended and strengthened the Freedom of Information Act (FOIA), Johnson-era legislation originally signed in 1966. Cheney was particularly concerned about the implications of FOIA on the presidency. As White House deputy chief of staff, he joined the chief of staff, Donald Rumsfeld, and Antonin Scalia—then head of the Justice Department's Office of Legal Counsel—in vigorously opposing the amendments. In their view, the FOIA amendments allowed too much access to presidential deliberations and could become a problem. Sitting with Ford in the Oval Office, each argued that Ford should veto the bill, which he did. But Congress stood its ground and sustained the legislation in an override. As Cheney predicted, the revised FOIA would later become a thorn in the sides of the president and the vice president.

In spite of the demands by Congress to reduce secrecy in government, particularly in the Oval Office, Cheney and Rumsfeld continued cloaking their decisions in secrecy as often as they could. When the Khmer Rouge captured an American merchant marine ship, the *Mayagüez*, off the Cambodian coast in May 1975, Cheney and Rumsfeld insisted that they, as part of a small closed group, should handle the issue.

After Cheney moved into the chief of staff's chair following Rumsfeld's appointment as secretary of defense, he continued to tightly control policy making. Vice President Nelson Rockefeller became an early casualty of Cheney's tightly run office. His dislike for Rockefeller, the independent-minded architect of Ford's domestic agenda, led to a series of secret meetings with Bo Calloway, who was running the Ford reelection committee. Cheney successfully urged Calloway and Ford to dump Rockefeller in favor of Kansas senator Bob Dole in 1976.

The Ford-Dole ticket, however, lost in a close election The secrecy of the Nixon-Ford years, promoted by Cheney, fueled Jimmy Carter's campaign for an "open administration" and a government "that does not spy on its citizens."[2] After eight years of Republican control of the White House, voters elected Carter, a Democrat, on his pledge of openness in government.

Ronald Reagan recaptured the Oval Office for Republicans in 1980, focusing his administration on containing, if not destroying, the Soviet Union. By that time, Cheney had won the lone Wyoming congressional seat, and Rumsfeld was CEO of an international pharmaceutical company. Reagan, however, asked both of them to oversee secret planning for "continuity of government" should the Soviet Union launch a nuclear attack on the United States. Rumsfeld and Cheney eagerly agreed.

Once a year throughout the Reagan presidency, Cheney and Rumsfeld met to brainstorm what James Mann calls "The Armageddon Plan"—how a shadow government would work in case of nuclear attack.[3] The ultra-secret plan, known as Project 908, was created by executive order, with Reagan to be regularly informed about the details, and with the mandate that the plan be carried out in total secrecy. Once operational, meetings for Project 908 began at Andrews Air Force Base, near Washington, D.C., where Cheney and Rumsfeld would gather with a team of forty or so federal officials and a single member of Reagan's cabinet, whoever was available that day. The team would then travel to a nearby bunker or military base.

During these meetings, Cheney and Rumsfeld created a detailed blueprint for continuity in government for Project 908. If a nuclear attack occurred, three teams—each with staff from the Defense, State, and Treasury Departments, the CIA, and several domestic agencies—would leave Washington and travel to different locations. Depending on which team managed to survive the nuclear attack, one of them would take control of the apparatus of government. To run the planning operation, the Reagan administration created a new agency, the National Program Office (NPO), with a budget that eventually reached billions of dollars by 1989.[4] The NPO worked closely with the National Security Council (NSC), including Oliver North, a Marine lieutenant colonel assigned to the NSC.[5] North, of course, was later caught in his own web of intrigue and secrecy as the architect of the Iran-Contra scandal.

As the Cheney-Rumsfeld group planned their operations for taking control of government, if necessary, they often used the National Emergency Airborne Command Post—a Boeing 747, based at Andrews Air Force Base, that was outfitted with secure communications equipment.[6] During their drills, the Cheney-Rumsfeld group practiced running the government from the airborne command center, designating one of the cabinet officers as president. Although cabinet members rotated during the exercises, Cheney and Rumsfeld were constant participants. Often the group would stay in the air for three days, based on the assumption that they would not be able to land during a nuclear attack.

After Reagan left office, planning exercises continued under George H. W. Bush, who had overseen Project 908 during the Reagan years. The details of the continuity in government planning in Project 908 remained relatively secret until 1989, when *U.S. News & World Report* raised the specter of the shadow government being planned. Other reports followed, including a CNN investigation in 1991 that broadcast a segment on the shadow government being assembled, opening with, "in the United States Federal Government there is a super-secret agency which controls this Shadow Government." When the Clinton administration took office, it shut down the super-secret Project 908.[7]

Soon after the Bush administration took office, however, Cheney reengaged himself in planning for an attack on U.S. shores, but by this time he had widened his conversation from one that focused on a nuclear attack to one that focused on weapons of mass destruction. Project 908 was dead, but Cheney found a new way to stay engaged in the federal government's response to a nuclear—or other—attack.

The opening for Cheney was provided in February 2001, with the release of the report by the U.S. Commission on National Security in the 21st Century. The commission, chaired by former senators Gary Hart (D-Colorado) and Warren Rudman (R-New Hampshire) and often known as the Hart-Rudman Commission, concluded that the federal response to a terrorist attack was uncoordinated and needed immediate attention. Cheney saw the perfect opportunity and grabbed it. "One of our biggest threats as a nation is no longer the conventional military attack against the United States," Cheney said, "but rather that it might come from other quarters. It could be domestic terrorism."[8] In May 2001, Bush assigned Cheney the role of coordinating how federal agencies responded to domestic terrorism. By its very nature, Cheney assumed, the planning operation would operate in secret, with its deliberations protected by executive privilege.

Cheney created the National Preparedness Review Task Force in his office and hired a retired four-star admiral, Steve Abbot, as its director. Cheney wanted someone he knew and trusted at the helm, and he had worked with Abbot, who had been deputy director of operations with the Joint Chiefs of Staff, in the first Bush administration. Among others tasks, the new task force was charged with developing guidelines for FEMA's new Office of National Preparedness. FEMA had been given primary authority in May to coordinate the federal response to a domestic terrorist attack. But Abbot did not move into his office until the summer of 2001—having waited months for his White House security clearance—and had only been working for a few weeks before the terrorist attacks of September 11 brought his planning work to a halt. Whatever the task force did during those weeks remained within the confines of the vice president's office and secret, as was everything else in the vice president's office.

The task force would have a short life, however, because the terrorist attacks of 9/11 changed Cheney's role in managing national security. Cheney's small task force and its recommendations would soon play an integral role after 9/11 as Cheney sought to integrate his office with the developing White House Office of Homeland Security. He would easily move Abbot into the key job of deputy director, ensuring that the new director, Pennsylvania governor Tom Ridge, would continue the work that Cheney's task force had initiated.[9]

Although Cheney had shifted gears from continuity in government to his national preparedness review, Cheney's years of secret planning in Project 908 paid off for him when terrorists struck New York City and Washington, D.C. On Tuesday, September 11, 2001, George W. Bush was in Florida talking to elementary school children when terrorists flew planes into the towers of New York's World Trade Center and the Pentagon. Cheney immediately phoned Bush and urged him not to return to Washington, D.C., but to fly instead to a secure military location. He then told Speaker of the House Dennis Hastert and the House and Senate leadership to evacuate their offices and move to the underground bunkers designed for senior government officials. Cheney himself did not evacuate, however, but instead remained in the underground bunker beneath the White House—the Presidential Emergency Operations Center (PEOC)—to run the government.

Within hours, Bush had landed at Offutt Air Force Base, near Omaha, Nebraska. At all times after the terrorist attacks, President Bush was safe and capable of acting as the nation's chief executive, but Cheney took control and made the important decisions. It was a role he had been planning for two decades. It didn't matter that everyone was still alive. Cheney was ready. A terrorist attack, not a nuclear attack, had knocked out the World Trade Center towers and the Pentagon, but Cheney took charge. There were no orders from Bush—only a taped message to the nation that he would "hunt down" whoever had attacked the country.

Responding to what he perceived to be a vacuum in leadership while Bush was out of town, Cheney jumped into action in his bunker beneath the East Wing to ensure continuity in government. He immediately began to create his shadow government by ordering one hundred mid-level executive officials to move to specially designated underground bunkers and stay there twenty-four hours a day. They would not be rotated out, he informed them, for ninety days, since there was evidence, he hinted, that the terrorist organization al-Qaʻida, which had masterminded the attack, had nuclear weapons. The shadow government, as a result, needed to be ready to take over the government from the bunkers.

After the White House evacuation that day, the East Wing bunker contained members of both the president's staff and the vice president's staff. With the vice president in the White House bunker were his wife, Lynn; his political advisor, Mary Matalin; and his national security advisor, Scooter Libby. Condoleezza Rice, Joshua Bolten, Karen Hughes, Nicholas Calio, and others were there from the president's staff.[10]

When the Cheneys finally left the underground bunker shortly after 10:00 P.M. on September 11, they boarded Marine Two—the vice president's helicopter—on the South Lawn of the White House, even though only the president traditionally leaves from the South Lawn. The Cheneys flew to Camp David, the president's retreat, where they settled into Aspen Lodge, the president's personal cabin. Dick Cheney was not just the vice president; as co-president, he felt he was entitled to these presidential privileges. On that day Cheney was not only running the shadow government, but also the government itself.

Soon Cheney left Camp David and moved seven miles west to the Alternative Joint Communications Center near Waynesboro, Pennsylvania, which housed an underground bunker under Raven Rock Mountain, known as Site R. Cheney stayed at the undisclosed location for several months, occasionally returning to Washington to meet with the president and his own aides on various national security issues.

As government returned to normal operations in the weeks after the terrorist attacks, Bush signed an executive order creating a Homeland Security Council and an Office of Homeland Security in the White House. Both, however, were largely Cheney's ideas. Jimmy Carter had first proposed creation of a central federal agency that would manage domestic crises, signing an executive order in 1979 that established the Federal Emergency Management Agency (FEMA). FEMA was originally envisioned as a central agency for overseeing national responses to natural disasters as well as to terrorist attacks that could leave water systems and the air quality at risk. Cheney, with his long institutional memory, built on Carter's plan for having a central federal agency coordinating disaster response in his recommendation for a White House office focused on homeland terrorism.

Bush quickly concurred, signing the executive order that created the White House Office of Homeland Security, and brought Ridge in to head the office, in October 2001. Still in his undisclosed location at Site R, Cheney intended to be closely involved in this critical national security function. Although Bush named Ridge to head the new office, Cheney easily persuaded Ridge to hire Abbot as deputy director.

As the Office of Homeland Security grew in size and responsibility, Congress considered replacing it with a cabinet-level Department of Homeland Security, which would move decision making on homeland security out of the White House into a cabinet-level department. It was an idea that the White House opposed, leading press secretary Ari Fleischer to say that "creating a cabinet-level post doesn't solve the problem" of homeland security.[11] By April 2002, the idea was supported both by Democrats, led by Senator Joseph Lieberman of Connecticut, and by Republicans, led by Senator Arlen Specter of Pennsylvania.

Cheney, with his penchant for secrecy, was the chief opponent within the White House. He opposed transforming homeland security functions into a cabinet-level agency, because that would give Congress oversight of its activities. Keeping Ridge's office in the White House would ensure that all its meetings and conversations remained privileged. Ridge was forbidden by Bush and Cheney to attend congressional hearings on how money was being spent on homeland security or to discuss internal conversations with members of Congress. Secrecy, for Cheney at least, was the coin of the realm.

Finally, however, mounting pressure from both sides of the aisle in Congress led the White House to develop its own proposal for a cabinet-level department. A five-member task force—organized by White House chief of staff Andy Card—determined which agencies should be absorbed into the proposed department.[12] Scooter Libby, although not a member of Card's core group, met regularly with them. After six weeks of meetings, the task force unveiled a proposal that called for a new Department of Homeland Security that would incorporate a broad array of agencies, including FEMA and the Coast Guard. This planning, of course, was done completely in secret. Not even cabinet officers whose departments would be dramatically affected had been consulted; as one task force member admitted, they "were just totally bamboozled."[13]

Cheney's distrust of career staff and their alliances with congressional committees was evident in the way the White House task force shaped the new department for homeland security. It made the stunning recommendation that some employees in the absorbed agencies lose their civil service status and be subject to political dismissals. As a result, the Department of Homeland Security that emerged was exactly what Cheney wanted: an agency that had fewer positions with civil service protections. Decision making could be cloaked in secrecy with the expanded politicization of senior staff.

The task force also recommended reorganizing the Department of Justice, creating a new division to handle national security cases. The new Justice superdivision would be immune from oversight. Its actions would be considered classified and protected from public or congressional scrutiny. Although it took several years, the reauthorization of the USA PATRIOT Act in 2006 provided for creation of a National Security Division in the Department of Justice, as the task force had wanted. A key component of the new division was the litigation division in the Office of Intelligence, which prosecuted terrorists. Prosecutions of the 9/11 terrorists, for example, could be handled in secret by a Military Commission jointly managed by the National Security Division and by the Department of Defense.[14]

Secret meetings and discussions had been Cheney's hallmark for decades. One of his central goals in building a single executive office was to ensure that he and his staff were covered by the shield of executive privilege generally reserved only for the president and his senior staff. Full transparency between the president's and vice president's offices presumably created an executive office with the full protections of executive privilege. Meeting discussions, and the participants in those meetings, would remain privileged and not subject to congressional or press scrutiny.

The Energy Task Force litigation became an early test of Cheney's assertions of executive privilege. Several organizations, including the General Accounting Office, sued the vice president's office to release the names of participants in the Energy Task Force. Each of the lawsuits asserted that the secrecy of the Energy Task Force prevented public disclosure of the participants, who were widely believed to be primarily energy executives. The lawsuits alleged that the absence of other voices, particularly from the environmental community, led to a one-sided energy plan.

The first lawsuit came in early 2002 when the General Accounting Office (GAO), sought to gain access to the task force's membership lists and records of the meeting dates. Carter Phillips, representing the GAO, argued in federal court that its comptroller general had authority to investigate how the task force used public funds. Phillips's argument centered on the GAO's legal authority to investigate any executive branch use of federal money.

Cheney's office countered that the GAO had no authority to investigate meetings held by the vice president and his staff—and that Congress had no right to any information about any conversations—under the principle of executive privilege. Paul D. Clement, the deputy solicitor general representing Cheney in the GAO case, argued that "no court that I'm aware of has ever ordered the executive branch to turn over a document to a congressional agent. This is unprecedented."[15]

That argument proved secondary, however, when U.S. District Court judge John D. Bates ruled against the GAO, noting that Congress had not tried to subpoena the documents before going to court. Bates did not address the separation of powers argument made by Clement, but rather focused on a procedural failing by Congress. They had to exhaust other procedural avenues before pursuing their court case. Under pressure from congressional Republicans, who never supported the lawsuit, Comptroller General David Walker did not appeal.[16] At the same time that the GAO was pressing its case, two private-sector litigants, Judicial Watch and the Sierra Club, filed lawsuits seeking the Energy Task Force information. After a four-year legal battle, the appeals court ruled in favor of Cheney and his argument for executive privilege. "In making decisions on personnel and policy, and in formulating legislative proposals, the president [and vice president] must be free to seek confidential information from many sources, both inside the government and outside," said Judge A. Raymond Randolph of the U.S. Court of Appeals for the District of Columbia.[17]

In yet another lawsuit, filed by the Natural Resources Defense Council (NRDC), the court ruled that the Federal Advisory Committee Act (FACA), better known as the open meetings law, only pertained if outside participants voted in the final outcome; since Cheney's task force involved input from—not votes cast by—outside sources, FACA, the court found, did not apply.[18]

Congress had also tried to secure documents from Cheney's Energy Task Force. John Dingell, the ranking Democrat on the House Energy and Commerce Committee, used the FACA approach to obtain the Energy Task Force documents, or at least the participants' names. But Cheney's legal counsel, David Addington, sent back a scathing letter to Dingell that tersely said, "Please be advised that the FACA does not apply to the task force."[19] In spite of these very different lawsuits, and a congressional inquiry, Cheney was able to preserve the secrecy of the Energy Task Force.

At times, the vice president's demand for secrecy took on comic proportions. In June 2007, ABC News posted a "Civics Quiz" on the Internet, which asked, "Is the vice president part of the executive branch?" adding, "You might think the answer is obvious but apparently not to Vice President Dick Cheney."[20] In one of the more bizarre twists of Cheney's efforts to protect his office from any scrutiny, he declared that the Office of the Vice President was not subject to an executive order that required all executive branch agencies to disclose the number of documents that had been classified and declassified during the year. Presumably, as the ABC News quiz noted, the vice president was subject to the mandate, since he was part of the executive branch. Cheney, however, did what no other vice president had done—he asserted that he was not part of the executive branch and therefore not subject to the terms of the executive order.

The issue surfaced because Executive Order 12958 (signed by Bill Clinton in 1995) required the Information Security Oversight Office (ISOO) in the National Archives and Records Administration to disclose the number of documents that had been classified and declassified during the year. The executive order was intended to ensure an automatic declassification of most government files after twenty-five years, in part because of the expanding demands for transparency in government. The executive order was amended by Bush in 2003—Executive Order 13292—to exempt much of the material on terrorism from declassification and to give extensions of five or more years to declassifying material such as audio and video tapes, which might require longer staff time to review.[21] All offices in the executive branch were required to provide the information. Presumably, the vice president was subject to the mandate, since his office was part of the executive branch.

This was a new tactic. In 2001, the vice president had done everything possible to transform the executive branch into a single executive office in which he and his staff had complete equality and access. The next year, he had the Office of Management and Budget change the federal budget to create a single appropriation for the Executive Office of the President, encompassing the Office of the Vice President. In defending the secrecy of the Energy Task Force against the GAO, Cheney had also argued that the vice presidency was part of the executive branch. Now, in the fight with the ISOO, he was suggesting that his office was not part of the executive branch.

The question of whether or not the vice president's office was part of the executive branch surfaced often in conflicts with the ISOO. In May 2006, David Addington sent a letter to J. William Leonard, the ISOO's director, stating that the vice president's office "does not consider itself an entity within the executive branch." Leonard retorted in early June 2006 that "it is entirely appropriate that security classification activity by OVP [Office of the Vice President] staff in supporting the vice president's performance of executive duties be reportable to this office in accordance with relevant sections of the [executive] order and directive."[22] Leonard added in his letter that the OVP had provided the information in past years.

Addington and Cheney had apparently reached the decision to exempt the OVP without any consultation with the National Archives or with the White House, which was following the president's executive order. Cheney's office, in isolation, had determined which rules applied to its own operations and its staff.

Addington then sent another letter to Leonard, stating that the vice president was not part of the executive branch because of his role as president of the Senate. The vice president had, according to Addington, a special constitutional role that exempted him from rules governing the executive branch. Meetings between Leonard's and Cheney's staff apparently became tense, with Cheney's aides threatening to abolish the Oversight Security Information Agency—although they denied it when the ISOO staff reported that threat to Congressman Henry Waxman.[23]

The issue between Cheney's office and ISOO remained unresolved until July 2007, when the Democratically controlled Congress sought to restrict Cheney's access to certain funds unless he observed the provisions of Executive Order 12958. The White House was now forced to become involved and, of necessity, to support Cheney. Fred Fielding, the White House counsel, informed the Senate that "the Office of the Vice President, like the President's office, is not an 'agency' for purposes of this [executive] order" and thus not subject to the executive order requiring the disclosure of the number of classified and declassified documents.[24] This was somewhat confusing, since Tony Fratto in the White House Press Office had issued a statement in June 2007 in which she said that "the White House complies with the executive order, including the National Security Council." When Leonard then sought a binding interpretation from the attorney general's office, Stephen Bradbury in the Office of Legal Counsel responded that his office would not be supplying an opinion, because Fielding's letter had resolved the matter. The ISOO was effectively overruled, and Leonard stopped asking the vice president to inform his office about how many documents it classified and declassified.

The vice president's press secretary, Lea Anne McBride, tried to explain to a cynical press why the vice president was not part of the executive branch. She argued that the distinction between the executive and legislative branches was irrelevant because the executive order did not apply to the president or vice president—only to agencies within the executive branch. "The executive order's intent," she asserted, "is to treat the vice president like the president, rather than like an agency."[25] Cheney was now, according to his office, part of the executive branch, although for other reasons. Addington had flatly stated that the vice president was not "an entity within the executive branch." The matter was unquestionably confusing to most who followed it.

Cheney's assertions of secrecy extended to travel costs. The Center for Public Integrity reported in 2005 that Cheney's office had not complied with the Ethics in Government Act of 1989, requiring federal employees to report all travel funded by private sources to the Office of Government Ethics (OGE).[26] Travel costs paid by private sources had been regularly reported by every executive agency, including the president's office. Alberto Gonzales, counsel to the president, and Karl Rove, director of the Office of Strategic Initiatives in the White House, had both provided information on their privately paid trips. David Addington wrote a letter to the OGE's director, Sandy Mabry, however, stating that the law applied to "the head of each agency of the executive branch," but that the OVP was "not an agency of the executive branch," and "hence the reporting requirement does not apply."[27]

Addington had written Mabry the same letter yearly since 2002. Following Addington's logic, it would seem that Gonzales, the president's lawyer, had determined that the White House itself was part of an agency of the executive branch and should thus comply with the regulations. Addington presumably disagreed with Gonzales on this point. Although Cheney had included the OVP in the White House appropriations for the federal budget, he now took the position that the vice president was "not an agency of the executive branch."

Cheney and his staff, it turned out, never took a single privately funded trip. When Cheney gave a commencement address at a university or spoke to a trade organization, he never accepted reimbursement for travel costs. During his entire tenure as vice president, he deemed every government-related trip to be official business, never seeking reimbursement for food, lodging, or travel. In contrast, during the period from 1997 to 2000, Vice President Gore returned $180,000 to the public coffers from travel reimbursements for speeches he gave to private groups and for commencements.

Cheney's classification of all of his travel as official, and the subsequent use of government funds for every trip, allowed him to avoid disclosing where he went or with whom he met. His calendar could be kept secret, and the speeches he gave could be shielded from public view if they were not privately reimbursed and open for scrutiny in the public filings of the Office of Government Ethics. Addington's clever wording—that the vice president was not an entity of the executive branch and, thus, was not subject to filing travel disclosure information—was part of a larger effort to protect the vice president's office from press and legislative oversight. But even the executive branch could not scrutinize the vice president, as the director of the OGE learned. Cheney had built a fortress-like wall of secrecy around his office and actions, which neither Congress nor other executive branch offices seemed able to penetrate.

Cheney's obsession with secrecy was evident in personal matters, too, including his hunting activities. On Valentine's Day 2006, he was quail hunting with friends on a Texas ranch when he accidentally shot Harry Whittington, a member of the hunting party, who was rushed to the hospital in serious condition.[28] Rather than release any information to the press, or even tell the White House what had happened, Cheney remained silent. The story only leaked after the ranch owner talked to the press. Cheney's attitude and silence were approvingly explained by Bill O'Reilly of Fox News in his column the next day. "The Cheney story," he wrote, "was unfortunate for the man accidentally shot, but who else was affected? No one."[29] Dick Cheney, however, was vice president of the United States, and he had shot someone; nevertheless, he saw no reason for that information to be made public.

Cheney's hunting trips were rarely disclosed to the press, or even the White House, because of his insistence that his travel remain private. In October 2007, for example, Cheney went to the exclusive Clove Valley Rod and Gun Club in New York, where members pay as much as $100,000 to shoot ducks and pheasants on four thousand acres. Only Cheney's staff knew where the vice president was; the president's staff was never informed. When reporters asked the White House Press Office about the trip, the response was a curt "no comment"; a White House spokeswoman could provide no details of the trip, because she didn't know any. Dick Cheney had demanded that his office be integrated into the White House staff, with "full transparency," but information flowed only in one direction.

Cheney's compulsion for secrecy took another twist in the fall of 2006, when he ordered the Secret Service to destroy all records of visitors to the vice president's official home on Massachusetts Avenue. Whether family members, staff, lobbyists, or others visited the residence, all logs, he instructed, were to be destroyed.[30] The issue surfaced in May 2006, when the Secret Service and the White House signed a memorandum of understanding designating visitor logs as presidential, including those of the vice president. They are "not records of an 'agency,' subject to the Freedom of Information Act. The records are at all times under the legal control of the White House," said the agreement. Addington then followed the agreement with a letter dated September 13, 2006, which ordered the Secret Service to destroy all but one copy of the logs, which they would turn over to the vice president. Since the logs, according to the letter, were covered by the Presidential Records Act, they were the personal property of the vice president; they could not be retained or released by the Secret Service.

The logs had, however, been part of information traditionally released to Congress and the press in past administrations. Openness in government had been the rule, not the exception, but it was not a rule that Cheney's office often chose to follow. Instead, Cheney's office asserted that the logs, like the Energy Task Force deliberations, were protected by executive privilege and were not subject to the Freedom of Information Act. Anyone seeking them through the act or other means would be turned down. Challenges to Cheney's interpretation of how visitor logs were to be controlled were first made in 2006, when the *Washington Post* sought copies of the Secret Service logs for a story on access that lobbyists, particularly Jack Abramoff, had to Dick Cheney and his staff. The newspaper speculated at the time that Cheney used his home for controversial meetings to avoid the logs that were carefully maintained at the White House and Old Executive Office Building. When Cheney's office refused the request for the logs, the *Washington Post* sued and won in federal district court. Judge Ricardo M. Urbina ordered the visitor logs released, noting that executive privilege did not apply, and that the logs were covered by the Freedom of Information Act.

As expected, Cheney appealed Urbina's decision, insisting that the vice president's office was not subject to FOIA requirements. The Department of Justice, now led by Alberto Gonzales, was an avid protector of presidential and vice-presidential privilege and said in its brief in the U.S. Court of Appeals that making the logs public would be an "unprecedented intrusion into the daily operations of the vice presidency."[31] The federal appeals court issued an emergency stay, blocking Urbina's order for release of the logs until the appeal was completed. The *Washington Post* chose not to pursue the litigation further and withdrew from the case.

The issue was not dead, however, since other organizations also had questions about who had been meeting with the vice president. Questions on who the vice president was meeting with were not new, as the litigation over the participants in the Energy Task Force indicated. Citizens for Responsibility and Ethics in Washington (CREW)—a government watchdog group funded by the liberal Democracy Alliance—filed another lawsuit against Cheney's office seeking the release of the logs. They sought information, through the FOIA, about visits that nine religious leaders—including James Dobson of Focus on the Family and Jerry Falwell, co-founder of the Moral Majority—had made to the vice president's home for private meetings. CREW sought the release of Secret Service logs as part of their contention that religious leaders had unduly influenced the administration's decisions in domestic and foreign policy.

Again, the federal court defended the relevancy of the FOIA and ordered the release of the logs. In December 2007, U.S. District Court judge Royce C. Lamberth ruled that "knowledge of these visitors would not disclose presidential communications or shine a light on the president's or vice president's policy deliberations."[32] The documents, he insisted, were public records and should be released. Lamberth, however, knew that the case dealt with many of the same issues as the *Washington Post* suit and blocked release of the documents until an appellate court had made its decision—giving the vice president's office a temporary victory. In 2008, the appellate court ruled against Cheney, sending the case back to Judge Lamberth and allowing his decision to stand.[33] The watchdog group was now free to submit requests for the Secret Service logs through the FOIA. Since Freedom of Information Act requests generally take months, if not years, to fulfill, however, Cheney had at least shielded his visitor logs for the remaining months of the administration, and likely longer.

As a result of the questions surrounding the FOIA, the White House created a web site that specifically noted that neither the president's nor the vice president's documents would be released. Neither office was, the web site asserted, subject to the requirements of the Freedom of Information Act. The web site had never been part of the White House web site nor any other official information until Dick Cheney began facing lawsuits concerning whom he had met with and why. The main purpose of the web site, evidently, was to deter more lawsuits against Cheney.

In its battle to keep every possible shred of information from public scrutiny, the vice president's office even refused to list the names of its staff in public and private directories. It had been a common practice for decades for administrations to release the names and titles of most members of the White House staff and the broader Executive Office of the President, including the vice president's office, to the Bureau of National Affairs (BNA), a privately held company, owned by *U.S. News & World Report*, which annually produced an exhaustive list of senior staff names, addresses, and phone numbers across the executive branch. The list was widely circulated inside and outside government and could be purchased for about $10 by anyone who requested it. After the Bush administration's first term, however, Cheney's staff refused to be included in the publications, extending the veil of secrecy to cover everyone and everything in the vice president's office.

By refusing to release information under the shield of executive privilege, as Nixon had often tried to do, Dick Cheney was returning to Nixon-era government practices. As the Pulitzer Prize–winning author Charlie Savage observed in his book *Takeover: The Return of the Imperial Presidency*, Cheney was trying to restore a system of government in which the president "consolidated government authority inside the White House."[34] For Cheney, shielding decision making in the vice president's office from prying eyes was part of a broader effort to restore presidential powers that he felt had been eroded by the post-Watergate press and Congress.

Throughout his tenure as vice president, Cheney successfully maintained the secrecy of his decision-making process and its participants. In many cases, Addington's assertion that the vice president would not provide requested material was enough to ward off further questioning, and Cheney rarely lost a court battle testing these claims. His penchant for secrecy in every aspect of the vice president's daily life became even more pronounced in national security policy decision making. Cheney secretly built the case for war in Iraq, circumventing the secretary of state, and developed policies for harsh interrogation of detainees and wireless surveillance. He legitimized his actions using the protective umbrella of the Constitution and an expansive interpretation of presidential power. Secrecy, after all, was essential to the imperial co-presidency he was creating.

CHAPTER 9

The Imperial Presidency

D ICK CHENEY'S aggressive assertion of presidential power led to frequent charges across the nation of an imperial presidency. Cover stories and headlines decrying presidential power grabs by Bush and Cheney were common in the press and reached a crescendo after 9/11. References to "King George" became routine, and critics decried an administration that often saw itself as above the law. A former Republican congressman went so far as to assert, "This administration is beyond the pale in terms of arrogance and incompetence. This guy thinks he's a monarch, and that's scary as hell."[1] Perhaps the references should have been to "King Richard."

Bush and Cheney rarely responded to charges of an imperial presidency. They maintained that their actions were essential to protecting the balance of power in the government and the president's constitutional authority. During eight years in office, Bush rarely commented on the expansive power that his administration accumulated. There is no question that he supported Cheney's drive to expand presidential authority, but it was Cheney who masterminded the plan. In the division of labor in the co-presidency, Cheney was the chief architect of the imperial presidency.

Speaking to NBC News's Campbell Brown in early 2002, Cheney explained his determination to rebalance the relationship between the president and Congress. "For the thirty-five years that I've been in town," he said, "there's been a constant, *steady erosion* of the prerogatives and the powers of the President of the United States."[2] The presidency itself was in danger.

For Cheney, the president's role as commander in chief was sacrosanct for the president, with absolute constitutional authority. Challenges to this role, he believed, began in 1973, when Congress passed the War Powers Resolution to insert Congress into military decisions in what it called a collective decision-making process. Speaking at a 1983 forum of the American Enterprise Institute, Cheney reasserted his concern that Congress was making unconstitutional intrusions into the president's ability to protect and defend the nation. "I very firmly believe" he said, "that the War Powers Resolution is an unwise and virtually unworkable intrusion by the legislative branch into the powers and prerogatives the president needs to lead the United States in a very dangerous and hostile world."[3]

Gerald Ford, too, had been critical of Congress's incursions. "Some people used to complain about what they called an imperial presidency [during the Nixon administration]," he wrote in a commissioned article for *Time* magazine; "now the pendulum has swung too far in the opposite direction." He warned of an "imperiled presidency," because of "misguided reforms" by Congress, and of the need to protect presidential authority.[4] Now with the Bush administration at the helm of government, Cheney was in a position to reverse the tide of encroaching congressional government that both he and Ford feared.

No one captured the parallels to the Nixon administration better than the Pulitzer Prize–winning historian Arthur Schlesinger Jr. It was Schlesinger who coined the phrase "imperial presidency" to define Nixon's expansive interpretation of presidential powers, which became synonymous with presidential power grabs.[5] Exactly thirty years after first writing about Nixon's imperial presidency, Schlesinger wrote an op-ed article for the *Washington Post* titled "The Imperial Presidency Redux," describing the Bush administration's expansive interpretation of presidential power.[6] For Schlesinger, the similarity to Nixon was unmistakable.

References to an imperial presidency first surfaced when Nixon ordered secret bombing runs against North Vietnamese in Cambodia, impounded congressional funds, and refused to release Oval Office audio tapes in the Watergate investigation. Nixon, for whatever reason, actively encouraged the image of an imperial presidency. For a while, he even dressed the White House security staff in uniforms reminiscent of palace guards, with gold-trimmed black vinyl hats and ceremonial trumpets.

After the Nixon years, presidents distanced themselves from any appearance of being above the law or of abusing the power of their office. Jimmy Carter, who billed himself as a simple peanut farmer from Georgia, went so far as to get out of the presidential limousine during inauguration ceremonies in 1977 to walk the parade route along Pennsylvania Avenue. He portrayed himself as a man of the people and, as part of his pledge of openness, shook hands with hundreds of visitors as they followed him into the White House. His presidency deliberately had no imperial trappings.

As the pendulum began to swing toward Congress in the Nixon and Ford years and later, Congress began to curb presidential power by passing laws such as the War Powers Resolution of 1973, the Budget and Impoundment Control Act of 1974, and the Boland Amendments in the early 1980s. Nearly a decade after Nixon, Congress was still carefully monitoring presidential actions, particularly in foreign policy.

MIDWAY THROUGH the Reagan presidency, allegations again surfaced about abuse of power, centering on secret funding that the Reagan administration provided to Nicaraguan insurgents—the Contras—in spite of legislation that Congress had passed to stop the funding. In very public hearings, Congress called a parade of Reagan's White House staff and others to testify. Television cameras carried the hearings from gavel to gavel, and the nation watched another test of wills over the limits of presidential power.

After weeks of testimony, new evidence surfaced that the administration—in a scheme hatched by Oliver North in the National Security Council—was also selling arms to Iran to help fund the Contra insurgents. Congress was outraged that Reagan had not only broken numerous laws banning aid to the Contras and the sale of arms to Iran, but had also seemingly lied to Congress and the American people in the process. Suddenly, calls for Reagan's impeachment began circulating in the halls of Congress in the Iran-Contra affair.

At the conclusion of the congressional hearings, a joint committee of the House and Senate issued a report sharply critical of Reagan for violating the law and overstepping his constitutional authority in foreign policy. Not everyone on the joint committee, however, was quite so willing to condemn Reagan and his staff. Several Republican members opposed the conclusions of the report and chose to release a Minority Report with a separate set of conclusions supporting Reagan. Congressman Dick Cheney of Wyoming joined five Republican members of the House (William Broomfield, Henry Hyde, Jim Courter, Bill McCollum, and Michael DeWine) and two Republican members of the Senate (James A. McClure and Orrin Hatch) in signing the report, issued on November 17, 1987.

The Minority Report was primarily written by Cheney and David Addington, the legal counsel for the House Intelligence Committee, in what was to become the first of their collaborations to expand presidential power. Cheney and Addington concluded that "there was no constitutional crisis, no systematic disrespect for the 'rule of law,' no grand conspiracy, and no Administration-wide dishonesty or cover-up."[7] Reagan, they said, was completely within his constitutional authority in his actions to fund the Nicaraguan Contras and allow the sale of arms to Iran. It was Congress, they said, that had overstepped its authority by trying to keep the president from engaging in his constitutional responsibility for national security. There was a distinct difference of opinion between the Minority and Majority Reports, which had polar opposite views of the limits of presidential power.

Buried within the Minority Report was perhaps its most important point. Cheney argued that unconstitutional statutes violate the rule of law. According to Cheney, "the fundamental law of the land is the Constitution. Unconstitutional statutes violate the rule of law every bit as much as do willful violations of constitutional statutes." The use of the phrase *unconstitutional statutes* implied that the president could decide whether or not a statute was unconstitutional.

Presidents, Cheney argued, do not have to follow a law or any part of a law they deem unconstitutional. The operative word was "they." "They," meaning presidents, could unilaterally decide whether a statute was unconstitutional. In the case of the Minority Report dealing with the Iran-Contra affair, Cheney believed that the laws that constrained the president were unconstitutional; as a result, Reagan had no obligation to follow them. The philosophy that *unconstitutional statutes violate the rule of law* was at the heart of Cheney's view of expansive presidential power, both then and as vice president.

The constitutional system, in Cheney's view, meant a governing structure in which the president could determine whether a statute violated his constitutional authority. There would be no recourse against his decision. It was not a view everyone shared. One editorial predicted that "when the Bush presidency ends, there will be a great deal of damage to repair, much of it to the constitutional system."[8] The system of checks and balances and constitutional assignments of power had not been under as much strain since the Nixon years.

Cheney's strategy for rebuilding presidential power usurped by Congress centered on building a wall of separation between Congress and the executive branch, using the Constitution as mortar. David Addington was the wall's chief builder, paying attention to the smallest details to prevent any gaps. Dick Cheney was the architect and construction foreman, overseeing broad plans for an impenetrable wall.

Signing statements would become the keystone of the wall. Addington reviewed every bill passed by Congress and sent to the president in order to remove any language that might open a chink in the wall. Cheney's staff, not the president's, took responsibility for monitoring bills for constitutional acceptability as they awaited the president's signature—determining whether any sentence, phrase, or paragraph implied that Congress was ignoring or overriding the president's constitutional authority. If Addington found language that *he considered unconstitutional*, he attached a signing statement to the bill for the president to sign asserting that certain parts were unconstitutional and therefore unenforceable.

Congress had no recourse once the signing statement was attached to the bill. During the eight years of his administration, Bush attached more than 800 signing statements to bills—an extraordinary number, which dramatically exceeded those in any previous administration. Reagan had 71 signing statements, George H. W. Bush had 146, and Bill Clinton had 105.[9] Cheney and Addington were using their power in the vice president's office to address the objections to an intrusive Congress that they had raised in the Minority Report of 1987.

Gaining control of signing statements in the White House proved relatively easy for Cheney and Addington. In the single executive office that Cheney created, the White House Office of Legislative Affairs routinely sent to the vice president's staff all enrolled bills that were ready for the president to sign or veto.[10] After Addington reviewed the bills, he circulated his recommendations for attaching signing statements among the entire White House senior staff to ensure that there were no objections, which there rarely were. No one in the White House objected to the role that Addington and Cheney had assumed as protectors of the president's constitutional authority.

Several signing statements, from the completely mundane to the contentious, illustrate the manner in which Addington and Cheney used them to bolster presidential authority. A mundane example involved a bill creating a commission to commemorate the fiftieth anniversary of *Brown v. Board of Education of Topeka*—the landmark 1954 desegregation decision by the Supreme Court. Congress had included a provision in the legislation that appointments to the commission should include representatives of specific organizations, such as the National Association for the Advancement of Colored People (NAACP). Bush signed the bill, but he (or rather Addington) included a signing statement asserting that only the president had the constitutional authority to appoint, and he would not take orders from Congress on whom to name to the commission. Although the signing statement insisted that the president alone would make all decisions on the appointments, two members of the NAACP were eventually included. Signing statements became a constant form of saber rattling by the administration, assailing Congress for intruding on its constitutional territory. Whether or not the administration followed the recommendations of Congress—in this case, with regard to appointments—was secondary to the principle it was asserting.

Signing statements repeatedly questioned Congress's constitutional authority to require a presidential action within the executive branch. Congress passed a law requiring the U.S. Customs Service and Border

Patrol to frequently relocate checkpoints in the Tucson, Arizona, area, for example. Members of Congress argued that moving the checkpoints more frequently would deter illegal immigrants from crossing the border. Bush signed the bill with a signing statement adding that decisions on how to manage the executive branch were his and his alone. Congress could not tell him how often to move the checkpoints or anything else in regard to how the Border Patrol did its job.

Signing statements were also used to give presidents more authority than the law specified. When Bush signed the Postal Accountability and Enhancement Act of 2006, he added qualifications in a signing statement that gave him authority to open mail under "exigent circumstances." Although the law did not address the issue of whether or not mail could be opened, Bush's signing statement raised it. Since the U.S. Postal Service was part of the executive branch, he told Congress in the signing statement, it could not control the president's management decisions. Opening mail, if necessary, was firmly within his authority to manage the executive branch, particularly as it fell within his responsibilities to protect national security.

Unlike many signing statements, which drew little response, this one touched a nerve. Members of Congress and the public vehemently objected to any interpretation that allowed the president to open mail. The director of the nonprofit Center for National Security Studies in Washington, D.C., assailed the administration. "The signing statement," the director said, "claims authority to open domestic mail without a warrant, and that would be new and quite alarming." The White House responded that the president had authority to open mail during a state of emergency or "in certain circumstances, such as the proverbial 'ticking bomb.' The Constitution does not require warrants for reasonable searches." This assertion was, of course, untrue. The Fourth Amendment of the Constitution requires warrants for all searches, and Congress created the Foreign Intelligence Surveillance Court for warrants that fell within the purview of national security, such as cases with a proverbial "ticking bomb."[11]

The issue of the signing statement became more complicated in August 2007 when Bush signed a Department of Homeland Security spending bill requiring the department's privacy officer to send Congress certain reports. Several months later, in January 2008, the Office of Legal Counsel (OLC)—overseen by Stephen Bradbury—directed the Department of Homeland Security not to apply this provision because it was unconstitutional for Congress to direct the president on any matter regarding personnel assignment. In other words, Congress could not require a privacy officer or any particular person to be responsible for sending material to Congress.

This, OLC argued, violated the president's constitutional responsibility for managing the executive branch. It was a cut-and-dried separation-of-powers question, and the president had the upper hand. "The statute must yield to the President's exercise of his constitutional authority to supervise subordinate Executive Branch officers and their communications with Congress," according to the OLC opinion. Although the bill had been signed without a signing statement, the issue was being revisited by the administration months later. After reexamining the issue, the administration said, they had decided that the bill violated the president's constitutional authority and would not be enforced. Arlen Specter, the ranking Republican on the Senate Judiciary Committee was enraged, calling the decision "unconstitutional." Specter added: "This is a dictatorial, after the fact pronouncement by him in line with a lot of other cherry picking he's done on the signing statements. To put it differently, I don't like it worth a damn."[12] The administration was now engaged in the retroactive signing statement.

Signing statements were drawing charges of an imperial presidency, and the chorus of outrage grew louder. How could the president alone decide that a sentence or phrase in a bill was not enforceable? Didn't this violate the requirement in the Constitution that a bill either be accepted or rejected in whole? Hadn't the Supreme Court ruled that the line-item veto process was unconstitutional? How could the president decide that he didn't need warrants to open mail?

These complaints apparently fell on deaf ears, for Cheney and Addington continued to oversee an aggressive strategy for rebuilding presidential power. It was, as one editorial pointed out, "Mr. Cheney's Imperial Presidency."[13] He and Addington relied on signing statements to enforce their view of the "unitary executive," in which the president was constitutionally empowered to make all decisions within the executive branch. The separation of powers, they argued, demanded the president's autonomy in managing the executive branch. According to this view, Congress could not tell the president whom to appoint to a commission, agency, or department, and Congress could not tell him how to manage any agency within the executive branch, which included his management of national security. Separation of powers demanded that the president was autonomous in managing the executive branch. Congress could not dictate management decisions, they said.

Signing statements first emerged as a tool for dealing with Congress during the Reagan administration. Previous administrations had attached signing statements to bills, but the Reagan administration began using them with more frequency and with greater focus on congressional usurpation of executive power. After watching an ascendant Congress after Watergate, Reagan's legal staff looked for ways to reassert presidential authority. They found signing statements to be a little-known tool that could be reworked around their needs.

It was, of course, not coincidental that, at the time, Reagan was being investigated by Congress in the Iran-Contra scandal, and his own Justice Department was trying to circumvent Congress. The creative band of Reagan lawyers who used signing statements in their increasingly combative relationship with Congress later moved into the Bush administration and continued their crusade to protect presidential power. When Cheney and Addington built the Bush legal team, they reached back in time to bring many of these same Reagan lawyers into their administration.

The Reagan administration had also skillfully built a team of conservative lawyers determined to withstand the challenges of an assertive Congress. At the helm of the Reagan legal team in the Department of Justice was Attorney General Edwin Meese.[14] Two young lawyers working for Meese, Steven Calabrisi and John Harrison, proposed in 1985 that signing statements be added to legislation to provide "interpretative statements" that a court could use.[15] The concept was only sketched out by Calabrisi and Harrison, but Meese assigned another young lawyer,

Samuel Alito in the Office of Legal Counsel within the Justice Department, to more fully develop the idea. Alito soon found that a more important use for signing statements was to include language that told the executive branch agencies that the president "interpreted" the law as being unconstitutional. Agencies could, as a result of this language in the signing statement, decline to enforce the statute.

But over the next twenty years, Alito's views evolved. By the time that the Bush administration took office, Alito—who was at that time on the U.S. Court of Appeals for the Third Circuit—advocated a slightly different role for signing statements. He now viewed a signing statement as the president's direct order to an agency on how to enforce a statute based on his interpretation of the constitutionality of a law or part of a law. Speaking in early 2006 to the annual dinner of Federalist Society lawyers at the Mayflower Hotel in Washington, D.C., Alito—now on the U.S. Supreme Court—argued that "the Constitution makes the president the head of the executive branch, but it does more than that. The president has not just some executive powers, but the executive power—the whole thing."[16]

Lawyers in the Federalist Society, formally the Federalist Society for Law & Public Policy Studies—many of whom held critical positions in the Bush administration—embraced this argument for a unitary executive and its new principle of absolutism. Signing statements became the vehicle for enforcing the unitary executive. According to Alito and lawyers in the Federalist Society, the president could decide what was and was not constitutional in any statute. His decision was final and absolute.

Alito's theory of the absolute nature of a president's right to determine the constitutionality of bills had been circulating among Federalist Society members for several years. Christopher S. Yoo, a Federalist Society member, wrote in a law review article that the unitary executive "holds that all three branches of the federal government have the power and duty to interpret the Constitution."[17] In other words, the president could apply his interpretation of the Constitution to managing the executive branch. The co-author of Yoo's article, Steven Calabrisi, a co-founder of the Federalist Society, was a longtime champion of signing statements from his years in Reagan's Justice Department.[18] "At its core," Calabrisi said, "the unitary executive is the notion that the Constitution gives the president the executive power, and it includes the power to superintend and control subordinates in the executive branch."[19] Congress, they argued, could not tell the president how to run his own house.

Other members of the Federalist Society, such as Professors Curtis Bradley of the University of Chicago Law School and Eric Posner of Duke Law School, added their weight to the discussion. They argued that "signing statements do not undermine the separation of powers" between Congress and the president, and "they can provide relevant evidence of statutory meaning."[20] For Bradley and Posner, the president was fully empowered to make decisions on the constitutionality of legislation.

The unitary executive became the underlying theme of the Bush administration. Critics, however, saw the imperial presidency resurrected in the unitary executive theory. Was Bush any different from Richard Nixon—who, in 1977, famously commented in an interview with David Frost, "when the President does it, that means it is not illegal"?[21] Not even Ronald Reagan had expanded the unitary executive theory to say that a president could choose not to enforce a law. Bush and Cheney appeared to be returning to the same principles that had guided Nixon's imperial presidency, where the president's decision and interpretation was absolute.

The long relationship between Addington and Cheney was a significant factor in the expansive interpretation of presidential power. Their lives had been intertwined since the mid-1980s, when they had collaborated on the Iran-Contra Minority Report. After Reagan left office, George H. W. Bush nominated Senator John Tower of Texas as secretary of defense and assigned Addington—who knew defense issues from his previous legal work at the CIA and with the House Intelligence Committee—to work with Tower in his confirmation hearings. When Tower withdrew, Addington then helped move Dick Cheney through the confirmation process, and Cheney subsequently brought Addington with him as his chief counsel in the Department of

Defense. While Cheney was out of office and working for Halliburton, Addington ran a political action committee, the Alliance for American Leadership—created to explore Cheney's run for the presidency in 1994—during a brief interlude in private law practice.

Addington continued to follow Cheney after the 2000 campaign. Only days after the election—as they sat together in the Four Seasons Hotel in Austin, waiting for the Florida vote tally to be decided—Cheney took charge of the transition and brought Addington onto his staff. One of Addington's roles during the transition was to recommend lawyers for key legal offices. It was Addington who recommended that White House counsel Alberto Gonzales hire Brett Kavanaugh, Noel Francisco, and Bradley Berenson, Federalist Society lawyers from Washington, D.C., who shared his expansive view of presidential power.

The circle of conservative Federalist Society lawyers who supported expansive presidential power now controlled both the president's and the vice president's legal offices. Senior staff in the Department of Justice were also members of the Federalist Society, including Attorney General John Ashcroft, Deputy Attorney General Larry Thompson, Solicitor General Ted Olsen, and Deputy Solicitor General Paul Clement. All endorsed expanding the parameters of the president's constitutional authority. Although Federalist Society members were a very small part of the national legal community, they gained significant influence in the Bush administration. Having built the legal framework in the White House and Department of Justice, Addington was now positioned to use signing statements to advance his expansive view of presidential powers.

But not everyone in the Beltway legal community agreed with Addington on the constitutional interpretations that were included in signing statements. One critic was Walter Dellinger, a former deputy attorney general. While working in Clinton's Department of Justice, Dellinger supported the use of signing statements—arguing in a formal memorandum to President Clinton that they were an acceptable use of presidential authority. However, after what he considered their abuse in the Bush administration, Dellinger publicly criticized Bush for his "dubious claim of unconstitutionality to sidestep a bill he simply doesn't like."[22] In the Bush administration, Dellinger argued, signing statements were pushing the envelope.

Other critics of the expansive use of signing statements were the American Bar Association (ABA) and the Government Accountability Office (GAO). In 2006, the ABA harshly criticized the administration's argument that the president could use signing statements to line-item veto parts of a bill he considered unconstitutional.[23] This was, they said, a violation of the checks and balances system and a violation of the constitutional requirement that bills be approved or disapproved in their entirety. In very emphatic terms, the ABA said, "the Constitution is not what the President says it is."[24] During the same year, the GAO also complained about how the administration was using signing statements. The harsh criticisms from the ABA and GAO, however, had no success in curbing their frequent use.

Having put legal staff in place who supported their expansive interpretation of presidential powers, Cheney and Addington turned their attention to filling the federal courts with judges who shared their views. Throughout the two terms of the administration, largely at their recommendation, a disproportionate number of nominations made to the federal appeals court were members of the Federalist Society, including lawyers whom Addington had placed in the administration. Among the nominees to the federal courts were White House counsel Brett Kavanaugh, who was confirmed to the U.S. Court of Appeals for the D.C. Circuit, and William Haynes—the Pentagon's chief counsel and an Addington protégé—who was nominated (but never confirmed) to the U.S. Court of Appeals for the Fourth Circuit. Among the many Federalist Society members named to the federal judiciary were Supreme Court Justices John Roberts and Samuel Alito.

Although nominations to the federal courts were largely managed through the White House counsel's office, Addington was a regular participant in its meetings and, more important, many members of Gonzales's staff had been placed there thanks to Addington's recommendation. His, and presumably Cheney's, suggestions on nominees for the judiciary had few dissenters. Although Cheney and Addington certainly did not have the final word—a role reserved for the president—they were clearly the most influential members of the vetting process.

Bush appeared to be detached from the appointment process, allowing the small group of lawyers in the White House counsel's office and from Cheney's staff, in consultation with Andy Card, to make the recommendations. For Cheney and Addington, the most important criterion for nominees was support for an expansive interpretation of presidential powers. For Bush, the primary criterion was to include women and minorities in the judicial pool (which may explain the unusual choice of Harriet Miers).[25]

When Supreme Court justice Sandra Day O'Connor announced her retirement, Cheney presented his five possible replacements to President Bush. The names, all drawn from the U.S. Court of Appeals, included four men and a woman: Alito, Roberts, James Harvie Wilkinson III, J. Michael Luttig, and Edith Brown Clement. Bush chose Roberts. When a second vacancy opened on the Supreme Court after the death of Chief Justice William Rehnquist, Bush chose Samuel Alito and named Roberts to the position of chief justice. Both justices were strong proponents of the unitary executive theory and championed expansive presidential powers.

One of the many Federalist Society members appointed to the court of appeals was Michael Chertoff, who, in 2003, was named to the U.S. Court of Appeals for the Third Circuit and would be named secretary of homeland security in 2005. At the Federalist Society annual conference in 2006, Chertoff reminded the audience in his luncheon speech of the success that the administration had had in bringing the society's members into key positions. "Some people," he quipped, "now have taken up the idea that, really, the Federalist Society is kind of like a modern day da Vinci conspiracy, a secret society that controls all the legal jobs and all the legal decision making in the administration. And of course," he added, looking around the room, "that is nonsense."[26] Other speakers that year included Justices Samuel Alito and Antonin Scalia and Vice President Dick Cheney.

To a significant degree, Cheney had gained control of judicial appointments by ensuring that Gonzales's White House legal staff shared his views. Since the single executive office that he created encouraged the full integration of the president's and vice president's staffs in meetings, Addington was able to guide discussions on judicial appointments as a full member of the White House legal team. Of all the decisions that were made involving appointments to the federal bench, however, none was more important than gaining control of appointments to the Supreme Court.

Recommendations for the high court, as well as nominations to the federal bench, had traditionally emerged from the Department of Justice, but in the Bush administration, recommendations came from the White House, in a process heavily influenced by Cheney. The vice president also altered tradition when he removed the ABA from its role in process. In past administrations, recommendations for Supreme Court nominations had been forwarded to the ABA. Since 1948, the organization's fifteen-member Standing Committee on the Federal Judiciary had reviewed the credentials of nominees to the Supreme Court, rating nominees as well-qualified, qualified, or not qualified on professional competence, judicial temperament, and integrity. The ratings were then sent to the Senate Judiciary Committee—which confirms all nominations to the federal bench—and to the Department of Justice.

Within two months of taking office, however, the Bush administration announced that it would no longer solicit the ABA's ratings. Refusing to be dismissed so easily, the ABA announced that it would continue to rate the nominees and provide the information to the Senate and the public. It rated Alito and Roberts as "well-qualified" in all categories in a letter to Arlen Specter, the Republican chairman of the Senate Judiciary Committee—dampening Cheney's argument that the forty-thousand-member American Bar Association had a liberal bias.

Cheney also took on the job of selling the Supreme Court nominations to the Senate and to the public. The confirmation process would now be managed, not by the Justice Department, or even the White House, but by the vice president's office. Steve Schmidt, Cheney's communications director and a former California political operative who had worked on the 2004 reelection campaign, oversaw the press campaign for both John Roberts's and Samuel Alito's confirmation hearings. Although Schmidt had the title of counselor to the vice president, with responsibility for press relations and communications, his primary job for months was to ensure that Roberts and Alito were confirmed.

Schmidt ran the confirmation process from a basement office in the West Wing. Even the president's staff at times answered to him as he designed the day-to-day strategy. Schmidt informed White House counsel Harriet Miers, in the 8:00 A.M. planning sessions, for example, that one of her roles would be to help prepare Roberts and Alito for courtesy calls with members of the Senate committee.[27] Similarly, Schmidt oversaw the role played by Ed Gillespie, a senior staff advisor to Bush, who had been added to Schmidt's group for the confirmation hearings. When Schmidt and Gillespie had different ideas on how to approach the hearings, Schmidt always won. Cheney's staff made the decisions.

Roberts easily coasted through the confirmation process. Alito ran into some trouble in the Senate hearings. At one point after intense Senate questioning, Mrs. Alito fled the Senate chambers in tears. Moments later, Schmidt led a media campaign portraying the Democrats opposed to Alito as out of control. Whenever the media needed to talk to someone in the administration, it was Schmidt they turned to.

In a live interview with CNN's Wolf Blitzer during the hearings, Schmidt attacked the Democrats on the Senate Judiciary Committee who were opposing Alito: "The American people who saw this hearing today are going to be troubled by some of the tactics of the Democrats," he said, "who I think didn't focus on law, didn't want to have an uplifting debate, but made a decision to try to attack Judge Alito and tear him down in the most unfair way."[28] Cheney had cannily put a political operative, not a legal expert, in charge of the hearings to deflect attention from any discussion of Alito's and Roberts's conservative views. By skillfully focusing media discussion on "fairness," Schmidt was able to sidestep Alito's views on the unitary executive and other constitutional issues.

Managed by Cheney's staff, the nomination process to the federal bench generally went smoothly for the administration, with Federalist Society members and conservatives dominating the list of names put forward to the Senate. When the Senate confirmation process did not go well, Cheney urged Bush to use a constitutional loophole called the recess appointment. Judge Charles Pickering of Mississippi and Alabama attorney general William H. Pryor Jr., both Federalist Society members, failed to win Senate confirmation in 2004, but Bush named both to positions on the U.S. Court of Appeals using recess appointments. According to the Constitution, the president could make appointments—including judicial appointments—when the Senate was not in session. Recess appointees, however, could only remain in their positions until the end of the existing Congress—which was January 2005 for both Pickering and Pryor.

Bush and Cheney took the position that Congress's constitutional role was only to advise and consent, not to deny a presidential nomination. In a statement in January 2004 announcing the appointment of Pickering to the federal appeals court, for example, Bush issued a statement that he "was proud to exercise my constitutional authority to appoint Judge Charles W. Pickering."[29] The phrasing was intended to bolster the president's image as the keeper of constitutional authority. Similarly, when Bush issued a statement announcing Pryor's appointment, he noted that he had exercised his "constitutional authority to appoint" Pryor and that the failure to confirm him had been "inconsistent with the Senate's constitutional responsibility."[30] Inserting statements on constitutional authority in these brief White House press releases was a tactic the administration used frequently to draw attention to the president's constitutional authority to act.[31] Not surprisingly, the phrasing was strikingly similar to Addington's language in signing statements.

When Pickering's term ended at the end of the recess appointment, he chose to retire from public life. When Pryor's recess appointment ended, however, Democrats threatened to filibuster his renomination, a strategy that would have required the Republicans to find sixty votes rather than a simple majority of fifty-one votes for Pryor's confirmation. In response, the Bush administration pushed Republicans in Congress to rewrite Senate rules to prohibit filibusters for judicial nominations. Since Republicans controlled the Senate by a slim majority, this rule change would have allowed their recess appointments, such as Pryor, to be confirmed.

In May 2005, Senator John McCain of Arizona brokered a one-time agreement between seven Republican senators and seven Democratic senators—the "Gang of Fourteen," as they called themselves—to allow a majority vote on Pryor and two other judicial nominees, Federalist Society members Priscilla Owen and Janice Rogers Brown, without a filibuster. McCain's bipartisan Gang of Fourteen stopped the Senate from permanently altering its rules for judicial confirmations—labeled the nuclear option—despite pressure from Cheney. All three judges were approved by razor-thin majorities.

Bush and Cheney were both comfortable with recess appointments to the federal judiciary, and Bush used the tool twice in one year without hesitation. It was a technique that previous presidents had rarely used for judicial appointments. Bill Clinton and Ronald Reagan each made only one judicial recess appointment in their two terms in office. Prior to Reagan, the last president to make a recess appointment to the bench had been John F. Kennedy, when he named Thurgood Marshall to the U.S. Court of Appeals for the Second Circuit in 1961, after Southern states balked at the nomination of an African American. Marshall was confirmed later that year.

Using recess appointments for the federal judiciary was only part of their generalized use. The Bush administration also made recess appointments to executive departments and agencies when Congress balked at confirming its nominees. Denying the president his choices for senior positions implied congressional oversight over the executive branch, according to Bush and Cheney. Any attempt at congressional oversight ran counter to Cheney's view of the constitutional balance between the branches.

Cheney was particularly protective of appointments to agency legal staffs. Cheney, for example, recommended Eugene Scalia, another Federalist Society member, and son of Supreme Court justice Antonin Scalia, as solicitor for the Labor Department.[32] When Scalia came under fire from organized labor and failed to win confirmation in the Senate, the administration gave him a recess appointment. Similarly,

Cheney favored Steven G. Bradbury, who co-founded the Federalist Society, to head the Office of Legal Counsel in the Justice Department.[33] After widespread publicity that Bradbury had authored the Justice Department memoranda allowing harsh treatment of terrorists during interrogations, he was given a recess appointment. Senate confirmation would have been impossible.

The nomination of John Bolton as United Nations ambassador proved to be another high-profile use of the recess appointment. When Bush and Cheney wanted to move Bolton into the vacancy created by John Danforth's resignation, both Democrats and Republicans on the Senate Foreign Relations Committee refused to confirm him. Secretary of State Colin Powell's own chief of staff, Lawrence Wilkerson, commented that Bolton would make an "abysmal" United Nations ambassador.[34] Failing to gain Senate confirmation, Bolton was given a recess appointment, which was heavily criticized. Senator Edward Kennedy, the ranking Democrat on the Senate Foreign Relations Committee, angrily charged that Bolton's recess appointment was a "devious maneuver that evades the constitutional requirement of Senate consent."[35] But Kennedy knew exactly what he was saying—he had cleverly turned the constitutional argument to favor Congress, rather than the president. After Bolton received his recess appointment and moved into his office at the United Nations Plaza in New York City, he continued to battle international delegations and staff in the Department of State, including Colin Powell's replacement, Condoleezza Rice.

By the end of 2006, when Bolton's recess appointment expired, he had still not been confirmed by the Republican-controlled Senate. The incoming Democratically controlled Senate—including the new chairman of the Foreign Relations Committee, Joseph Biden—made it clear that Bolton would not be confirmed in the new term. Cheney, Bolton's staunch supporter and longtime friend, examined other ways to keep him in the job and to circumvent the confirmation process. One option was to give him another recess appointment, but second recess appointments could not carry a salary. Another option would be to give Bolton a different position at the United Nations that did not require Senate confirmation. When Bolton chose to leave the Department of State rather than accept a demotion or a position without a salary, Bush publicly complained that Congress had pursued "stubborn obstructionism" in blocking his nomination. Congress, Bush said, was "obstructing" the president's constitutional right to build an administration. Constitutional issues, as Cheney wanted, now framed the discourse between the president and Congress, even when disputes were merely political.

In his eight years in office, Bush made recess appointments more than 165 times, including 17 on one day in January 2006. His recess appointments included Julie Myers, the wife of the chief of staff for Homeland Security secretary Michael Chertoff, whose own appointment Cheney had orchestrated. Myers had previously held a mid-level political appointment in the Department of Commerce, but she was named to head the Homeland Security's Bureau of Immigration and Customs Enforcement, which had fifteen thousand employees and a $4 billion budget. Myers also had ties to Cheney through her uncle, General Richard B. Myers, former chairman of the Joint Chiefs of Staff. General Myers had served under Cheney, in a different capacity, in the first Bush administration. In spite of support from Cheney, Julie Myers failed to win confirmation when both Democratic and Republican members downplayed her experience in immigration affairs and called her completely unqualified for the position.[36] She was later given a recess appointment.

Undeterred by Congress's growing impatience with administration appointments, Cheney moved another ally, Gordon England, into office using a recess appointment. England, a former executive with General Dynamics and George W. Bush's secretary of the Navy, originally received an acting appointment as deputy secretary of defense in 2005, after Paul Wolfowitz resigned. England never gained the confidence of the Senate, however, and moved from an acting appointment to a recess appointment in 2006. Recess appointments had become a routine tool for combating Congress.

The Bush administration used acting appointments as often as recess appointments when it needed to circumvent Congress. The Justice Department was perhaps the agency most aggressive in using acting appointments to fill positions. At one point, more than a quarter of the

Justice Department's ninety-three U.S. attorneys were serving under acting status, without Senate confirmation. In addition to the U.S. attorney slots, the Justice Department had two senior deputy attorneys general with acting status.

As the administration drew to a close, the tendency of the executive departments to circumvent the Senate confirmation process became an increasing trend. Under the 1998 Vacancies Reform Act, political appointees who require Senate approval can fill their positions for 210 days without confirmation. In October 2007, with fifteen months to go before the end of the administration, these temporary appointments included an acting attorney general, an acting secretary of agriculture, and an acting secretary of veterans affairs, in addition to numerous lower-level appointments.

The use of signing statements and recess and acting appointments were only part of the clash of wills between Congress and the executive branch during the Bush administration, most of which were orchestrated by Dick Cheney. Executive privilege was another battleground. Both the president and the vice president continually asserted that their communications—including meetings, letters, memos, and e-mails within the White House—were protected under the Constitution. Through letters written by David Addington, the White House regularly informed Congress that requests for documents would not be honored. Irritated, Senator Patrick Leahy of Vermont—chair of the Senate Judiciary Committee, which was seeking certain documents—charged that "increasingly, the president and vice president feel they are above the law."[37]

For the Bush administration, executive privilege was an institutional prerogative that could not be violated by Congress. Bush and Cheney did not view themselves as above the law, as Leahy had claimed, but rather saw executive privilege as their constitutional right. The Supreme Court provided some constitutional support for executive privilege in its 1974 decision *United States v. Nixon*, in which Nixon was ordered to turn over the audio tapes from his Oval Office discussions about the Watergate break-in and subsequent cover-up. The Supreme Court acknowledged that there was a need for presidents to have private conversations that would not be available to Congress or the courts as long as matters of state were being discussed. During the Clinton administration, the Supreme Court reestablished the right of executive privilege. Oval Office discussions on national security and matters of state were protected, unless criminal activity was involved. Executive privilege did not, however, protect personal matters, such as the issue of Clinton's relations with Monica Lewinsky.[38]

Dick Cheney had been a first-hand observer of Nixon's battles with Congress over executive privilege. When he moved into the Oval Office as Gerald Ford's deputy chief of staff, he had supported the decision to pardon Nixon. Not only would the pardon help heal the nation, as Gerald Ford liked to say, but it would signal that Nixon had not completely violated the trust of the American people. Some of his actions, such as protecting executive privilege, were essential, Cheney believed, in managing the presidency. Extending executive privilege to the vice president, however, was a novel concept. Cheney argued that all White House memos and all conversations—even the vice president's—were privileged, since there was a single executive office in the White House.

The issue of executive privilege surfaced again not long after the terrorist attacks of September 11, 2001. Families of the victims and members of Congress clamored for an investigation into security breaches that allowed terrorists to fly planes, and the administration finally acquiesced. But there were limits to what the administration would accept. Bush and Cheney opposed creation of an independent commission and instead wanted any investigation to be managed by congressional intelligence committees—allowing the administration to cherry-pick the information its intelligence operations provided the committees and protecting the White House from demands for material.[39] Arguments of executive privilege and separation of powers would deny Congress access to all of the information it might want.

Bush stonewalled the creation of an independent commission for more than a year, until the public's outcry forced a change of position. He finally said he would accept legislation creating a presidential commission; however, he would name all of the members, since only the president, he argued, had the constitutional power of appointment. After signing the act creating the 9/11 Commission—formally titled the National Commission on Terrorist Attacks after 9/11—Bush appointed Thomas H. Kean, a former Republican governor of New Jersey, as the commission's chair and former congressman Lee Hamilton, a Democrat, as the commission's vice chair, as well as all of the commission's members.

Creation of the presidential commission led to both benefits and problems for the administration. On the plus side, it prevented assertions of executive privilege as a means of protecting confidential conversations within the White House, since a presidential commission fell within the realm of the executive branch. On the negative side, however, commission members had no standing to demand information from the president or vice president, for whom they technically worked, and would not have access to all of the material they would need. As a result, the president had a public relations problem. If the commission didn't have access to key material, it would fail at its job, and Congress would reinsert itself into the issue. To appease the commission, Bush and Cheney volunteered to meet in the White House with commission members in November 2003. They demanded that there be no recording of the conversation and that no oaths be taken, however, and that both the president and vice president meet with the commission at the same time. The demand went unchallenged by Congress.

The president also allowed National Security Advisor Condoleezza Rice to meet with the commission, but he drew the line at material to which they would have access. After negotiations had gone on for months over access to the President's Daily Brief (PDB)—which included the highly classified intelligence material that the president and vice president received every morning—the White House finally allowed four members of the commission to review, but not copy, the material. The White House asserted that the president could invoke executive privilege over the PDB, and Congress did not challenge that assertion.

The thorny issue of executive privilege surfaced once again, late in the administration, when Attorney General Alberto Gonzales fired eight U.S. attorneys. Instead of accepting their dismissal as a routine matter in a political environment, many of the fired U.S. attorneys began a public relations campaign, arguing that their dismissal was purely political. Some, like New Mexico's U.S. attorney David Iglesias, regularly gave interviews to the national media.

Thomas DiBiagio, the U.S. attorney for Maryland, also very publicly protested his dismissal. DiBiagio claimed that Gonzales had fired him for purely political reasons, since he had been investigating Maryland's Republican governor, Robert L. Ehrlich Jr., for public corruption. "There was direct pressure [from the Department of Justice] not to pursue these investigations," DiBiagio charged, and there were questions about whether Karl Rove and others in the White House were involved in the firings.[40]

When evidence surfaced, in e-mails between the White House and the Justice Department, that presidential advisors Karl Rove and Harriet Miers might, in fact, have been involved in the dismissals of the U.S. attorneys—or at least in discussions about hiring criteria—Congress subpoenaed Rove and Miers to testify. Later, the Democratically controlled Senate Judiciary Committee also subpoenaed the White House chief of staff, Joshua Bolten, the political director, Sara Taylor, and her deputy, J. Scott Jennings, for all documents related to the firings. Congress, by this time, was convinced that the White House had colluded with the Department of Justice to remove the eight U.S. attorneys for political rather than professional reasons.

Furious that members of Congress would subpoena members of his staff, Bush stated, in what the *New Yorker* described as "his most petulant self-dramatizing mode," that testimony by the White House staff would amount to "show trials."[41] Meeting the press in the White House Diplomatic Reception Room, he angrily insisted that executive privilege protected his staff from having to talk to members of Congress. They would not respond to subpoenas and had no obligation to enter into conversations with any member of Congress. Citing the Constitution and his constitutional authority, as he always did in matters relating to confrontations with Congress, Bush declared, "the President relies on his staff to provide him candid advice. The framers of the Constitution understood this vital role when developing the separate branches of government."[42] Again, Cheney's fingerprints were on the constitutional argument that Bush put forward.

After his formal remarks on the staff subpoenas, Bush answered several questions from the press, insisting that Congress had no constitutional authority to question his staff. "They ought to accept what I proposed," Bush said, "and the idea of dragging White House members up there to score political points, or to put the klieg lights out there, will harm the President's ability to get good information."[43] The phrase "ought to accept what I proposed" reinforced a theme repeated throughout the administration—that once the president and vice president had determined an issue's constitutionality, that decision was final and not subject to discussion with Congress.

It is unclear whether any of the White House staff had discussed Department of Justice staffing with the president or vice president. The position taken by Bush, however, was that the White House staff were protected in their conversations with one another and with agency members. Staff were acting on the president's behalf and had the same protections of executive privilege in conversations in their official capacity as they did as presidential advisors. This was a more expansive interpretation of executive privilege than had been articulated by any other administration, including the Nixon administration, and was vintage Cheney.

Bush's official response to Congress was communicated by Fred Fielding, who had replaced Alberto Gonzales as counsel to the president when Gonzales replaced John Ashcroft as attorney general. Fielding formally refused the committee's request, saying, "The president feels compelled to assert executive privilege with respect to the testimony sought" by Congress.[44] He added that executive privilege fell within the "constitutional prerogatives of the Presidency," maintaining the position established by Addington and Cheney. Although the White House refused to allow its staff to testify, it finally reached a compromise. The staff could testify under oath with transcripts, but in private. The issue of executive privilege was defused for the moment.

Still, there were allegations that the Department of Justice had become the administration's political tool, with staff hired for their political connections and views, rather than merit. The politicization of the Justice Department—particularly in the firing of the U.S. attorneys—finally led to pressure for Gonzales to resign as attorney general or be censured by Congress or dismissed by the president. Two of Gonzales's staffers, evidence revealed, had been in direct contact with the White House over political credentials for lawyers hired in the department.[45] The issue became increasingly polarized after one Justice Department witness noted before the Senate Judiciary Committee that he had actively recruited lawyers from the Federalist Society and Heritage Foundation. The department's own inspector general began an investigation to determine if Gonzales had lied under oath to the Senate Judiciary Committee about his involvement in politicizing departmental staff.

Although there was certainly potential for a major confrontation over the president's constitutional authority to keep his staff from testifying, Congress backed away from the fight—calculating that it would have more success fighting a political, rather than constitutional, battle with the president. Congress was less interested in a constitutional showdown over executive privilege than in demanding the resignation of Alberto Gonzales. Attorney General Gonzales finally resigned, and Congress turned its attentions from executive privilege and the politicization of the Department of Justice to the search for a new attorney general. When Michael Mukasey, a retired federal judge, was confirmed in late 2007 to replace Gonzales, Congress backed away from further efforts to make former and current White House staff testify about the firings and department staffing.

As a result, both the president and Congress scored a degree of victory in this battle over constitutional authority. The president had successfully asserted that his staff was protected by executive privilege. Congress had successfully forced the resignation of the attorney general. On balance, however, the president scored the more important win, although he sacrificed his attorney general to deflect a constitutional showdown.

With the appointment of Mukasey—a jurist respected on both sides of the aisle, who was neither a Cheney loyalist nor a member of the

Federalist Society—the Department of Justice began to return to its nonpartisan role to enforce the law. But the damage had been done. By the time Mukasey took office, the public and the Congress had lingering doubts about the department's independence from the White House.

In general, however, the drive for the expansion of presidential powers was extraordinarily successful. Cheney's use of signing statements went unchallenged by the Republican-controlled House and Senate, allowing for unprecedented assertions of presidential power. Acting and recess appointments were regularly used to circumvent the confirmation process. But the legal framework that supported these assertions of presidential power was perhaps Cheney's greatest accomplishment. Without an internal support structure that constantly affirmed the assertions, they would certainly not have stood.

During his eight years in office, Cheney successfully created a business-friendly regulatory structure, encouraged the outsourcing of tens of thousands of federal jobs, and changed the relationship of Congress and the presidency for years to come. The Bush administration left the presidency in a stronger position in its relationship with Congress and the executive agencies than when it took office, largely due to the aggressive efforts of Cheney in the co-presidency's division of labor.

CHAPTER 10

Cheney's War

NOTHING DEFINED Dick Cheney's role as co-president more than his involvement in the wars in Afghanistan and Iraq. He was the architect of the policies to go to war and of how the wars were prosecuted. Less well known, however, was how Cheney and his fellow hawks Donald Rumsfeld, Paul Wolfowitz, Richard Perle, Douglas Feith, and others had long assessed the military options for toppling Iraq's leader, Saddam Hussein. The terrorist attacks of Tuesday, September 11, 2001, opened the door for their long-developed plans to invade Iraq.[1]

Even before the World Trade Center towers and the Pentagon were hit by the al-Qaʻida suicide mission on 9/11, Cheney and Rumsfeld were trying to sell Bush on the necessity of removing Saddam Hussein from power. Within days after the administration came into office, Cheney was directing the conversation at the meeting of the National Security Council (NSC) to focus on Iraq. He adroitly steered discussion away from the agenda to a conversation on Iraq. No one challenged him, and no one challenged the idea that Iraq was a threat to the United States.

It was not a hard sell. Bush, after all, was a Texas governor with no foreign policy experience and little interest in matters of national security. The Bush agenda centered on domestic issues such as education reform, tax cuts, and faith-based initiatives. They were issues within his comfort zone, and he eagerly pursued them in his new administration. For national security, he had Dick Cheney, and he would follow Cheney's recommendations. When Cheney focused on Iraq, so did Bush.

Bush readily admitted his lack of foreign policy experience throughout the presidential campaign of 2000. When a Boston television reporter, Andy Hiller, quizzed him before the New Hampshire primary, Bush could not name leaders in the Middle East or Asia, including those of India and Taiwan. He could not name the leader of Pakistan—General Pervez Musharraf—who had just led a military coup d'etat, ousting the elected prime minister. When Bush turned the tables on the interviewer, asking if he knew the name of Mexico's foreign minister, the reporter replied, "No, sir, but I would say to that, I am not running for president."[2]

This was not an isolated gaffe on Bush's part, but a pattern of regular foreign policy stumbles throughout the campaign. Bush never pretended to be well versed in foreign policy matters. "The only thing I know about Slovakia," he told a reporter from that country, "is what I learned first-hand from your foreign minister that came to Texas, and I had a great visit with him."[3] Bush had, however, in fact met, not Slovakia's foreign minister, but Slovenia's prime minister. Bush referred to Greeks as Grecians, Kosovars as Kosovians, and the East Timorese as the East Timorians. His foreign policy team seemed unable to coach him enough to improve his understanding of foreign policy. One close advisor, Richard Perle, acknowledged that Bush "didn't know much," but said he had "good instincts" when it came to foreign policy issues.[4]

His instincts during the presidential campaign had been to avoid foreign policy as much as possible. One of his few significant statements was a pledge not to engage in nation-building, as he suggested the Clinton administration had done in Bosnia and Kosovo. His understanding of nation-building appeared to be limited, however. Discussing the issue with Vice President Gore in a Boston debate, he rambled: "They said we could, even though we're the strongest military, that if we don't do something quickly, we don't have a clearer vision of the military, if we don't stop extending our troops all around the world in nation-building missions, then we're going to have a serious problem down the road. And I'm going to prevent that."[5] His administration, Bush suggested, would use the military cautiously around the world, and steer clear of nation-building.[6]

Once in office, Bush relied heavily on Cheney for foreign policy advice. His own lack of foreign policy knowledge and experience had been painfully evident throughout the campaign. Thus when Cheney wanted to turn attention to Iraq, he easily could. Ten days after the inauguration, at the first meeting of the National Security Council (NSC), Bush, Cheney, Colin Powell, Condoleezza Rice, Donald Rumsfeld, CIA director George Tenet, White House chief of staff Andy Card, Treasury secretary Paul O'Neill, and General Hugh Shelton, chairman of the Joint Chiefs of Staff, gathered in the Situation Room in the White House basement. By the end of the meeting, Cheney had sidelined the original points on the agenda—Israeli-Palestinian peace talks and Russian nuclear weapons—to focus the discussion on the dangers of Iraq and Saddam Hussein.[7]

The second NSC meeting on February 1, 2001, dealt only with Iraq. Other more pressing issues in the Middle East, such as the Israeli-Palestinian question and instability in Iran, vanished from the National Security Council agenda. The cover sheet of the briefing material, circulated to NSC members, explained that the purpose of the February 1 meeting was "to review the current state of play (including CIA briefing on Iraq) and to examine policy questions on how to proceed."[8] The influence that Cheney wielded in national security discussions was becoming evident.

And it was not a hard sell for the vice president to turn Bush's attention toward Iraq. Bush routinely followed Cheney's recommendations. After the 2001 terrorist attacks, he became increasingly receptive to Cheney's circumstantial case for going to war against Saddam Hussein and, later, for urging harsh policies against detainees.[9] Bush acquiesced to all of Cheney's recommendations, even agreeing that prisoners taken by U.S. forces in Afghanistan and Iraq should not be referred to as "prisoners of war" but rather as "enemy combatants." This slight change in terminology allowed the administration to deny prisoners the legal protections of the Geneva Conventions and the military's own Uniform Code of Military Justice.

Cheney was the "800 pound gorilla whose views carry much more weight than the others and which therefore skew discussions and quash open dissent, inadvertently or otherwise," David Rothkopf thought.[10] Richard Haas, president of the Council on Foreign Relations and a former director of policy planning under George W. Bush, echoed that view, remarking that "Cheney had three bites of the apple. He had his staff at every meeting. He would then come to the principals' meeting and then he'd have his one-on-ones with the president. And given the views that came out of the vice president's office, it introduced a certain bias to the system."[11]

As promised during the campaign, the first nine months of the administration were devoted to domestic issues. Education and tax-cut legislation in particular dominated Oval Office time. Although Cheney was deeply involved in lobbying for these bills in both the House and the Senate, he was also focused on ways to remove Iraq's leader from power. His network of like-minded hawks, equally eager to topple the Iraqi leader, dominated the senior levels of national security policy. Among this group of hawks—whom Cheney had placed strategically in the administration—was his old mentor and ally, Donald Rumsfeld, with whom he had spent the 1980s developing plans for a shadow government in the event of nuclear attack.

Cheney and Rumsfeld had moved their own allies into senior positions in the administration. Paul Wolfowitz, a top aide to Cheney during his four years as secretary of defense, became Bush's deputy secretary of defense, and Wolfowitz's former student and protégé I. Lewis "Scooter" Libby became Cheney's chief of staff. Steven Hadley, another Wolfowitz protégé from the first Bush administration, became deputy national security advisor to the president. John Bolton, another ally, was placed in the State Department, where he became a constant thorn in the side of Secretary of State Colin Powell, who had long suspected that Cheney had placed Bolton in the State Department to spy and report back on him and his deputy, Richard Armitage. Richard Perle also found his way to a senior position, although he purposely chose to remain outside the bureaucracy as head of the quasi-governmental Defense Planning Board. Each of the Cheney appointees had been a member of Bush's foreign policy team during the campaign. They called themselves the Vulcans—named after the statue of the Roman god Vulcan in Birmingham, Alabama, the hometown of Condoleezza Rice.[12]

Powell had never been a member of Bush's foreign policy team during the presidential campaign. He was neither involved in their meetings nor invited to their strategy sessions. He had joined the campaign reluctantly, as a public speaker, not as a private advisor. John McCain, Bush's chief rival, had actively courted him, stating that, if elected, he would ask Powell to join his cabinet. But during the primaries, Powell had remained noncommittal, sending the Bush and McCain campaigns each a check for $1,000. When the primaries were over, Powell finally embraced the Bush candidacy, becoming the keynote speaker at the Republican convention in Philadelphia. But he never embraced Dick Cheney. Their relationship had been rocky since the earliest days of the George H. W. Bush administration. Cheney had refused to support the nomination of Powell's close friend Richard Armitage to be secretary of the Army when conservative Republicans in Congress opposed the appointment.[13]

Their relationship throughout the Bush years was often distant, at best, including during the Gulf War. Although Cheney publicly supported the decision not to enter Baghdad, which Powell, Brent Scowcroft, and Norman Schwarzkopf all endorsed, Cheney apparently had lingering doubts about that choice. Only months after the withdrawal of U.S. troops, Cheney and Wolfowitz started to plan for further military action in Iraq if the region's oil reserves came under threat. A revealing 1992 memo written by Wolfowitz—then undersecretary of defense for policy, the third-ranking appointment in the Pentagon—and his deputy, Scooter Libby, underscored their view that the United States should have continued into Baghdad during the Gulf War. They argued in the Defense Planning Guidance memo that the first military objective of the United States should be to "prevent any hostile power from dominating a region whose resources would, under consolidated control, be sufficient to generate global power." They urged that a policy of preemption be pursued, and, under certain circumstances, a course that included unilateral action: "the United States should be postured to act independently when collective action cannot be orchestrated."[14] Their influence was clear years later when George W. Bush proclaimed the Bush Doctrine of Preemption as the underlying theme of his foreign policy agenda.

Cheney did not refute their recommendations, which were intended to address the possibility that Saddam Hussein might dominate the region and "consolidate control" over production and distribution of Middle East oil. "Our overall objective," the Defense Planning Guidance memo continued, "is to remain the predominant outside power in the region and preserve U.S. and Western access to the region's oil. . . . Therefore, we must continue to play a strong role through enhanced deterrence." Access to oil, Wolfowitz and Libby asserted, should guide American foreign policy in the Middle East.[15] The assertion that the United States should use military resources to protect the region's oil was shared by a wider group of conservative Republicans involved in foreign policy assessments.

The most vocal were a small group of neoconservatives who had urged President Clinton to change his policy for dealing with Saddam Hussein from containment—prescribed by George H. W. Bush—to regime change. A relatively unknown think tank of neoconservatives, the Project for the New American Century (PNAC), sent a forceful letter to Clinton in 1998 arguing that toppling Saddam Hussein was essential to national security.[16] The letter urged Clinton to implement immediately "a strategy for removing Saddam's regime from power"— a regime, they stated, that was harboring "weapons of mass destruction," threatening the stability of the region and, possibly, the United States.[17] The eighteen who signed the letter included Donald Rumsfeld, Paul Wolfowitz, Stephen Cambone, and John Bolton.[18]

These were friends of long standing, with a shared vision of the world. The relationship among them—particularly Cheney, Rumsfeld, and Wolfowitz—began during the Ford administration and continued through the George H. W. Bush and Clinton administrations, through a series of interwoven jobs. Cheney first became familiar with Wolfowitz in 1976, when Cheney was running the Ford White House and Rumsfeld was running the Defense Department. Both Cheney and Rumsfeld were at war with Secretary of State Henry Kissinger—who was also national security advisor—and constantly challenged his policy of détente with the Soviet Union, which they saw as more of a threat than did either Kissinger or the career staff at the State Department.[19] However, the

National Intelligence Estimate (NIE)—which incorporated data from the entire intelligence community—supported Kissinger.

Unbowed, Cheney and Rumsfeld challenged the NIE conclusions as unreliable and tried to persuade William Colby, director of the Central Intelligence Agency (CIA), to prepare an independent intelligence estimate. After Colby refused, Cheney and Rumsfeld engineered his firing on November 4, 1975, in what was known as the Halloween Massacre. Ford fired not only Colby but also Secretary of Defense James Schlesinger—who was replaced by Rumsfeld—and he removed Kissinger from his position as national security advisor (although he retained Kissinger as secretary of state). Colby was replaced as CIA director by the more cooperative George H. W. Bush, who agreed to Cheney's and Rumsfeld's demand to prepare a secret counterintelligence analysis of the Soviet Union.

To do this, George H. W. Bush quietly assembled a secret planning team of ten, known as Team B, which included Paul Wolfowitz, a young Yale professor on leave at the U.S. Arms Control and Disarmament Agency. Team B looked at the same data included in the NIE, but it drew different conclusions. It determined that "all the evidence points to an underlying Soviet commitment to what is euphemistically called the 'worldwide triumph of socialism,' but in fact connotes global Soviet hegemony."[20] Cheney and Rumsfeld believed that they were vindicated by the findings of Team B. Its different set of conclusions, drawn from the same data, resulted from differing analyses of satellite photographs and an essentially reverse view of how the Soviet Union was interacting with the world. Members of Congress who had questioned Kissinger's efforts at détente saw Team B's conclusions as a confirmation of their trepidation about U.S.–Soviet relations.

Team B's effort to demonstrate that the intelligence community was not the final word in intelligence analysis provided the opening for Republicans in Congress during the Clinton administration to challenge intelligence estimates about the threat of a ballistic missile attack. To analyze the nuclear capabilities of the former Soviet Union and other countries, the Republican-dominated Congress created a missile defense commission, chaired by Donald Rumsfeld and including Wolfowitz. As its executive director, the commission hired Stephen Cambone, who would later become Rumsfeld's undersecretary for intelligence in the Defense Department, a newly created position that broadened the department's intelligence operation. The commission, as expected, given its leadership, determined that the threat of a successful missile attack on the United States was greater than the CIA indicated, which fueled new talk of expanding the missile defense system. As with Team B, an outside investigation involving Wolfowitz challenged information from the CIA.

Circumventing the intelligence community had become commonplace for Cheney and Rumsfeld by the time the George W. Bush administration took office. Nine years earlier, Cheney had tried unsuccessfully to circumvent Colin Powell, chairman of the Joint Chiefs of Staff—the chief military officer of the U.S. government—and Norman Schwarzkopf at the Central Command (CENTCOM), as the plans for military action were drawn up. During the Gulf War, it was Powell's responsibility to devise a military plan for the coalition forces, but it was a plan that Cheney disliked. Instead of consulting with Powell and pursuing alternate military options, Cheney quietly developed another plan with Department of Defense staff, bypassing Powell. Employing the same clandestine planning process with the Pentagon that he and Rumsfeld had used in the Ford administration to create Team B, Cheney formed Operation Scorpion to develop an alternate U.S. military strategy for removing Iraqi forces from Kuwait. Cheney asked his deputy, Paul Wolfowitz, to prepare the alternate plan, instructing him, "don't tell Powell or anyone else."[21]

Cheney brought the Wolfowitz-devised plan from Operation Scorpion to George H. W. Bush while Powell was in Saudi Arabia, during the buildup to the Gulf War. The plan, which Bush quickly rejected, would have taken American troops into western Iraq, far from Kuwait, whose rescue was the intended mission of the United States. Potentially, the presence of American troops in western Iraq, near Baghdad, could have led to fighting within the capital city, a civil war, and the breakup of the country—an outcome opposed by American allies such as Saudi Arabia and Turkey. Powell, in contrast, had designed a military operation in which American forces attacked Iraqi forces in Kuwait, drove them north across the desert, captured them, and left. Baghdad and Saddam Hussein would not be touched.

By 2001, the Cheney-Rumsfeld-Wolfowitz alliance had been involved in Plan B, the missile defense planning commission, and Operation Scorpion—all of which challenged the information developed by career military and intelligence operations. In the George W. Bush administration, this reassembled team saw Saddam Hussein as a threat that the intelligence community was not adequately addressing—in the same way that they had viewed the Soviet Union and, later, ballistic missiles as a threat that the intelligence community underestimated. For Cheney, Rumsfeld, and Wolfowitz, Saddam Hussein had to be removed, and they would now use all of the resources at their disposal to do so—despite mounting opposition from George Tenet's CIA and Colin Powell's Department of State.

George W. Bush never understood this extensive network of relationships around Cheney and Rumsfeld, their long-held distrust of the intelligence community, or the depth of their interest in removing Saddam Hussein from power. By raising the issue of Iraq during that first meeting of the National Security Council in January 2001, Cheney and Rumsfeld opened the door to begin planning military action.

Throughout the winter and spring of Bush's first year in office, while the administration concentrated on domestic issues, the Cheney-Rumsfeld-Wolfowitz team was quietly developing plans to launch a strike against Saddam Hussein. In August 2001, Bush left for a month-long vacation at his ranch in Crawford, Texas, returning to Washington, D.C., after Labor Day to begin a week-long tour of speeches about reading in order to promote his signature agenda item, the No Child Left Behind Act.[22] Laura Bush remained in Washington, D.C., to testify before a Senate committee on early childhood development.

After spending Monday, September 10, visiting an elementary school in Jacksonville, Florida, Bush traveled to Sarasota, Florida, to visit another elementary school the following day. On Tuesday, September 11, at 8:46 A.M., while he was reading a children's story, "My Pet Goat," in Mrs. Sandra Kay Daniels's second-grade classroom at the Emma E. Booker elementary school in Sarasota, the first plane hit the North Tower of the World Trade Center in New York City. Seventeen minutes later, a second plane hit the South Tower; minutes later, a third plane hit the Pentagon.

The Secret Service moved immediately to protect the president from unknown terrorists and threats, quickly returning him to the safety of Air Force One. By 9:55 A.M., the 747 was in the air, flying the president back to Washington, D.C. On the advice of the vice president, however, the decision was made to change course.[23] By 10:10 A.M., instead of heading to the nation's capital, Air Force One was on its way to Barksdale Air Force Base in Louisiana, a destination selected by the military aide aboard the plane.

But it was soon determined that Barksdale had neither the needed command and control facilities nor the needed secure housing for the president. The decision was made to move to another military base. After landing at Barksdale at 11:45 A.M., the plane took off again at 2:50 P.M. for Offutt Air Force Base in Nebraska, headquarters of the U.S. Strategic Command. Offutt, as the Defense Department's command and control center, would provide both the requisite security and the requisite communications structure. It would also have the space to house the fifty staff and Secret Service agents aboard the plane.[24]

At the same time that agents were whisking the president from the elementary school into a waiting limousine and putting him safely aboard Air Force One, other agents were taking the vice president from his office in the Old Executive Office Building to the bunker—the Presidential Emergency Operations Center—underneath the White House. "They came in and said, 'Sir, we have to leave immediately,' and grabbed me," Cheney recalled. "They hoisted me up and moved me very rapidly down the hallway, down some stairs, through some doors, and down some more steps into an underground facility under the White House."[25]

From that point, it was the vice president, not the president, who took control of the nation's military response. Cheney directed Bush not to return to Washington, D.C., immediately, but instead to fly to Offutt Air Force Base, where he would be out of danger. Cheney was now setting in motion the shadow government that he and Rumsfeld had planned during the Reagan years. The nation was under attack, the president was in jeopardy, and Cheney needed to take command of the crisis.

Soon after he moved to the underground bunker beneath the White House and assumed control of the Presidential Emergency Operations Center, Cheney faced a "horrendous decision," as he called it. He ordered military jets to shoot down commercial passenger planes heading toward Washington, D.C.—fearing that more planes manned by terrorists were in the air to attack the Capitol and the White House, as they had the Pentagon. But Cheney later denied giving the order, suggesting that he had only confirmed Bush's order to shoot down the passenger planes. As vice president, Cheney had no authority to give orders to the military. Only the president, as commander in chief of the armed forces, is constitutionally authorized to do so.

The controversy over whether or not Cheney had initiated the order was publicly raised in 2004 when the 9/11 Commission investigated whether Cheney had overstepped his constitutional authority. When the 9/11 Commission questioned the vice president on the shoot-down order, he responded that Bush had in fact given the order, on his recommendation. But the commission could not verify this assertion and found that Cheney had not sought approval from Bush before issuing the order.

The president's phone logs, according to the commission, did not show a phone call between Bush and Cheney. In addition, other phone logs showed no evidence of a telephone call. According to Philip Shenon, a *New York Times* reporter who interviewed the commission staff, there were seven logs maintained of the president's and vice president's phone calls—"one maintained by the White House telephone switchboard," Shenon wrote, "one by the Secret Service, one by the Situation Room, and four separate logs maintained by military officers working in the White House."[26] The 9/11 Commission also reviewed Scooter Libby's notes, which were meticulously written. According to these notes, in the time period from 10:15 A.M. to 10:18 A.M. on September 11, 2001, commercial aircraft were within a sixty-mile range of Washington, D.C., and Cheney gave the order to shoot them down. "Aircraft 60 miles out, confirmed as hijack—engage? VP? *Yes*," Libby recorded in his notes.

Joshua Bolten, the deputy chief of staff, was in the room when Cheney gave the shoot-down order. According to Libby's notes, Bolten then said that the president needed to confirm the engage order that Cheney had just issued. Libby's notes read: "JB [Joshua Bolten]: Get President and confirm engage order."[27] Cheney very clearly had given the order—a scenario that he and Donald Rumsfeld had practiced for years during the Reagan administration, to ensure continuity of government if the president was dead or unavailable to make decisions. But this was a different situation. George W. Bush was safely aboard Air Force One and available to take command, constantly linked to the White House by secure phone.

At 3:15 P.M. on September 11, Bush spoke from Offutt Air Force base by secure video conferencing with Cheney, Condoleezza Rice, and others in the White House bunker. His message was short: "We're at war." The vice president had no doubt Iraq was involved, whoever the terrorists were. For Cheney, all roads led to Iraq.

The next day—Wednesday, September 12—with the immediate danger past, Bush returned to Washington, D.C. He spent the day meeting with religious leaders he called to the White House, proclaiming a National Day of Prayer and Remembrance, and working on his nationally televised address for the memorial service at the Washington National Cathedral. At the same time, Cheney was meeting with CIA director George Tenet, Secretary of Defense Donald Rumsfeld, Deputy Secretary of Defense Paul Wolfowitz, National Security Advisor Condoleezza Rice, his own national security advisor, Scooter Libby, and others to determine who the terrorists were and how to respond.

Within hours after the attack, Tenet and the CIA had built a convincing case that those most likely to be responsible were individuals from the al-Qaʻida terrorist network, which was protected by the Taliban government in Afghanistan. Tenet did not suggest that Iraq or Saddam Hussein had been involved with either the terrorist attacks or with al-Qaʻida. Afghanistan, not Iraq, according to Tenet and the

CIA, was the group's training location and center of operations. Others, however, immediately accused Iraq.

On Wednesday, September 12, in a tense National Security Council meeting—the first formal planning meeting after the attacks that included Bush—Rumsfeld pushed for broadening the discussion to include "getting Iraq." According to Richard Clarke, the White House terrorism expert who participated in the meeting, Wolfowitz argued that a terrorist group could not have "pulled off" the attack without a state sponsor. Rumsfeld was adamant that Iraq—the likely state sponsor of al-Qa'ida, according to him—had to be included in any military action.[28]

For Rumsfeld, "getting Iraq" would rectify what he viewed as the missed opportunity to remove Saddam Hussein during the Gulf War. A longtime political rival of George H. W. Bush, Rumsfeld still considered the former president a "political lightweight." Now, as secretary of defense, he wanted the chance to fix what Bush had failed to do in Iraq in 1991. Bob Woodward, writing in *Plan of Attack* on White House decision making in the run-up to the Iraq war, gives a glimpse into Rumsfeld's determination to go after Saddam Hussein and his personal dislike of George H. W. Bush. "One night in 1995, on a trip to Vietnam with his friend Ken Adelman," Woodward wrote, "Rumsfeld kept Adelman up until 3:00 A.M., giving him an earful on how badly the elder Bush had screwed up. 'He never should have agreed to a cease-fire that let Saddam survive in power,' Rumsfeld said. 'He should have destroyed more of the Iraqi military while they still had the cover of war.'"[29]

Rumsfeld, like Cheney and Wolfowitz, saw the Gulf War as a hollow victory for the United States, since Saddam Hussein had remained in power. According to notes from a Pentagon meeting on the afternoon of the terrorist attacks, Rumsfeld ordered General Richard B. Myers, acting chairman of the Joint Chiefs of Staff, to develop plans to go after Osama bin Laden, leader of the al-Qa'ida network in Afghanistan, and Saddam Hussein.[30]

Several days after the terrorist attacks, when Bush had returned to the nation's capital, he and his national security team—which by this time was dubbed the war council—met at Camp David, Maryland. Wolfowitz, who as deputy secretary of defense had the second-highest position at the Pentagon, floated the idea that U.S. forces should simultaneously invade Iraq and Afghanistan.[31] The war council kept this suggestion a closely guarded secret, and it only came to light years later, when the investigative staff of the 9/11 Commission uncovered the transcripts of the Camp David meeting.[32]

But there was even more early evidence, uncovered by the investigative staff of the 9/11 Commission, that invading Iraq was on the table in all of the national security meetings after September 11. On September 17, 2001, at a meeting of the National Security Council, Wolfowitz and Rumsfeld again raised the issue of toppling Saddam Hussein. In a memo earlier that day, Wolfowitz argued that if there was a 10 percent chance that Saddam Hussein was involved in the attacks, the United States had to respond militarily.[33] At every opportunity, Rumsfeld and Wolfowitz—fully supported by Cheney—pushed the Iraq connection to the September 11 attacks and urged a military response by the United States.

George W. Bush listened to Rumsfeld and his other advisors, but he decided, instead, to focus military action in Afghanistan. George H. W. Bush had chosen a strategy of containment, not regime change, in Iraq, and it would be a difficult decision for Bush to change the course his father had embarked on during the Gulf War. But Cheney soon devised a way to allow George W. Bush to move past his father's decision, by framing the war in Afghanistan as part of a larger war on terror. Iraq, Cheney and others argued, harbored terrorists with weapons that jeopardized America's national security. Once the vice president positioned the issue around a larger war on terror that included Iraq, Bush believed he was fighting a different set of problems than those his father had faced—a terrorist network, with ties in Iraq, that threatened the very security of the United States. By changing the language and the mission, Cheney persuaded Bush to move to his camp and abandon his father's position.

Speaking on the weekly news commentary *Meet the Press* on September 16, 2001, Cheney laid out his case to the American public that the first Gulf War was very different than the present situation. He was, in a subtle way, reinforcing for Bush the view that the terrorist attacks on American soil had transformed the way the United States should deal with terrorism. The world, he told the program's host, Tim Russert, was now a different place and required different decisions than it had during the George H. W. Bush administration:

MR. RUSSERT: When the president went to the World Trade Center on Friday he said, "The people who did this will hear from all of us soon." There's an expectation in the country that we're about to pay back big time, quickly. What should the American people think or feel about that?

VICE PRES. CHENEY: I think the important thing here, Tim, is for people to understand that, you know, things have changed since last Tuesday. The world shifted in some respects. Clearly, what we're faced with here is a situation where terrorism is struck home in the United States. We've been subject to targets of terrorist attacks before, especially overseas with our forces and American personnel overseas, but this time because of what happened in New York and what happened in Washington, it's a qualitatively different set of circumstances.

It's also important for people to understand that this is a long-term proposition. It's not like, well, even Desert Storm where we had a buildup for a few months, four days of combat, and it was over with. This is going to be the kind of work that will probably take years because the focus has to be not just on any one individual, the problem here is terrorism. And even in this particular instance, it looks as though the responsible organization was a group called al-Qaʻida. It's Arabic for "The Base."[34]

Less than a month after the terrorist attacks, the United States launched a military strike on Afghanistan. Contingency planning for military action against the Taliban—though not al-Qaʻida terrorists—had already been under way for several months inside the Pentagon. After September 11, those plans were implemented. Congress accepted Bush's decision to send troops into Afghanistan as well within the scope of the president's duties as commander in chief. To emphasize that Bush was constitutionally empowered to send the military into Afghanistan to protect and defend the nation, the administration called the military strike "Operation Enduring Freedom." An invasion of Iraq, however, was not part of the Pentagon's contingency planning.

By December 2001—two months into the campaign to topple the Taliban regime and capture Osama bin Laden—Bush had turned his full attention to national security issues. His domestic agenda fell to a distant second place. "Defending the American people," Bush stated, "is my highest priority as Commander in Chief."[35] The war on terror, as he called it, was his only focus.

A brief encounter that Bush had with Secretary of State Colin Powell and retired four-star Marine Corps general Anthony Zinni in November 2001 revealed how few other policy issues Bush apparently engaged in beyond the ongoing war in Afghanistan. With the president's approval, Powell had named Zinni to serve as a special envoy to work with Israel's Ariel Sharon and the Palestinian Liberation Front's Yasir Arafat on a permanent cease-fire.

On November 21, 2001, Powell brought Zinni to the White House to meet with Bush and receive final instructions before leaving for Israel. When Powell and Zinni arrived at the Oval Office, Cheney was at the president's side, as he always was when foreign policy issues were being discussed. Bush, however, seemed to know little about Zinni or what he would be doing in the Middle East. Instead of giving Zinni direction, Bush quizzically asked him, "What's your mission?" Bush seemed unprepared to talk about the approach that Zinni should take with Sharon and Arafat. "Well, Colin, this is your baby," he remarked to Powell about the Middle East peace process. "You convinced me, now it's your show."[36] The Arab-Israeli conflict was no longer a prime concern for George W. Bush; his focus had been terrorism since September 11.

The decision to use military force against Afghanistan, rather than any diplomatic or economic tool, reflected the power that Cheney and his Defense Department colleagues—rather than Powell and the State Department—wielded in the administration. Cheney scored another victory in December 2001, soon after the start of the Afghan war, when Bush terminated the Anti–Ballistic Missile (ABM) treaty with Russia.

The treaty, originally signed in 1972, capped the number of strategic weapons, banned space-based weapons, and limited the number of ABM sites maintained by each country to one.[37]

Terminating the treaty—which had a clause providing for withdrawal on notice—would allow the United States to introduce new weapons programs, such as space-based systems, and expand the number of ABM sites. In June 2002, just days after the United States formally withdrew from the treaty, the government started construction on a new missile defense network site in Alaska.[38] Fears of the Russian bear—which Cheney and Rumsfeld acted on during the Ford administration, when they challenged Kissinger's proposals for détente—apparently were being resurrected. The new missile defense system in Alaska would help tame the bear.

Not surprisingly, as early as the 2000 presidential campaign, Bush had adopted the foreign policy position, crafted by Rumsfeld and Wolfowitz, of terminating the ABM treaty. In his acceptance speech at the Republican national convention, Bush stated that he might terminate "outdated treaties" like the ABM accord.[39] Wolfowitz, in particular, had ardently advocated expansion of the missile defense system for years. As Bob Dole's foreign policy advisor in the 1996 presidential campaign, he had urged Dole to include a platform statement that supported terminating the ABM treaty and installing a new anti–ballistic missile network. Dole and his advisors had bought Wolfowitz's argument and posted their new position on the campaign's web site, stating, "as President, Bob Dole will deploy an effective national missile defense system which will keep Americans free from nuclear intimidation and reduce the incentive of rogue regimes to acquire weapons of mass destruction."[40]

When Wolfowitz was advising George W. Bush on foreign policy four years later, he again pressed for expanding the anti–ballistic missile system and terminating the ABM treaty with Russia. When Bush finally announced in December 2001 that he was abrogating the treaty, his language closely resembled the phrases Wolfowitz had crafted for Dole. "The greatest threats to both our countries come not from each other, or other big powers in the world," Bush said of the United States and Russia, "but from terrorists who strike without warning, or rogue states who seek weapons of mass destruction."[41] The themes of rogue states and weapons of mass destruction had reemerged.

Although the NATO countries and Moscow angrily protested, there was relatively little public outcry in the United States about the ABM treaty's termination. What limited response there was came from congressional Democrats, led by Senator Russell Feingold of Wisconsin, who argued that Bush lacked the constitutional authority to terminate the Senate-confirmed ABM treaty.[42] But Feingold's challenge had no support from congressional leadership and no chance of success in federal court. With the Republican majority firmly behind Bush and Cheney, Congress as an institution would not oppose the treaty's termination. The U.S. Supreme Court had already decided in 1979 that members of Congress needed broad support from both political parties to have standing to sue the president of the United States.

The ABM treaty's termination, like the war on terror, fell within Cheney's definition of the president's unbounded constitutional authority to protect and defend the nation. "I believe in a strong, robust executive authority," Cheney told reporters aboard Air Force Two, adding that "the world we live in demands it . . . and in wartime the president needs to have his constitutional powers unimpaired."[43] Terminating the ABM treaty was an early volley in a broadening war to establish the president as the final arbiter in matters regarding national security—a war that led the Pulitzer Prize–winning author Charlie Savage to charge Cheney and the Bush administration with "the subversion of American democracy."[44]

Nothing gave Bush and Cheney more robust executive authority than cloaking an issue in national security and broader issues of foreign policy. Writing in 1940, the presidential scholar Edwin Corwin noted that the Constitution was silent on certain issues involving national security and foreign affairs. The Constitution, he argued, provided "an invitation to struggle for the privilege of directing American foreign policy," because it was silent or unclear on so many issues—such as which branch was responsible for recognizing foreign governments, terminating a treaty, creating a foreign policy, or making national security decisions.[45] This invitation to struggle led to various attempts, over the years, by the executive and legislative branches to control decision making.

As this struggle continued into the twenty-first century, Cheney acted to control the process and stem the intrusion of Congress into national security and foreign policy decision making. For Cheney, the issue was clear: the president had the responsibility and the constitutional authority to act, and he easily convinced Bush that there were few limits to the president's constitutional authority when national security was involved.

The war in Afghanistan proved to be an early test of Cheney's expansive interpretation of presidential war powers. One of the first assertions orchestrated by the vice president was the manner in which the United States dealt with prisoners of war. Weeks after American troops entered Afghanistan, thousands of prisoners were being held at a crumbling and overcrowded prison at Sheberghan. At one point, the prison, designed to hold eight hundred people, held more than thirty-six hundred, and special operations forces were culling through the prisoners for suspected terrorists.

Some prisoners—who were considered part of al-Qa'ida or a Taliban terrorist network—were moved out of Sheberghan into separate detention centers, where they were further interrogated on the whereabouts of Osama bin Laden, the names of other terrorists, and plans potentially under way for future terrorist attacks on the United States or elsewhere. At the end of December 2001, the Pentagon announced that it was holding 136 Taliban and al-Qa'ida terrorists in detention centers in southern Afghanistan, including the Bagram Air Base, the Kandahar airport, and even a naval vessel, the amphibious assault ship USS *Peleliu*.[46] Some of these sites were frequently targets of sniper attacks, and Taliban fighters overran one facility, killing a CIA agent. After the Pentagon argued that the detention centers were not secure, and with the number of prisoners increasing daily, Bush signed an executive order to move the most dangerous prisoners to the forty-five-square-mile U.S. naval base at Guantánamo Bay, Cuba, where they would be held outside any established legal authority and, eventually, would be tried by specially created military tribunals.

The order to transfer the prisoners to Guantánamo Bay attracted little criticism, but the decision to try them in special military tribunals did. These tribunals, the Pentagon stated, would be conducted under special rules and would not be subject to the Uniform Code of Military Justice. According to an executive order prepared by Cheney's office and signed by the president, they would be held in secret courts without the press and neutral observers; under the new rules, the Pentagon's military lawyers from the Judge Advocate General's Corps would not represent the prisoners in the prosecutions.

David Addington prepared the executive order after talking with John Yoo in the Office of Legal Counsel at the Justice Department. Remarkably, the order, which detailed how prisoners captured in Afghanistan were to be treated, had been written without consultation with either Secretary of State Colin Powell or National Security Advisor Condoleezza Rice. Instead, Addington consulted with Rumsfeld at the Department of Defense on the order's wording.

Once it was written, Cheney personally walked the order into the Oval Office for President Bush to sign. Bush did not read it; he simply pulled his felt-tipped pen out of his pocket and signed the order. Trust was the coin of the realm, and Cheney clearly had Bush's complete trust on national security matters. The director of the CIA, George Tenet, didn't know about it. The legal advisor to the National Security Council, John Bellinger III, didn't know about it. Powell only learned that Bush had signed the executive order while watching CNN News. "What the hell just happened?" he fumed after the newscast. Condoleezza Rice, equally furious at being kept out of the loop, hastily dispatched her staff to find out what Cheney had done.[47]

According to Cheney's expansive view of presidential powers, the president had complete constitutional authority to create the military tribunals and bypass the military's legal procedures. Rather than following existing rules, which called for convening military commissions, the tribunals were created by a small group of administration lawyers, which Cheney controlled. The executive order that Bush authorized created a separate process in which prisoners considered terrorists would be labeled enemy combatants. As a result, they would be denied basic protections guaranteed under the Uniform Code of Military Justice and the Geneva Conventions—a set of treaties, formulated between 1864 and 1949 and ratified by nearly every country in the world, including the United States, that, among other points, established international rules for the treatment of prisoners of war.

Terrorists, the administration argued, were not prisoners of war, because they did not represent or wear the uniforms of their countries.[48] Because they were part of a nonstate entity, the administration concluded, they were not entitled to legal due process or the protections of international agreements between nations. But this interpretation flew in the face of international law and the Third Geneva Convention, which requires prisoners of war, without condition, to have counsel and be charged with a crime. Prisoners at Guantánamo Bay would have no such protection under George W. Bush's executive order.

Throughout the fall of 2001 and spring of 2002, Cheney was building the legal arguments for expansive presidential war powers to protect the nation against terrorist attacks. Moving militarily against al-Qaʻida in Afghanistan proved relatively easy, since George Tenet and the CIA provided intelligence that linked the terrorists to training facilities in Afghanistan. Linking Saddam Hussein to the terrorist attacks, however, proved more difficult. Tenet refused to support Cheney's contention that there was a connection between the September 11 terrorists and the Iraqi leader. As a result, Cheney set out to build his own evidence by creating a data-gathering unit in the Department of Defense that circumvented career intelligence and military staff. Working with Wolfowitz, Cheney created a secret planning unit, like Team B, called the Office of Special Plans (OSP) and run by political appointees, to assess intelligence information. The OSP, controlled by Cheney, Rumsfeld, and Wolfowitz, would create its own data when the information from the CIA and other intelligence agencies failed to support their objectives.

The OSP operated for a little over a year in 2002 and 2003 under Douglas Feith, who reported directly to Wolfowitz. Under Cheney's orders, the OSP looked at raw intelligence data coming out of Iraq and used it to build a separate set of intelligence assumptions. Cheney moved William Luti from the vice president's staff to the Office of Special Plans to handle the team's day-to-day work.[49] Although the assumptions made by Luti and the OSP often contradicted information developed by the CIA, Cheney used their data to persuade Bush to move against Saddam Hussein. Five years later, reviewing the material that Luti and Feith assembled for Cheney, the Defense Department's inspector general said that the OSP's conclusions on Iraq's relationship with al-Qa'ida were "inconsistent with the consensus of the Intelligence community."[50] Saddam Hussein was not supporting the al-Qa'ida terrorists in Afghanistan, was not harboring any in his country, and did not have any weapons of mass destruction.

The U.S. Senate was harsher than the inspector general in its criticism of the Cheney-Wolfowitz Office of Special Plans. According to a June 2008 report issued by the Senate Select Committee on Intelligence, chaired by Senator Jay Rockefeller of West Virginia, the OSP had orchestrated "clandestine meetings between Pentagon officials and Iranians in Rome and Paris" that were "inappropriate and mishandled from beginning to end." More important, the Senate report indicated, "potentially important information collected during the meetings [with Manucher Ghorbanifar and Michael Ledeen] was withheld from intelligence agencies." According to the Senate committee's findings, Cheney and Wolfowitz had used the Office of Special Plans to circumvent George Tenet and the CIA, as well as Colin Powell and the State Department, as they presented the case to Bush to invade Iraq.[51] When Powell resigned at the end of Bush's first term, it was quiet testimony to his frustration in dealing with Cheney, Rumsfeld, and Wolfowitz.

The decision to expand the war on terror from Afghanistan to Iraq appears to have been the product of two somewhat different sets of priorities. Bush's priorities were to protect and defend the nation from acts of aggression by terrorists and, he would later say, to ensure that democracy allowed freedom of religion. Cheney's priorities, however, seemed to be protecting America's access to the region's oil reserves.

Wolfowitz laid the groundwork for the invasion of Iraq in his 1992 Defense Planning Guidance memo, stating that the first military objective of the United States should be to "prevent any hostile power from dominating a region whose resources would, under consolidated control, be sufficient to generate global power." Others in the administration within Cheney's network argued that removing Saddam Hussein from power would end a threat to Israel, a position that Douglas Feith and Richard Perle championed. It would, moreover, ensure that Iraq—labeled a rogue state by Wolfowitz and Cheney—would not acquire or use weapons of mass destruction or serve as a safe haven for terrorists.[52]

The term "rogue state" had often been used during the administration of George H. W. Bush, and Cheney had based President George W. Bush's abrogation of the ABM treaty on the threat of rogue states possessing nuclear weapons.[53] By framing the government's challenge as protecting the nation from rogue states that possessed weapons of mass destruction, Cheney eventually won Bush's support in his drive to topple the regime of Saddam Hussein.

Using the 9/11 attacks as an opening for military strikes against Iraq, Cheney began to build an argument for Bush that Afghanistan was only the first step in defeating the terrorist network. He argued that the terrorists were supported by Saddam Hussein, and that Iraq— a rogue state like North Korea and Iran—had developed chemical, biological, and nuclear weapons that could easily be used against the United States. The only recourse, Cheney insisted, was to remove Saddam. If they did so, he suggested in an interview, the Iraqi people would welcome the U.S. military with open arms.

Cheney, Addington, and Libby had to convince Bush that Iraq possessed chemical, biological, and nuclear weapons of mass destruction and was therefore an immediate threat to the United States. Although the intelligence community was not persuaded that Iraq posed an imminent threat, by January 2002—only weeks after the invasion of Afghanistan—Cheney had persuaded Bush to remove Saddam Hussein and his regime from power. Bush then began a public campaign to convince the nation and the world that the United States had to deal forcefully with Iraq.

In his 2002 State of the Union address—the first public discussion of the danger presented by Iraq—Bush addressed the issue of weapons of mass destruction that three "rogue states" had hidden from the international community. Embedded in this address was the now-famous reference to the "axis of evil" countries—North Korea, Iran, and Iraq—and the first major assertion by the White House that Iraq had weapons of mass destruction:

Iraq continues to flaunt its hostility toward America and to support terror. The Iraqi regime has plotted to develop anthrax and nerve gas and nuclear weapons for over a decade. This is a regime that has already used poison gas to murder thousands of its own citizens, leaving the bodies of mothers huddled over their dead children. This is a regime that agreed to international inspections, then kicked out the inspectors. This is a regime that has something to hide from the civilized world.

States like these and their terrorist allies constitute an axis of evil, arming to threaten the peace of the world. By seeking weapons of mass destruction, these regimes pose a grave and growing danger. They could provide these arms to terrorists, giving them the means to match their hatred.[54]

Cheney, meanwhile, emphasized the argument that rogue states, particularly Iraq, were an imminent danger. In a speech he gave in Nashville in August 2002, six months after Bush's reference to the axis of evil, he asserted, with chilling precision, that "there was no doubt" that Iraq had weapons of mass destruction. He went even further, predicting that Saddam would "seek domination of the entire Middle East."

Bush took another step toward war in Iraq in January 2003, when, in his State of the Union address, he warned with absolute authority, "if Saddam Hussein does not fully disarm, for the safety of our people and for the peace of the world, we will lead a coalition to disarm him."[55] Bush also announced that Secretary of State Colin Powell would present "information and intelligence about Iraq's illegal weapons program, its attempt to hide those weapons from inspectors, and its links to terrorist groups" to the United Nations.

What was so remarkable about this statement was that Bush and Cheney had never mentioned the UN speech to Colin Powell—who was furious, once again, that Cheney had used his influence with Bush to keep him out of the loop.[56] For Powell, this was beyond reason. Nevertheless, he handled the job like the soldier he was. He sent his chief of staff, Colonel Lawrence Wilkerson, to the CIA to work with John McLaughlin, its deputy director, to review information that might be included in the U.N. speech.[57]

Cheney had already developed the material he wanted Powell to present. John Hannah, Cheney's national security advisor, handed the secretary of state a script on Iraq's weapons of mass destruction and directed Wilkerson to use the 48-page document as the basis for the speech. Wilkerson discovered, however, that the script had little sourced material and no CIA evidence to support it, and he chose, therefore, to look elsewhere for material.

Upon Tenet's advice, he turned first to the National Intelligence Estimate (NIE) that had been prepared only three months earlier, in October 2002. The NIE had information on Iraq's possible nuclear capabilities, but Powell and the CIA viewed the information as unreliable. Although neither Tenet nor McLaughlin could confirm that Iraq had nuclear capabilities, Cheney and his staff insisted that the National Intelligence Estimate was the definitive word on the subject.[58] Two days before Powell was to deliver his speech, the State Department's research and intelligence bureau objected to its assertions that Iraq possessed nuclear arms capabilities. Those objections, however, were overturned by the remainder of the U.S. intelligence community.

Under pressure from Bush and Cheney, Powell delivered the speech in February 2003 to the Security Council of the United Nations. "My colleagues," Powell told council members, with George Tenet sitting behind him, "every statement I make today is backed up by sources, solid sources."[59] Weeks after the Security Council speech, on March 19, 2003, U.S. military aircraft began their assault, paving the way for the invasion.

How Cheney maneuvered Powell into giving the United Nations speech, and manipulated the information in the speech, is a remarkable illustration of the power that he had in the administration. Cheney's reach was even more remarkable. By the time Powell gave the speech,

Cheney and Bush had already asked General Tommy Franks, commander of U.S. Central Command to create plans for invading Iraq. In February 2002, Franks had been directed to create the plans.

As American forces marched on Baghdad, Cheney justified the war by saying, "we believe that he [Saddam Hussein] has in fact reconstituted nuclear weapons."[60] With his customary use of the words "in fact," Cheney reassured the nation that there was no question about the accuracy of his assertion. His language echoed the arguments that he, Rumsfeld, and Wolfowitz had used for years to promote military action against Saddam. Several months earlier, in September 2002, the administration's *National Security Strategy of the United States of America* declared that "given the goals of rogue states and terrorists, the United States can no longer solely rely on a reactive posture as we have in the past. . . . We cannot let our enemies strike first."[61] The administration was arguing for preemptive action.

In order to convince the American public that Saddam Hussein possessed weapons of mass destruction, Cheney shifted the national discourse from terrorism, the original context of military action in Iraq, to the threat of chemical, biological, and nuclear weapons. The reason was simple: Cheney believed that Bush had a stronger argument for using his constitutional authority under the "protect and defend" clause if the nation was threatened with weapons of mass destruction. The use of preemptive action, later known as the Bush Doctrine of Preemption, would be easier to frame within the scope of presidential powers if that were true. In this way, Cheney successfully built the case for the use of military force against Saddam.

New questions, however, would be raised about the limits of presidential powers as the war progressed and reports surfaced about wireless surveillance, harsh interrogations of prisoners, and closed military tribunals. To justify these policies, Cheney drew on the extensive network of lawyers he had built within the administration—especially the Department of Justice's Office of Legal Counsel (OLC) and the White House Counsel's office, headed by Alberto Gonzales. Gonzales defended Bush's authorization to tap phone conversations between U.S. citizens and suspected terrorists outside the country without warrants, asserting that the president "has the inherent authority under the Constitution, as commander-in-chief, to engage in this kind of activity."[62] The legal team that Addington had built in Gonzales's office and the OLC joined him in crafting arguments in defense of the administration's war policies.[63]

Addington became the driving force behind the expansive legal interpretation of presidential war powers. He formed a White House legal team known as the war council—a name that mirrored that of the military war council that Bush and Cheney were convening at the same time—which included Gonzales; William Haynes, general counsel from the Department of Defense; Tim Flanigan, Gonzales's deputy; and John Yoo, a deputy in the OLC.[64] Yoo was the only member of the group empowered to render official decisions that bound the executive branch. His decisions were critical to building the constitutional justification for the conduct of the wars in Afghanistan and Iraq.[65]

When Bush and Cheney decided to initiate a war on terror, Yoo prepared an opinion from the OLC asserting the "president's plenary authority to use force" when necessary to protect and defend the nation. He expanded his opinion, adding that the Constitution allows for "the centralization of authority in the president alone . . . in matters of national defense, war and foreign policy."[66] In other words, the decision to attack the Taliban and terrorists in Afghanistan did not require any action from Congress. The president, Yoo stated, had "the plenary authority" from the Constitution to act unilaterally, without congressional assent.

Questions soon arose about the use of military tribunals for prisoners taken from the battlefields of Afghanistan who were being held at Guantánamo Bay without trial or counsel. Yoo's memoranda supported the administration's position, which had been crafted by Addington and Cheney. According to an OLC opinion written in January 2002, Yoo stated that the Geneva Conventions—adopted by more than 180 nations—"do not protect members of the al-Qaʿida organization, which as a non-State actor cannot be a party to the international agreements governing war. We further conclude that these treaties do not apply to the Taliban militia."[67]

The United States was now denying the protections of the Geneva Conventions to the Afghan fighters. This decision intensified the friction between Cheney and Powell. Only days after Yoo's opinion, the general counsel of the Department of State, William H. Taft IV—one of the few lawyers who had not been vetted by the vice president's office—sent a scathing memo to Gonzales and Ashcroft saying that the State Department disagreed with the OLC's interpretation of the applicability of the Geneva Conventions and that the conventions did apply to prisoners at Guantánamo Bay.[68] Bush ignored these objections, choosing to abide by Cheney's position, which Yoo had endorsed.

The first real challenge to the legal control wielded by Addington and Yoo came when an opening arose for a new director of the Office of Legal Counsel in 2003. Jack Goldsmith had been recommended for the post by an Addington protégé, William Haynes, in the Department of Defense. As a first step in the interview process, Goldsmith met with Gonzales and Addington in Gonzales's office.[69] The two quizzed him about whether he was an expert on presidential war powers, the laws of war, terrorism, and international law. Once they had cleared him, Goldsmith went for a second round of interviews with Attorney General John Ashcroft at the Justice Department. His appointment was approved, and he was confirmed by the Senate.

Despite Addington's influence in his hiring, however, Goldsmith proved to be independent and challenged positions written by Yoo—who had left by this time to return to the Boalt School of Law at the University of California at Berkeley. Goldsmith, at one point, met with Gonzales and Addington to revisit Yoo's decision about whether the Geneva Conventions protections were applicable in military tribunals. "If Gonzales seemed puzzled and slightly worried [about revisiting the opinion]," Goldsmith recalled, "David Addington was just plain mad. 'The president has already decided that terrorists do not receive Geneva Conventions protections,' he barked. You cannot question his decision."[70] The unspoken principle was that the president had absolute authority in matters pertaining to national security—and suddenly that principle was being questioned.

Yoo had authored another opinion, that prisoners of war could be subjected to harsh interrogation techniques. Acts of torture, he argued, caused a level of pain that was associated with serious physical conditions or injury, such as death, organ failure, or serious impairment. Any interrogation that did not meet that standard was not torture according to the administration. To many, however, the administration's harsh interrogation techniques were, in fact, torture, or close to it. When photos were leaked of abusive interrogation techniques and miserable conditions at the Abu Ghraib prison in Iraq, broader questions arose about the treatment of enemy combatants. The issue of torture—a word that had not been current since the Vietnam War—erupted, with charges that prisoners were being subjected to waterboarding, sleep deprivation, beatings, and other extreme interrogation methods.[71]

When the Abu Ghraib scandal erupted in 2004, Bush declared to the nation, "we do not condone torture. I have never ordered torture."[72] He had not specifically authorized torture, nor was he involved in any of the discussions on CIA interrogation techniques, he declared. As it turned out, however, he had known about the harsh interrogations and approved them, saying in 2008, "I'm aware our national security team met on this issue. And I approved."[73]

Cheney, however, had been deeply involved in these discussions. Tenet briefed only Cheney and a small group of others on the harsh treatment that prisoners were receiving.[74] This was the vice president's war, and he would work to protect whatever interrogation techniques he believed necessary for its prosecution. Congress, he argued, could not tell the administration how to conduct it.[75] After Abu Ghraib, however, Congress reasserted its opposition to torture. In the 1990s, Congress had been so concerned about the international treatment of prisoners in the Bosnian civil war that it passed the War Crimes Act of 1996, which made it a felony to engage in any acts of torture as defined by the Geneva Conventions.

Nine years later, in the wake of Abu Ghraib, Congress, led by Senator John McCain, proposed the Detainee Treatment Act of 2005, which banned the "cruel, inhuman, or degrading treatment or punishment of detainees."[76] McCain had endured torture during his five years in captivity in Hanoi, North Vietnam; when he returned home, he was unable to lift his arms over his head or comb his hair. He demanded an end to the use of harsh interrogation techniques.

Cheney battled the bill, regularly traveling to Capitol Hill to lobby members of his party to oppose it. At one point, he unexpectedly walked into a luncheon of Republican senators to persuade them to oppose the ban on torture. Although Congress passed the legislation, that wasn't the last word on the subject. When Bush took out his pen to sign the bill, he added a signing statement, clearly orchestrated by Cheney, declaring that the president did not have to abide by the statute. "The executive branch," it read, "shall construe [the law] in a manner consistent with the constitutional authority of the president . . . as commander in chief," adding that this decision was "consistent with military authority." This phrase was part of the broader argument that the president was in charge of all decisions within the executive branch. Bush had full authority, and Congress could not direct his decision making, on interrogation techniques or other matters, within the military.

Although Bush and Cheney viewed harsh interrogation as an acceptable means of building intelligence from captured al-Qaʻida prisoners of war, others in the administration found the practice abhorrent. Chief among them were Secretary of State Colin Powell and his staff, as well as many within the Department of Defense. Lawrence Wilkerson, Powell's chief of staff, sharply criticized Bush's interpretation of the words "military authority" in his signing statement:

Military necessity means that if I'm detaining you, and you threaten me or my buddies, I can [pistol-whip] you; I can even shoot you. I'm not going to kill you, but I can. It doesn't mean that I can hang you by your shackles in a dungeon in Bagram [Air Base in Afghanistan], subject you to 50-degree temperature day after day after day, fail to feed you except the bare minimum to live, introduce your body to hypothermia, and then beat the crap out of you and kill you, which clearly happened on December 10, 2002, in Bagram to two detainees and apparently that has happened to a number of others. That's not what that means.[77]

The Office of Legal Counsel, however—which Addington and Cheney again controlled after Goldsmith left in 2005—determined that Bush's signing statement was constitutional. The law, it said, violated the president's ability to gain "the intelligence he believes necessary to prevent attacks upon the United States." According to the OLC opinion, "*Any* effort by Congress to regulate the interrogation of battlefield detainees would violate the Constitution's sole vesting of the Commander-in-Chief authority in the president." As even Goldsmith later commented, this was an "extreme conclusion" with "no foundation in prior OLC opinions, or in judicial decisions, or in any source of law."[78] It was another victory for Cheney and Addington in their expansive interpretation of presidential power.

The head of the OLC was now Steven G. Bradbury, one of the original Federalist Society lawyers whom Addington had hired for Gonzales's staff. Unlike Goldsmith, who often challenged legal arguments seeking to justify expanded presidential power, Bradbury tended to support these legal positions. One of his first opinions at the OLC authorized the CIA to use harsh interrogation techniques on terrorists under the president's protect-and-defend constitutional authority as commander in chief. Since harsh interrogation methods offended both Republicans and Democrats in Congress, Bradbury failed to gain confirmation as head of the OLC in a Republican-controlled Senate. When Democrats took control of the Senate in 2007, they continued to block Bradbury's confirmation.[79]

Eventually, the Bush administration was charged with abuse of power in its expansive interpretation of presidential war powers. Such accusations erupted in 2005 over its use of warrantless wireless surveillance. In 2002, by executive order, Bush had authorized the National Security Agency (NSA) to conduct e-mail and phone surveillance of suspected terrorists without seeking a court warrant, as required by the Fourth Amendment to the Constitution. Congress had authorized NSA surveillance in 1978 through the Foreign Intelligence Surveillance Act (FISA), a law that included a provision for creating a special court, known as the FISA court, to review requests for surveillance warrants and to act immediately if necessary. Bush's executive order exempted the NSA from having to seek a warrant from the FISA court, or any other court, when dealing with terrorists.

For Cheney and Addington, the FISA court was an unconstitutional intrusion by Congress on how the president managed his responsibility for national security. As Goldsmith noted, Addington "and the Vice President had abhorred FISA's intrusion on presidential power ever since its enactment in 1978."[80] Soon after Bush signed the executive order, Cheney called congressional leaders into his office in the White House to inform them that warrantless surveillance had been initiated. By holding the meeting in the White House rather than in his office in the Old Executive Office Building, Cheney lent an aura of executive authority to the decision and his own role in national security.

For three years the warrantless surveillance program was kept from the public. Not until the winter of 2005 did the *New York Times* break the story that the president had secretly issued the executive order and that the NSA was conducting warrantless wireless surveillance. Its reporters stated that "the White House asked the *New York Times* not to publish this article, arguing that it could jeopardize continuing investigations and alert would-be terrorists that they might be under scrutiny."[81]

By the time the newspaper made its revelations, the chief judge of the FISA Court and some of the administration's own lawyers had become uncomfortable with the legality of the program. David S. Kris, a national security lawyer in the Justice Department, was one member of the department's staff who believed that the federal courts would rebuke the Bush administration, and he was one of the few who went public with his concerns after leaving the administration.[82] The Bush administration eventually revised the warrantless surveillance program after the executive order became public, and it came under greater control of the FISA court.

Cheney and Bush, however, were both disdainful of congressional criticism. When critics of the war in Iraq—particularly the vice president's role—voiced their concerns, Cheney, in an uncharacteristic display of emotion, called the criticism "dishonest and reprehensible." In response, Senator Edward Kennedy of Massachusetts declared, "the only thing dishonest and reprehensible is the way the administration distorted, misrepresented, and manipulated the intelligence to justify a war America should never have fought. It defies belief."[83] As congressional criticism of the war mounted, Bush and Cheney insisted that the debate "sends exactly the wrong message to our troops, to the Iraqis, and to our terrorist enemies."

In mid-2006—as war casualties increased and the government of Iraq was mired in internal conflict and unable to control a growing insurgency—there were increasing calls among both Democrats and Republicans for the administration to review its Iraq policy. One of the most vocal critics of the administration's decisions on Iraq was David Abshire, president of the Center for the Study of the Presidency, former ambassador to NATO during the Reagan administration, and former president and founder of the Center for International and Strategic Studies.

Abshire saw Cheney as overly influential in the national security decision process, bypassing both Rice and Powell. "Cheney broke the National Security Council, largely because of his personal animosity for Colin Powell," Abshire bluntly stated.[84] The NSC had been created by statute in 1947 to assess the available national security information and provide the president with unbiased information for making decisions. By centralizing decision making in the vice president's office and failing to work with the national security advisor, Condoleezza Rice, Cheney undermined the president's established structure for receiving national security advice.

Abshire was instrumental in creating the congressionally mandated, bipartisan Iraq Study Group, co-chaired by former secretary of state James Baker and former chair of the House Intelligence Committee Lee Hamilton. The group's five Republicans and five Democrats prepared bipartisan recommendations about how long the American military should remain in Iraq. Their 160-page report to Congress, with seventy-nine recommendations, called the situation in Iraq "grave and deteriorating." The group urged diplomatic talks with Iran and Syria about Iraq and the withdrawal of most U.S. combat troops by 2008.[85]

Bush and Cheney summarily dismissed the recommendations. Instead, they created their own internal review of U.S. policy in Iraq, led by National Security Advisor Stephen Hadley, a Cheney ally. Hadley's review urged continuing, even escalating the war. Only a year earlier, the administration had released its 38-page *National Strategy for Victory* in Iraq, which included eight goals—pillars as the strategy called them—necessary to declare victory. Hadley's review endorsed the goals established by the *National Strategy for Victory* and ignored the Iraq Study Group's recommendations.

Defeating terrorists was one of the eight pillars of victory. Months after the Iraq Study Group released its report, the administration began to escalate the war, in what it called a surge, to destroy terrorist enclaves. By sending 20,000 additional troops into Iraq, it raised the number of battle zone troops from 130,000 to 150,000. When questioned about Bush's authority to escalate the war, Cheney repudiated any possibility that Congress could block the surge. Its efforts, he shot back, "won't stop us."[86]

The war in Iraq continued to divide the electorate. Most apparently agreed with the Iraq Study Group's conclusion that the situation was "grave and deteriorating." When Democrats took control of Congress in the 2006 midterm elections, they began to revisit administration practices such as harsh interrogation techniques, military tribunals, and the issue of a timed withdrawal. Points made by the Iraq Study Group were again open for discussion within Congress.

The road to war in Iraq—which had been poorly planned and executed by Cheney, Rumsfeld, and Wolfowitz—had cost the United States more than 4,000 lives, 30,000 casualties, and $100 billion a year. Cheney's assertion that the Iraqis "would welcome us with open arms and greet us with flowers" was a miscalculation of Iraqi support for the U.S.-led invasion. As the sun set on the administration's two terms in office, Dick Cheney was one of the few proponents of the Iraq war who still held office. Most of the leadership team of the war council had left, many in disgrace. The war ended the career of Secretary of Defense Donald Rumsfeld, who was forced from office over Cheney's objections.[87] Colin Powell, who resigned after the first term, had become increasingly marginalized after the terrorist attacks. Rumsfeld resigned after the 2006 midterm elections resoundingly showed the nation's disapproval of the war's prosecution. Wolfowitz resigned as the number-two person at the Defense Department in 2005 to become president of the World Bank; but two years later, he resigned under pressure from that post after negotiating a favorable salary increase for his girlfriend, a bank employee. John Bolton, who was rebuffed by the Republican-controlled Senate in his confirmation as ambassador to the United Nations, moved to the American Enterprise Institute, where he remained unabashedly political.[88]

Scooter Libby was found guilty in 2007 of lying to a grand jury and obstruction of justice in an investigation to determine who in the White House or vice president's office had leaked the name of a CIA agent, Valerie Plame, to the press. Bush commuted Libby's two-and-a-half-year prison sentence, without ruling out a full pardon before his term ended, and Libby paid a $250,000 fine.[89] Bush, however, left office without giving Libby a pardon. Alberto Gonzales, one of the strongest advocates for expansive war powers, resigned under pressure in 2007, after allegations that he had lied to Congress about political hiring and firing in the Department of Justice.

Cheney remained unbowed by the decisions he had made.[90] He was still committed to protecting access to Iraq's oil supply and the president's unbounded war powers. In the end, responsibility for the war in Iraq rested squarely on Dick Cheney's shoulders. As Michael Duffy of *Time* magazine concluded, "everyone knows that Bush and Cheney took the country into a deadly, costly war on flimsy evidence of weapons of mass destruction. But no one was more responsible than the Vice President for pushing the limits of prewar intelligence that did all the convincing."[91] His arguments were supported by intelligence emerging from Douglas Feith's OSP in the Pentagon and by opinions written by the Justice Department's Office of Legal Counsel and the president's own counsel, Alberto Gonzales. Cheney ended his term in office with an abysmal approval rating of only 18 percent—reflecting the public's understanding that the costly, intractable, five-year-long quagmire in Iraq was Dick Cheney's war.

Epilogue

The Cheney Legacy

Dick Cheney left his mark on the presidency in a way that no other vice president had. He was, without question, the most powerful vice president in U.S. history. But perhaps more important, the legacy of the Bush presidency will be inextricably tied to Cheney. The legacy of Cheney is not his role as vice president, but his role as co-president, where he crafted decisions in energy, environmental, economic, and national security policy; asserted absolute constitutional authority for the president; created an anti-regulatory structure; and initiated a mammoth outsourcing of the federal government.

Whether he left the Office of the Vice President itself stronger is doubtful. A more substantive case can be made that he weakened the office, because he ensured that future presidents will be cautious about the roles that their vice presidents are given. White House staff and cabinet officers, the traditional homes of presidential advisors, will reclaim their roles as the principal sources of advice and information in presidential decision making. Vice presidents will constantly be watched, reviewed, and checked by the White House.

The Obama administration in particular will check the role of the vice president, in part to distance itself from the policies of the Bush administration. The new vice president, Senator Joseph Biden of Delaware, who was sharply critical of his predecessor's broad reach in the administration, called Cheney "the most dangerous vice president in history." Neither he nor Obama will continue the role that Cheney created for the vice president.

Rather, Biden's role will be one of confidant and advisor to President Barack Obama, offering candid advice in their weekly private lunches. Weeks before taking his oath of office, Biden carefully said that he would "restore the balance" to the office and that his primary role would be to offer the president "the best, sagest, most accurate, most insightful advice" he could.[1]

But his voice as an advisor will only be one of many heard by the president, and his role in policy making will be sharply limited. Biden will return to the more traditional role of recent vice presidents, who have been given specific assignments by the president, such as his role in overseeing the newly created White House Task Force on Working Families.

Conscious of the free-wheeling nature of Cheney's portfolio, the Obama administration gave Biden clear markers for his vice presidency. He would have specific assignments, in the same vein that Vice President Al Gore had with his assignment to manage the National Performance Review and policies regarding global warming. To reinforce that limited role, Obama tapped Ron Klain, Gore's former chief of staff, as Biden's chief of staff. Unlike Cheney, who brought his own staff, such as David Addington and Scooter Libby, into the vice president's office, Biden's senior staff would be controlled by the White House. Decisions regarding staff and assignments for the Biden vice presidency were in sharp contrast to the Cheney years, another marker that the office had not been inalterably changed.

The Office of the Vice President is, after all, only what the president wants it to be. In Cheney's case, Bush wanted a strong vice president to provide counsel and to oversee a segment of the policy apparatus of government. Bush's limited agenda and his untested Texas support staff left a hole in governance, which Cheney easily filled for the administration.

Cheney did change the character of the vice presidency in one significant way. He asserted that the vice president was part of the executive office and entitled to the rights and privileges of that office. He was not merely part of the executive branch (which he at times questioned), but specifically part of the executive office. That designation freed him from explaining his decision-making conversations to Congress, which he asserted were covered by executive privilege. And the designation freed him from an assortment of other mandates in the broader executive branch, such as providing information on the classification and declassification of his documents. These assertions were made solely by Cheney, who never sought the approval of the White House. However, future vice presidents will most likely seek the same protections for their conversations, asserting that they too have executive privilege. Whether they will assert broader protections for their office is uncertain. The assertion of executive privilege for the vice president, however, may be one of the changes in the office that remains in future administrations.

Yet Cheney will best be remembered for his role as the architect of the war in Iraq. His legacy will be that of managing the post–9/11 policies, from the war in Iraq to harsh interrogation of the newly designated "enemy combatants" to wireless surveillance to military commissions at Guantánamo Bay. As the mastermind of the war in Iraq and all the war-related policies that followed, Cheney led the administration to the lowest approval ratings in modern history, with Bush registering a paltry 28 percent and Cheney an even worse 18 percent. But as Cheney often commented, polls didn't matter. Their decisions were made based on other factors.

The war defined the Bush presidency. Both Bush and Cheney will be inextricably tied to the decision to send over 100,000 troops into Iraq in March 2003—a decision that led to the deaths of over 4,000 American soldiers, to the wounding of over 30,000 American soldiers, to 100,000 Iraqis killed and wounded, and to record federal deficits from the costs of going to war. America's standing in the world was dramatically diminished, as former allies robustly admonished the United States for invading a sovereign nation and for the manner in which prisoners were treated.

There is overwhelming evidence that Cheney led Bush into the war in Iraq based on his own agenda. A decade earlier, as secretary of defense, Cheney had fought with Colin Powell and Brent Scowcroft over the necessity of sending troops into Baghdad during the Gulf War. The first meeting of the National Security Council only days after the inauguration gave ample evidence of Cheney's focus on Iraq, where he reframed the discussion from the Israeli-Palestinian conflict to the necessity of removing Saddam Hussein from power. For Cheney, ensuring access to Middle East oil was critical. As vice president, his national energy plan would reinforce the nation's dependence on oil, eschewing alternative energy sources and conservation as prime energy goals.

Once Bush declared that the war on terror would be the focus of his administration, he essentially abrogated his presidency and handed it over to Cheney. And, what was worse, Bush didn't even know what had happened. Cheney so thoroughly controlled the foreign policy apparatus—with the exception of Colin Powell's Department of State—that every policy recommendation that Bush saw came from Cheney loyalists. Even the deputy director of the National Security Council was a Cheney loyalist. Cheney loyalists went so far as to create a new intelligence office in the Defense Department to evaluate raw intelligence, circumventing the CIA when it met their needs to do so.

Cheney's control of the flow of foreign policy information stemmed from his control of the appointment process as director of the post-election transition. This was Bush's fatal error, which allowed Cheney to establish himself as a power-broker in the administration. Not only did Cheney put his loyalists into key cabinet and subcabinet positions across the administration, but he and his staff became equal partners in all White House policy discussions. It is almost comical to remember that Cheney was in charge of the vice-presidential selection process in 2000, but could find no one, except himself, who met the criteria he established. And no one vetted Cheney once Bush suggested that he take the job.

Future presidents will certainly be leery of allowing their vice presidents to control the transition process. Neither the Obama campaign nor the McCain campaign in the 2008 presidential race tasked their vice-presidential nominees with transition roles. Both campaigns carefully avoided assigning their running mates with managing the transition, preferring to keep their vice presidents well outside of the process. After the election, staffing the new administration was managed by a transition team controlled by the Obama staff, with little interaction with the vice president. Clearly, both of the 2008 presidential candidates had seen the damage done by a vice president in charge of a transition.

The lesson learned from the Bush-Cheney years ran deeper, however, in how the relationship between the president and the vice president should be managed. Cheney's insistence that a single executive office be created in which information flowed freely between the two offices, memos were routinely shared, and integrated staffs participated in policy meetings was not one that future presidents are likely to replicate. Future presidents will certainly continue to share information, and certain material will routinely be shared, but certainly not to the degree that occurred between the Bush and Cheney staffs.

Had Cheney and his staff been less involved in the daily policy discussions within the White House, he would have had less influence in the administration. However, ironically, what gave Cheney the most power was not his involvement in the policy discussions but his involvement in policy matters that were not being discussed in the White House. Cheney knew where the policy vacuums were.

Cheney never stepped on the toes of the White House staff, thus minimizing friction between the two offices. Bush's interest in pro-life policies, faith-based programs, volunteerism, and education were the focus of White House policy discussions. Armed with this information, Cheney was free to address other policy areas, such as environmental regulations, energy policy, outsourcing, and national security policy. He had the staff, the connections, and the institutional resources to move forward his own policy agenda.

Traditionally, vice presidents have served as spokesmen for presidents and represented the administration in second-tier international events. Nelson Rockefeller tried to craft such a role, but he failed when the White House staff blocked him. With the blessing of Gerald Ford, Rockefeller had taken responsibility for managing the broad domestic agenda while Ford traveled the country to, as he said, "heal the nation" after the Watergate revelations. But Ford's White House chief of staff, Dick Cheney, had been the one to demand an end to the free-wheeling policy responsibility of the vice president. Using covert warfare, Cheney persuaded Ford to strip Rockefeller not only of managing the domestic agenda but of his place on the 1976 Republican ticket. On Cheney's recommendation, Rockefeller was replaced by Bob Dole.

The battle over who controlled the domestic agenda was won by Cheney in the White House staff when it was threatened by the vice president. White House staff view themselves as the keepers of the president's agenda and rarely acquiesce to having their role minimized or circumvented by others. When Cheney captured such a significant part of the policy agenda in the Bush administration, he knew from his own role in history that he couldn't threaten the role in making policy that the White House staff had carved out for itself.

Unlike the 1975 battle with Rockefeller, who threatened his place in the policy-making scheme, Cheney would carve out a territory that did not threaten the Bush loyalists on the White House staff. As long as their territory wasn't threatened, he felt reasonably assured that they would not interfere with his policy activities. Changing the landscape of the regulatory process to favor business and industry was fully supported by the White House staff, but they lacked Cheney's passion for doing so or the knowledge of how to accomplish it. At no point did Cheney endeavor to push a policy that either Bush or the White House staff found out of sync with their own agendas. Cheney's policies were simply not at the top of their list.

Twenty years earlier, Walter Mondale had watched Cheney destroy Nelson Rockefeller. When the Carter-Mondale administration took office, Mondale chose not to confront the Carter team that moved into the White House from the Georgia-based campaign. He didn't know them and had only been added to the ticket for his Beltway experience. As vice president, to ensure that he did not alienate the White House staff, Mondale refused to be responsible for any specific policy areas. Rather, he chose to become an informal advisor to Carter, meeting once a week in the White House to offer his candid assessments of how administration policies were playing on Capitol Hill and in Peoria.

Similarly, when Ronald Reagan was elected president, he gave his vice president a limited role, with the White House chiefs of staff James Baker and Edwin Meese firmly in command of the domestic and foreign policy agendas. As president, George H. W. Bush gave his own vice president, Dan Quayle, a similarly limited role. Quayle's role in the administration was largely limited to work on the Space Council and in coordinating the Competitiveness Council. Both were created by Bush to keep Quayle outside of the policy discussions in the White House, but to give him some role in the administration.

Bill Clinton chose his good friend Al Gore to join him on the Democratic ticket in 1992, but Gore too was kept within certain boundaries. Gore would have broader assignments than any vice president before him. Clinton placed him in charge of environmental and telecommunications policy, and he would later take charge of a newly created task force to find efficiencies in the federal government.

In retrospect, the model that Cheney created for a vice president with policy responsibilities had been slowly emerging since Rockefeller. When Gore's chief of staff, Roy Neel, gained access to the president's staff as an equal partner in senior staff meetings, it further expanded the relationship that the vice president had within the White House.

Yet Cheney expanded the relationship far beyond the bounds of any previous vice president. Keenly aware of the turf battles that could arise between the White House and the vice president's office from his own experience with Rockefeller, Cheney pursued a strategy that built on the expanding role for vice presidents that had been emerging in recent administrations. However, he took both roles far beyond the natural evolution that had been under way for over twenty-five years. Vice presidents had been slowly gaining a role in the policy process and had been expanding their involvement in decision making.

Cheney was unwilling to stay within the boundaries of that natural progression and pursued his own picture of what the relationship should be between the two offices. In Cheney's world, the president and the vice president were equal partners, with each taking responsibility for certain areas of policy.

The process that Cheney developed worked because he and Bush had different agendas, because Cheney's agenda didn't distract from Bush's agenda, and because Cheney knew how to make the government work for him. After serving as a member of Rumsfeld's staff in the Office of Economic Opportunity, as White House chief of staff, as a five-term member of Congress, and as secretary of defense, Cheney was well versed in the inner workings of the federal government. He knew how to get things done.

How Cheney captured so much of the policy process remains an open book, which future administrations will have to carefully evaluate. It is unlikely that future vice presidents will have substantive policy responsibilities that do not fall within strong White House oversight, nor will future staff in the vice president's office be completely integrated into the White House.

One role that will not be continued in future administrations is Cheney's control of signing statements. In future administrations, this will be managed in the White House counsel's office or in the Office of Legislative Affairs. The White House staff will want full control over the thorny relationship that the White House maintains with Congress, of which signing statements are a significant part. The experience of a pliant Congress failing to challenge presidential assertions of constitutional authority is unlikely to continue. Having a Republican Congress, with relatively weak leaders in both the House and the Senate, allowed the Republican Bush administration to make assertions of presidential power that went unchallenged. Future Congresses, even those that share party control with the president, are unlikely to allow presidents to refuse to enforce legislation that they view as unconstitutional. Rather, they will argue, the remedy for presidents is to veto the entire piece of legislation rather than to line-item pieces that they will not enforce.

So where does that leave us? What exactly is the legacy of the Cheney vice presidency? Cheney's remains a unique vice presidency, one that was never seen before and will never be seen again. Future presidents will ensure that the role played by their vice presidents is limited and controlled. But Cheney's influence in the larger scheme of executive-legislative relations will be more enduring than the role he carved out in the vice presidency. While the Office of the Vice President will return to its pre-Bush functions, the Office of the President has been given abundant new powers because of the aggressive efforts of Dick Cheney.

Notwithstanding that Cheney failed in his own quest to capture the White House in his run for office in 1994, his legacy involves the presidency, not the vice presidency. It lies in the contribution that he made to the Office of the President. His expansive interpretation of presidential power is likely to persist for years to come as future presidents and futures Congresses tackle the new parameters of presidential power.

There is, of course, the war in Iraq, for which Cheney will also be remembered. The misinformation that was put forth by Cheney, Rumsfeld, and others in the months before the war has been widely discredited, leaving the public angry at being misled—hence the abysmal poll numbers. The slightly higher approval ratings that Bush maintained reflected the public's distaste for a vice president whose personal agenda led the nation to an unnecessary and failed war.

Cheney will not be remembered for the way he inserted himself into the White House policy apparatus, which can be easily dismantled in future administrations, but for the arrogance of power that he carried into office. While that arrogance broadened the institution of the presidency, it destroyed the presidency of George W. Bush and any expansion of power that the Office of the Vice President might have carried forward.

Reference Matter

Notes

CHAPTER 1: INTRODUCTION

1. By the time Florida Secretary of State Katherine Harris certified Bush the winner of Florida's electoral votes on November 27, 2001, "Cheney was already overseeing the transition," according to Scott McClellan, *What Happened: Inside the Bush White House and Washington's Culture of Deception* (New York: Public Affairs, 2008), p. 58.

2. Steve Schmidt joined John McCain's presidential campaign in July 2008 and soon became the senior political strategist.

3. Seymour M. Hersh, "Preparing the Battlefield," *New Yorker*, July 7–14, 2008.

CHAPTER 2: THE BUSH-CHENEY TICKET EMERGES

1. Karl Rove is called a "boy genius" as the architect of the successful political campaigns for governor of Texas in 1994 and 1998, and for the presidency in 2000, in Carl Cannon, Lou Dubose, and Jan Reid, *Boy Genius: Karl Rove, the Architect of George W. Bush's Remarkable Political Triumphs* (New York: Public Affairs, 2003). The authors attribute Bush's victory over popular incumbent Texas governor Ann Richards to Rove for crafting the merger of the compassionate agenda of George Bush with the more conservative agenda of most Texans. The ideological merger of these two agendas proved successful for the 2000 presidential election when Cheney's conservative political philosophy became a perfect fit with Bush's compassionate (religious) political philosophy.

2. Ron Suskind, "Without a Doubt," *New York Times Magazine*, October 17, 2004.

3. Carl Leubsdorf, *Dallas Morning News*, telephone interview by author, April 2007.

4. Robert Draper, *Dead Certain: The Presidency of George W. Bush* (New York: Free Press, 2007), p. 39. In writing this book, Draper had broad access to both George W. Bush and Laura Bush. Laura Bush's discussions with Draper about her husband's decision to stop drinking are framed around more practical explanations than a religious conversion.

5. The November 8, 1994, election for governor resulted in a win for George W. Bush with 53.48 percent of the votes cast to 45.08 percent for the incumbent, Democrat Ann Richards.

6. In *Boy Genius*, Cannon, Dubose, and Reid chronicle the relationship of George W. Bush and Karl Rove throughout Bush's two campaigns for governor and his campaign for president.

7. Scott Pendleton, "Stetson-Size Agenda for Texas," *Christian Science Monitor*, December 15, 1994.

8. Proposition 187, passed by California voters in 1994, denied state benefits to illegal immigrants; it was subsequently overturned by the federal courts for violating the constitutional control of immigration issues by the federal government.

9. Pendleton, "Stetson-Size Agenda."

10. Prison Fellowship Ministries mission statement.

11. An NBC News–*Wall Street Journal* poll revealed that Bush was favored by 40 percent of Republicans. Dan Quayle and Steve Forbes polled as the best vote-getters

after Bush. See G. Ratcliffe, "Bush Thinking About Presidency: Speech to Movie Industry Heavy with Political Overtone," *Houston Chronicle*, April 24, 1998.

12. R. G. Ratcliffe, "Bush Defends Closing Events to News Media," *Houston Chronicle*, April 21, 1998.

13. Ibid.

14. Ratcliffe, "Bush Thinking About Presidency."

15. Ratcliffe, "Bush Defends Closing Events to News Media."

16. Cannon, Dubose, and Reid, *Boy Genius*, p. 114.

17. Candy Crowley, "Days Away from Re-Election, Will Texas Gov. Bush Run for President Next?" CNN.com, October 29, 1998, www.cnn.com/ALLPOLITICS/stories/1998/10/29/texas.gov.

18. When Bush decided to write a presidential campaign autobiography, he commissioned the Texas journalist Michael Herskowitz as the ghostwriter. Bush was dissatisfied with the direction that Herskowitz took, however, and fired him. Karen Hughes, his close friend and communications director in the governor's office, rewrote sections that Bush found to be unfavorable. Hughes was given full credit on the back jacket of the book, which states that the book was "written with his longtime communications director, Karen Hughes." Herskowitz is not mentioned. See, e.g., www.nytimes.com/2008/02/01/books/chapters/1st-chapter-bush-tragedy.html?pagewanted=12&_r=1. However, in a surprising twist to the story, the British web site of Amazon.com (amazon.co.uk) has *A Charge to Keep* listed with Herskowitz as the co-author.

19. George W. Bush, *A Charge to Keep* (New York: William Morrow, 1999), pp. 228, 232, 235.

20. Rick Lyman, "Bush Blends Optimism and Challenge in Texas Inaugural," *New York Times*, January 20, 1999.

21. Paul Kengor, *God and George W. Bush: A Spiritual Life* (New York: HarperCollins, 2004), p. 34.

22. Governor George W. Bush, inaugural address, Austin, Texas, January 20, 1999.

23. Ken Herman, "Select Few Earn Spots on Bush's First Team; Small Group of Trusted," *Austin American-Statesman*, February 28, 1999.

24. Bradford Freeman was a partner in the Los Angeles investment firm of Freeman Spogli and Co., which he founded in the 1980s with former Los Angeles mayor Richard Riordan, who left the firm in 1988, and Ron Spogli. The firm focused on leveraged buyouts over $100 million. Ken Herman, "Select Few Earn Spots on Bush's First Team; Small Group of Trusted," *Austin American-Statesman*, February 28, 1999.

25. Burt Solomon, "Issues & Ideas: George W. Bush's New Hooverville," *National Journal*, March 27, 1999.

26. John B. Taylor, author interview, November 2007. Martin Anderson and John Cogan, author interviews, Stanford University, October and November 2007.

27. Robert McGrew and Henry Tosner, "Bush Finds Core Advisors at Hoover," *Stanford Review*, October 29, 1999. As Martin Anderson, a Hoover Fellow, noted in a 1998 interview with the *Stanford Review*, "Over the years, we've invited most candidates from both parties. When they come, they don't ask for advice."

28. The official White House biography during the Bush administration of Condoleezza Rice noted that she was "a Fellow (by courtesy) of the Hoover Institution" (www.whitehouse.gov/nsc/ricebio.html).

29. McGrew and Tosner, "Bush Finds Core Advisors at Hoover."

30. Richard L. Berke, with Rick Lyman, "Training for a Presidential Race," *New York Times*, March 15, 1999.

31. Ibid.

32. Ibid. An editor's note at the bottom of this article reads:

March 19, 1999, Friday. An article on Monday about the prospect of a Presidential campaign by Gov. George W. Bush of Texas described a series of tutorials aimed at helping him study issues he would face. As published, the article included an opinionated sentence casting doubt on his mastery of those issues. The sentence was sent as a message between editors after the article was written, and the reporters were never aware of it. The comment was typed in a nonprinting computer script, but converted into print through a command error.

33. John Cogan, author interview, Stanford University, November 2007. Cogan met regularly with Bush on Social Security individual accounts, which became one of the main campaign agenda items. Although Cogan declined a position in the administration, preferring to remain at Stanford University, he was appointed in 2001 to chair a Social Security commission.

34. Whether or not Ronald Reagan would have supported George W. Bush or encouraged his advisors to support his candidacy is unknown, but Reagan's diary of May 17, 1986, reveals the following:

A moment I've been dreading. George [Vice President George H. W. Bush] brought his ne'er-do-well son around this morning and asked me to find the kid a job. Not the political one who lives in Florida [future Gov. Jeb Bush]. The one who hangs around here all the time looking shiftless. This so-called kid is already almost 40 and has never had a real job. Maybe I'll call Kinsley over at the *New Republic* and see if they'll hire him as a contributing editor or something. That looks like easy work.

35. Among the numerous articles on Cheney's selection as vice president, see Nicolas Lemann, "The Quiet Man," *New Yorker*, May 7, 2001.

36. "Bush Introduces Cheney as Running Mate," *USA Today*, July 25, 2000.

37. Fred Barnes, "The Second Bush White House," *Weekly Standard*, December 25, 2000.

38. Eric Schmitt, "The 2000 Campaign: The Running Mate," *New York Times*, July 26, 2000.

39. When Cheney mentioned to George H. W. Bush that he was considering a run for president in 1996, Bush encouraged him and connected Cheney with Mel Sembler, a fundraiser for the Bush campaigns. See Peter Schweizer and Rochelle Schweizer, *The Bushes: Portrait of a Dynasty* (New York: Doubleday, 2004), p. 445.

40. Ibid., p. 445.

41. Nelson Rockefeller's papers are housed at Rockefeller University. Among them are several interviews. In an interview with Hugh Morrow on November 22, 1977, Rockefeller blamed Rumsfeld and Cheney for destroying him in the Ford administration. According to Rockefeller, their actions were self-serving rather than based on philosophical disagreement. Rumsfeld, who wanted to run for president in 1980, sought to ensure that Rockefeller was not a sitting vice president to challenge him in 1980. Rumsfeld's "entire strategy was designed as to how he could eliminate all competition that might be vice president in the next election, after President Ford had had a term, could then be a potential candidate in 1980," Rockefeller said. Asked by Morrow if he didn't think that Ford should have selected Rumsfeld as vice president instead of him, Rockefeller answered, "He certainly did" (p. 27). In responding to subsequent questions, Rockefeller referred to Cheney as "very cagey" (p. 40).

42. "Reports of the Iran-Contra Committees: Excerpts from the Minority View," *New York Times*, November 17, 1987.

43. Later in his career, when Addington followed Cheney into the executive branch in the vice president's office, he would become the architect of the unitary executive that Cheney championed. Addington, for example, would write signing statements that were appended to legislation. Bush would sign the legislation sent over by Congress, making it the law of the land—except for the small matter of Addington's signing statement, which listed those portions of the bill that the president could not enforce. Rather than veto the entire bill, Addington reviewed every bill signed by Bush for any legislative encroachment on presidential authority and prepared a signing statement. The signing statement only invalidated, or effectively vetoed, a paragraph or two. Those unenforceable parts, according to Addington, were unconstitutional. Congress, he argued, could not tell the president how to act in certain circumstances.

44. Alison Mitchell and Frank Bruni, "The 2000 Campaign: The Arizona Senator: McCain Said to Be Willing to Run as Bush's No. 2," *New York Times*, July 21, 2000.

45. "How Bush Selected Cheney," July 26, 2000, *Philadelphia Inquirer*.

46. Karen Hughes, *Ten Minutes from Normal* (New York: Viking, 2004), p. 142.

47. Ibid.

48. Richard Cohen and James Kitfield, "Cheney: Pros and Cons," *National Journal*, July 29, 2000.

49. Richard Cohen and James Kitfield, "Bush's List of Running Mates Getting Shorter, but Not Clearer," *New York Times*, June 19, 2000.

50. Robert Draper, *Dead Certain: The Presidency of George W. Bush* (New York: Free Press, 2007), p. 89.

51. Sidney Blumenthal, *How Bush Rules: Chronicles of a Radical Regime* (Princeton, N.J.: Princeton University Press, 2006), p. 80.

52. The column "Washington Whispers," *U.S. News & World Report*, June 10, 2007, reported that Cheney said of the offer: "Running for my current job as vice president in 2000 was . . . somebody else's idea. I was not a volunteer."

53. Stephen Hayes interviewed Cheney for his book *Cheney: The Untold Story of America's Most Powerful and Controversial Vice President* (New York: HarperCollins, 2007). Cheney was on the treadmill when Bush called, Hayes says. After a brief interchange, Cheney hung up and said to Lynne Cheney, "Honey, let's sell the house. I quit my job. We're going back into politics" (ibid., p. 284).

54. "Bush Introduces Cheney as Running Mate," *USA Today*, July 25, 2000.

55. John Sheridan, "Religion at Core of Cheney Talk," Missouri Digital News, August 30, 2000.

CHAPTER 3: TRANSITION PLANNING

1. Stephen Hayes, *Cheney: The Untold Story of America's Most Powerful and Controversial Vice President* (New York: HarperCollins, 2007), p. 297. Based on an interview with Cheney.

2. Karen Hughes, *Ten Minutes from Normal* (New York: Viking, 2004), p. 172. She recounts the phone call to her from Governor Bush to inquire if she was going to go to the Four Seasons to join him and his family in his suite. She noted: "my phone rang again. 'Are you coming?' Governor Bush asked. I had stayed away to give him some privacy, but hurried over now." At that point, she left Rove's office to join the Bush family at the governor's mansion.

3. Hughes, *Ten Minutes from Normal*, p. 176.

4. Hayes, *Cheney*, p. 298. Related by Cheney to Hayes in an interview.

5. Robert Draper, *Dead Certain: The Presidency of George W. Bush* (New York: Free Press, 2007), pp. 306–7.

6. Peter Schweizer and Rochelle Schweizer, *The Bushes: Portrait of a Dynasty* (New York: Doubleday, 2004), p. 494.

7. Cheney told Stephen Hayes that Libby "had two sets of qualities, one in terms of substantive interest, but also, he was a guy that was well organized in terms of being able to get things done" (Hayes, *Cheney*, p. 299).

8. John Podesta, Clinton's White House chief of staff, ordered the General Services Administration to abide by the law and to await final election results until providing government-funded transition space. Podesta issued a statement on November 13, 2000, that stated that "because of the uncertainty over election results, no President-elect has been identified to receive federal funds and assistance under the Presidential Transition Act of 1963" (Executive Office of the President, Memorandum from Chief of Staff John Podesta for the Heads of Executive Departments and Agencies, "Presidential Transition Guidance," November 13, 2000).

9. Clay Johnson, "The 2000–01 Presidential Transition: Planning, Goals, and Reality," *PS Political Science and Politics* 35, 1 (March 2002). The need to raise money for the transition was actually expected, although using it for the McLean headquarters was not part of the plan. It was expected that the transition would cost $8.5 million, which was over the allotted transition allocation from the General Services Administration, and they were fully aware that private money would be needed to supplement the transition. It appears that the IRS designation had been established by Johnson prior to the election.

10. "Contesting the Vote: Excerpt from Statement by Cheney on the Transition," *New York Times*, November 28, 2000. Cheney also noted that he would not accept contributions from corporations or political action committees.

11. Clay Johnson had been a classmate of George W. Bush's at Phillips Academy in Andover, Massachusetts, and was his roommate at Yale. After graduating from Yale and the Sloan School of Management at the Massachusetts Institute of Technology, Johnson held senior management positions in PepsiCo's Frito-Lay, Wilson Sporting Goods, and Citicorp; he was president of Horchow Mail Order Inc. from 1983 to 1991.

12. John P. Burke, *Becoming President: The Bush Transition, 2000–2003* (Boulder, Colo.: Lynne Rienner, 2004). See also Martha Joynt Kumar, *PS: Political Science and Politics* 35, 1 (March 2002). According to Kumar's interview with Johnson, Johnson moved into the position of appointments secretary in 1999 when Bush created a campaign staff. Joe Allbaugh, the appointments secretary at the time was moved to manage the campaign.

13. James Traub, "The Bush Years: W.'s World," *New York Times*, January 14, 2001.

14. Johnson, "2000–01 Presidential Transition."

15. Martin Anderson, author interview, October 2006, Stanford University. For a detailed discussion of the 1976 convention, see Martin Anderson, *Revolution: The Reagan Legacy* (Stanford, Calif.: Hoover Institution Press, 1988, 1990), p. 69.

16. Gerald R. Ford, *A Time to Heal: The Autobiography of Gerald R. Ford* (New York: Harper & Row, 1979), p. 400.

17. Martin Anderson, author interview, November 2007, Stanford University.

18. Alan Greenspan, *The Age of Turbulence: Adventures in a New World* (New York: Penguin Press, 2007), pp. 89–90.

19. Ibid., p. 90.

20. Chase Untermeyer, interview with John Robert Greene, 1996, quoted in John Robert Greene, *The Presidency of George Bush* (Lawrence: University of Kansas Press, 2000), p. 46.

21. E. Pendleton James, author interviews, Washington, D.C., and New York City. Research for Shirley Anne Warshaw, *The Domestic Presidency: Policy Making in the White House* (Boston: Allyn & Bacon, 1997), p. 119.

22. Fielding would be named counsel to the president in the second term of the administration, replacing Alberto Gonzales, who was confirmed as attorney general (to replace John Ashcroft).

23. Jo Becker and Barton Gellman, "Angler: Leaving No Tracks," *Washington Post*, June 27, 2007.

24. Steven A. Holmes, "Counting the Vote: The Republican Running Mate; Bush Takes Appeal to U.S. Supreme Court; Cheney in Hospital with Mild Heart Attack," *New York Times*, November 23, 2000.

25. Questions later arose as to the thoroughness of the exam. Dr. Gary Malakoff was relieved of his duties as chairman of George Washington University Hospital Medical Center's Internal Medicine Division in 2004 for abusing prescription drugs. Jane Mayer, "In the Beltway: The Vice President's Doctor," *New Yorker*, July 12, 2004.

26. Tom Raum, "Bush Staff Chief Steps Up Work on Transition," AP, December 5, 2000.

27. James Bennet, "The Bush Years: CEO, USA," *New York Times*, January 14, 2001.

28. "Cheney Talks Transition with GOP Lawmakers on Capitol Hill," December 13, 2000, CNN.com, edition.cnn.com/2000/ALLPOLITICS/sotires/12/13/cheney.hill.

29. The Department of Homeland Security, statutorily created as a result of the terrorist attacks of September 11, 2001, was the fifteenth cabinet department.

30. The task force that Cogan put together included Tim Morris, Glen Hubbard, Keith Hennessy, Clark Judge, and Amy Smith. John Cogan, author interview, November 2007, Stanford University.

31. Press Release of the National Association for Convenience and Petroleum Retailing, "NACS Named to Bush-Cheney Transition Advisory Teams Giving Convenience Story Industry a Voice in Forming New Administration," January 17, 2001, www.nacsonline.com.

32. John Mintz, "Transition Advisers Have Much to Gain," *Washington Post*, January 17, 2001.

33. Howard Fineman and Michael Isikoff with Martha Brant, "Right from the Start," *Newsweek*, January 22, 2001.

34. Jack Goldsmith, *The Terror Presidency: Law and Judgment Inside the Bush Administration* (New York: Norton, 2007), p. 17. Goldsmith recounts that when he went to Ashcroft's fifth floor conference room with his wife and two young sons for his swearing-in ceremony on October 6, 2003, "Ashcroft asked me to swear on the black Bible in his hand."

35. Ibid., pp. 160–62. According to Goldsmith, Cheney told Ashcroft directly that the interrogation opinion was "deeply flawed." Goldsmith also notes that he had broad support for positions he took as director of the Office of Legal Counsel, except for David Addington, the vice president's legal counsel. "No one except Addington disputed that the opinions I had withdrawn and redone (or started to redo) were deeply flawed," Goldsmith said.

36. Peter Baker, "An Exit Toward Soul-Searching," *Washington Post*, October 7, 2007.

37. See Richard L. Berke, "Bush Is Providing Corporate Model for White House," *New York Times*, March 11, 2001. While the corporate model provided for delegation of authority by Bush to the cabinet, it also strengthened the business-friendly administration that Cheney created.

CHAPTER 4: FULL TRANSPARENCIES

1. Sheryl Gay Stolberg, "In Glimpses, Private Soul Contemplates Public Legacy," *New York Times*, August 31, 2008.

2. Eric Schmitt, "Cheney Assembles a Formidable Team," *New York Times*, February 3, 2001.

3. Dana Milbank, "For Number Two, The Future Is Now; Cheney Has Historically Broad Agenda," *Washington Post*, February 3, 2001.

4. Schmitt, "Cheney Assembles a Formidable Team."

5. These were policies that attracted national support from conservatives as Bush moved through the primaries and needed to recapture the Reagan coalition. Not surprisingly, the principal advisors on Social Security and tax policy were the Stanford University economists Michael Boskin, John Cogan, and John Taylor. Overseeing foreign policy were Donald Rumsfeld, Paul Wolfowitz, Richard Perle, and Condoleezza Rice. All were former Reagan or George H. W. Bush staffers.

6. Stephen Hayes, *Cheney: The Untold Story of America's Most Powerful and Controversial Vice President* (New York: HarperCollins, 2007). According to Hayes, Cheney met with Libby and Addington two days after the election at the Four Seasons to discuss their jobs in the vice president's office. However, a somewhat different interpretation is offered by Ron Christie, who says that when Libby hired him during the transition, Libby suggested in the interview that he had not yet been offered a job in the vice president's office. Christie recounts his job interview with Libby as follows: "Scooter noted that he had been asked by the vice president–elect to help staff the various offices with policy experts to carry out President Bush's agenda. At this point, Scooter confessed even he didn't know whether or not he would be offered a position himself (an assertion I didn't entirely believe)." See Ron Christie, *Black in the White House: Life Inside George W. Bush's West Wing* (Nashville, Tenn.: Nelson, 2006), p. 9.

7. The FY 2003 budget includes a line that reads, "As part of the FY 2003 Budget, the Administration is again requesting a consolidation and financial realignment for the EOP. The initiative would consolidate 15 EOP components and fund them with a single appropriation for a total of $336.2 million. This proposal will give the President maximum flexibility in allocating resources and staff in support of his office." For Cheney, this would keep his staff from being a separate line item in the budget and minimize scrutiny of its size or cost.

8. Schmitt, "Cheney Assembles a Formidable Team."

9. The Bureau of National Affairs publishes a staff list for the Executive Office of the President and the Office of the Vice President. The June 2005 list, which was essentially a 2004 compilation, has eighty-five staff in the Office of the Vice President. For a list of the titles and names of senior staff in the vice president's office on a yearly basis, see *The Capitol Source*, an annual publication of *National Journal*, Washington, D.C. Providing staff for vice presidents was a relatively new idea. It began with a small staff in Nelson Rockefeller's office during the Ford administration. Rockefeller only accepted the job of vice president on the understanding that he could play a role in domestic policy decisions. Although he had few of his own staff in the vice president's office, he selected staff such as James Cannon, a former editor of *Time* magazine, to oversee the Domestic Council staff. When Walter Mondale left

the Senate to be Jimmy Carter's vice president, he did so on the understanding that there would be an expanded role for the vice president. He would be an advisor to Carter, using his weekly luncheons to discuss policy matters, and he relied on a small staff to prepare him for those weekly luncheons. George H. W. Bush, whose relationship with Ronald Reagan did not improve after the divisive primaries, maintained a low profile during the eight years of the administration. When George H. W. Bush became president, his vice president, Dan Quayle, was assigned the job of overseeing the newly created Competitiveness Council. Quayle's job was to determine how intrusive the federal regulatory process was on the competitiveness of business and industry. Al Gore, Bill Clinton's vice president, following in Quayle's path, focused primarily on his National Performance Review, assigned by Clinton, and on environmental issues. For both Quayle and Gore, each of whom had as many as ninety people working for them, the staff in the vice president's office worked on specific assignments and did not stray into the broader issues being addressed by White House staff.

10. Christie, *Black in the White House*, pp. 38–47.

11. After the September 11, 2001, terrorist attacks, Cheney's expertise in national security matters added another dimension to the co-presidency, and again it would be based on his information. Cheney would become the principal architect of the administration's response to the terrorist attacks, which encompassed both Afghanistan and Iraq, partly because he and his staff had the policy expertise. His national security staff would become the key players in the White House as decisions were made on removing Saddam Hussein from power. John Hannah, Cheney's deputy national security advisor, for example, prepared the speech for Secretary of State Colin Powell to deliver (but that he rejected) in the United Nations.

12. Schmitt, "Cheney Assembles a Formidable Team." For a lengthy discussion of the staffing process in the vice president's office, see Christie, *Black in the White House*, pp. 38–47.

13. Cheney did, however, nudge Republicans in Congress to support the bill. But the bill had strong bipartisan support, led by Senator Edward Kennedy of Massachusetts, giving Cheney only a minimal role in Republican arm-twisting.

14. Christie, *Black in the White House*, p. 7.

15. Ron Suskind, "Mrs. Hughes Takes Her Leave," *Esquire*, July 30, 2002.

16. Karen Hughes, *Ten Minutes from Normal* (New York: Viking, 2004), p. 184.

17. David Frum, author interview, April 2007, Washington, D.C. According to Frum, Rove wanted to reinvent the Republican Party to create a permanent governing coalition. To do so, Bush needed to bring lower- and moderate-income voters into the party. Compassionate conservatism was a strategy designed to appeal to Roman Catholics and urban African Americans, who traditionally voted for Democrats. Using the federal government to fund faith-based organizations would appeal to both groups and would eventually lead to a permanent change in their voting behavior from the Democratic to the Republican Party.

18. Nicholas Calio, author interview, October 2007, Washington, D.C.

19. At times, Hughes consulted with David Frum, whom Cheney had hired as a speechwriter, but Hughes always initiated the requests, and Frum was more of an exception than the rule. Frum, author interview, Washington, D.C., April 2007.

20. Robert Draper, *Dead Certain: The Presidency of George W. Bush* (New York: Free Press, 2007), p. 90.

21. Nicholas Thompson, "Dick Cheney's Dick Cheney," *Washington Monthly*, July–August, 2001.

CHAPTER 5: GOD AND GEORGE W. BUSH

1. In addition to Bush, Forbes, and Keyes, the candidates were Senator John McCain (R-Ariz.), Senator Orrin Hatch (R-Utah), and Gary Bauer, president of the Family Research Council. When Bauer was asked which philosopher had the most influence on his life, he responded "Jesus." Bush followed Bauer's response with his answer, "Christ, because he changed my heart." John Bachman then interrupted before the next respondent, asking Bush, "I think the viewer would like to know more about how he's changed your heart." At that point, Bush gave the expanded answer: "When you turn your heart and your life over to Christ, when you accept Christ as the savior, it changes your heart. It changes your life. And that's what happened to me." Frank Bruni, "Bush Tangles with McCain over Campaign Financing," *New York Times,* December 14, 1999.

2. Howard Fineman, "Bush and God," *Newsweek*, March 10, 2003. See also Paul Kengor, *God and George W. Bush: A Spiritual Life* (New York: Regan Books, 2004), p 62. Kengor recites other instances in which Bush said, "God wants me to run for president."

3. Frank Bruni, "A Nation Challenged: White House Memo: For President, a Mission and a Role in History," *New York Times,* September 22, 2001.

4 Ron Suskind, "Without a Doubt," *New York Times Magazine*, October 17, 2004.

5. "Governor George W. Bush Delivers Remarks," cnn.com, December 13, 2000, www.cnn.com/ELECTION/2000/transcripts.121300/bush.html.

6. George W. Bush, *A Charge to Keep* (New York: Morrow, 1999), pp. 44–45. Jacob Weisberg was among the first to uncover the disparity between the artist's intent and Bush's interpretation of the painting, which Weisberg noted was "not the title, message, or meaning of the painting" (Weisberg, *The Bush Tragedy* [New York: Random House, 2008], p. 90). Scott Horton writes of Bush's mistaken interpretation of the origins of the painting: "So Bush's inspiring, proselytizing Methodist is in fact a horse thief fleeing from a lynch mob. It seems a fitting marker for the Bush presidency. He [Bush] is completely convinced he knows what things are, so he shuts down all avenues of inquiry about them and disregards the information that is offered to him. The president of the United States has identified closely with a man he sees as a mythic, heroic figure. In fact, that man is a wily criminal one step out in front of justice. It perfectly reflects Bush the man . . . and Bush the president" (Horton, "The Illustrated President," *Harper's*, January 2008, www .harpers.org/archive/2008/01/hbc-90002237).

7. Jack Brubaker, "My Visit with President Bush," *Lancaster* [Pennsylvania] *New Era*, September 26, 2006. Brubaker reports this as said to Jacob S. Stoltzfus during a visit by President Bush in the summer of 2004. Stoltzfus described his meeting with President Bush and quoted this remark in *Die Botschaft*, a weekly publication of letters written by and for the Amish.

8. Robert Draper, *Dead Certain: The Presidency of George W. Bush* (New York: Free Press, 2007), p. xiii.

9. Suskind, "Without a Doubt."

10. David Frum, *The Right Man: The Surprise Presidency of George W. Bush* (New York: Random House, 2003), p. 18. Frum discussed the religious nature of the domestic agenda during his two years on the White House staff. David Frum, author interview, April 2007, Washington, D.C.

11. Stephen Mansfield, *The Faith of George W. Bush* (Lake Mary, Fla.: Charisma House, 2003), p. 120.

12. *Tammy Kitzmiller, et al. v. Dover Area School District, et al.*, 400 F. Supp. 2d 707 (M.D. Pa. 2005). The Dover, Pa., school board did not appeal the case because

all of the school board members who had supported including intelligent design in the curriculum were unseated in an election a few months after the decision. The newly elected school board members declined to appeal, having run on the platform to return to the science-based curriculum. U.S. District judge John E. Jones III presided over the case in the federal courthouse in Harrisburg, Pa. Jones was appointed to the bench in 2002 by George W. Bush.

13. Bush, *A Charge to Keep*, p. 10.

14. White House, Office of the Press Secretary, "President Delivers Remarks on Healthy Forests Initiative," August 13, 2003.

15. White House Office of the Press Secretary, "President Unveils Nation's Founding Documents at National Archives," August 17, 2003.

16. White House, Office of the Press Secretary, "President Bush Discusses Faith-Based Initiative with Urban Leaders," July 16, 2003.

17. Peter Wehner, author interview, October 2007, Washington, D.C.

18. Michael J. Gerson, *Heroic Conservatism: Why Republicans Need to Embrace America's Ideals* (New York: HarperOne, 2007), p. 42. Gerson, a graduate of Wheaton College in Illinois, a conservative Christian college, had been the head speechwriter for the 2000 presidential campaign before his appointment to the White House staff.

19. Ibid., p. 51.

20. Jean Bethke Elshtain, "An Extraordinary Discussion," *Sightings* (online academic religious forum), October 3, 2001, http://divinity.uchicago.edu/martycenter/publications/sightings/archive_2001/sightings-100301.shtml.

21. White House, Office of the Press Secretary, "National Day of Prayer and Prayer Service at the Washington National Cathedral," September 14, 2001.

22. White House, Office of the Press Secretary, proclamation of "National Day of Prayer and Remembrance," August 31, 2002.

23. White House, Office of the Press Secretary, "Statement by the President in His Address to the Nation," September 11, 2001. See also Thomas M. Freiling, *George W. Bush on God and Country* (Fairfax, Va.: Allegiance Press, 2004), p. 47.

24. Randall Balmer, *God in the White House, A History: How Faith Shaped the Presidency from John F. Kennedy to George W. Bush* (New York: HarperOne, 2008), p. 219. For an excellent discussion of religious conflict during the Crusades, see Steven Runciman, *A History of the Crusades* (New York: Cambridge University Press, 1987).

25. "A Nation Challenged: President Bush's Address on Terrorism Before a Joint Session of Congress," September 20, 2001.

26. White House, Office of the Press Secretary, "Remarks on the War on Terror and a Question and Answer Session, Wheeling, West Virginia," March 22, 2006.

27. Peter Wehner, interview with Collin Hansen, *Christianity Today*, September 20, 2007. *Christianity Today* is, according to its masthead, "a magazine of evangelical conviction."

28. Matthew Scully, "Present at the Creation," *Atlantic*, September 2007. Scully's article takes aim at chief speechwriter Michael Gerson, whom he accuses of constantly taking credit for the material in Bush's speeches. Scully notes that there was a speechwriting team, which circulated all major speeches and each of whom contributed to the speeches. Scully disputes the statement made by Frum in his book that Gerson alone changed the phrase from "axis of hatred" to "axis of evil." Scully notes, among other points, that Bob Woodward writes in *State of Denial* (New York: Simon & Schuster, 2006) that Gerson wrote all of the post–9/11 speeches by himself, which Scully says is absolutely wrong.

29. David Frum, *The Right Man: The Surprise Presidency of George W. Bush* (New York: Random House, 2003), p. 238. Frum confirmed this view in an interview, Washington, D.C., April 2007.

30. White House, Office of the Press Secretary, "Remarks to Employees at the Army Tank Plant, Lima, Ohio," April 24, 2003.

31. Howard Fineman, "Bush and God," *Newsweek*, March 10, 2003.

32. Rajiv Chandrasekaran, *Imperial Life in the Emerald City: Inside Iraq's Green Zone* (New York: Knopf, 2007), p. 10.

33. White House, Office of the Press Secretary, "Remarks by the President at Bush-Cheney 2004 Luncheon," August 21, 2003.

34. During the 2004 reelection campaign, Karl Rove went so far as to work with state Republican leaders to put referendums against same-sex marriage on the ballot to increase the evangelical vote.

35. Dr. Douglas Jacobsen, author interview, Grantham, Pennsylvania, November 2007. Dr. Jacobsen, an expert on evangelical Christianity, is professor of religion, Messiah College, Grantham.

36. Executive Order 13199, January 29, 2001, created the White House Office of Faith-Based and Community Initiatives.

37. "Groups Now Receive More than $2.1 Million from the Federal Government," *USA Today*, March 10, 2006. For a broad discussion of faith-based initiatives, see Jo Renee Formicola, Mary C. Segers, and Paul Weber, *Faith-Based Initiatives in the Bush Administration: The Good, the Bad, and the Ugly* (Lanham, Md.: Rowman & Littlefield, 2003).

38. For a discussion of how faith-based programs were used in the prison system, see Amy E. Black, Douglas L. Koopman, and David K. Ryden, *Of Little Faith: The Politics of George W. Bush's Faith-Based Initiatives* (Washington, D.C.: Georgetown University Press, 2004).

39. Diana B. Henriques and Andrew Lehgren, "Religion for Captive Audiences, with Taxpayers Footing the Bill," *New York Times*, December 10, 2006. See *Ams. United for Separation of Church & State v. Prison Fellowship Ministries*, 432 F. Supp. 2d 862 (S.D. Iowa 2006). This was subsequently reversed in part and remanded on the issue of damages.

40. *Moeller v. Bradford County*, No 3:05cv334, M.D. Pa. (August 10, 2006). See Neela Banerjee, "Court Rejects Evangelical Prison Plan over State Aid," *New York Times*, June 3, 2006.

41. White House Office of Faith-Based and Community Initiatives, "Los Angeles FBCI Conference Highlights Prisoner Reentry Initiatives," November 27, 2007. The prisoner reentry programs were highlighted in the 2004 State of the Union Address. White House, Office of the Press Secretary, "State of the Union Address," January 20, 2004.

42. The mission statement of Teen Challenge says: "we believe that there is hope for recovery of every individual who is bound with life controlling problems such as addiction to illegal drugs or alcohol by establishing a relationship with Jesus Christ. Teen Challenge offers a safe place for recovery for eligible individuals based on Biblical principles" (www.teenchallengetc.com).

43. Paul Singer and Brian Frist, "Leaps of Faith," *National Journal*, January 6, 2007. See also Biblical Concepts in Counseling mission statement, which begins "In 1996 God began Biblical Concepts in Counseling . . ." (www.biblicalconccepts.org/ministry.htm).

44. Jay Parsons, "Spellings Lauds Dallas Program: U.S. Needs Faith-Based Initiatives Like Oak Cliff Model, She Says," *Dallas Morning News*, October 5, 2006.

45. Clay Johnson, who had worked on the transition with Cheney, first served as director of the White House Personnel Office before moving to OMB as deputy director, with primary responsibility for the President's Management Agenda.

46. Kate O'Beirne, "Church (Groups) and State: The Problem with the Faith-Based Bit," *National Review*, February 19, 2001.

47. The Robertson School of Law, founded in 1986, was originally named the CBN School of Law, after Robertson's Christian Broadcast Network.

48. "In our written request to the interim U.S. Attorneys, we cited political affiliation and religion as examples of improper or illegal hiring criteria" (U.S. Department of Justice, Office of Inspector General, "An Investigation of Allegations of Politicized Hiring by Monica Goodling and Other Staff in the Department of Justice," July 28, 2008, p. 28).

49. Chris Mooney, *The Republican War on Science* (New York: Basic Books, 2005), pp. 251–52.

50. Seth Schulman, *Undermining Science: Suppression and Distortion in the Bush Administration* (Berkeley: University of California Press, 2006), p. 114.

51. Chandrasekaran, *Imperial Life in the Emerald City*, p. 92.

52. Don Eberly, the founder of the National Fatherhood Initiative, was named the deputy director of the White House Office of Faith-Based and Community Initiatives, under John DiIulio. DiIulio and Eberly had different views of how the office should operate, with DiIulio seeking a nonreligious perspective.

53. "Interview: Wade Horn—Let's Get Married," *Frontline*, PBS, July 12, 2002, www.pbs.org/wgbh/frontline/shows/marriage/interviews/horn.html.

54. Wade Horn, "Wade Horn on Marriage," *National Review Online*, August 2005. For detailed material on the Healthy Marriage Initiative, see Roundtable on Religion and Social Welfare Policy, Rockefeller Institute of Government, State University of New York.

55. Administration for Children and Families, U.S. Department of Health and Human Services, Fact Sheet, Section 510, State Abstinence and Education Program, Acting Associate Commissioner Curtis Porter.

56. Richardo Alonso-Zaldivar, "Abstinence Approach Gets an Unlikely Ally," *Los Angeles Times*, October 14, 2007.

57. "Sex, Science, and Savings," *New York Times*, editorial, December 2, 2007.

58. House Committee on Government Oversight and Reform, "Experts: HHS Teen Health Website Inaccurate and Misleading," July 13, 2005.

59. Mathematica Policy Research, Inc., "Impacts of Four Title V, Section 510 Abstinence Education Programs," April 2007, www.mathematica-mpr.com/publications/PDFs/impactabstinence.pdf.

60. White House, Office of the Press Secretary, "President Bush Participates in Joint Press Availability with President Yayi of Benin," February 16, 2008.

61. White House, Office of the Press Secretary, "President Calls for Constitutional Amendment Protecting Marriage," February 24, 2007.

62. Jake Tapper, "Homosexuality Isn't Natural or Healthy," ABC News, June 7, 2007, http://abcnews.go.com/Politics/Story?id=3251663&page=1.

63. Gerson, *Heroic Conservatism*, p. 166.

64. White House, Office of the Press Secretary, "President Discusses Schiavo, WMD Commission Report," March 31, 2005.

65. White House, Office of the Press Secretary, "National Sanctity of Human Life Day," January 20, 2004.

66. The Mexico City policy was named after the city where the United Nations

International Conference on Population was being held in 1984 when President Ronald Reagan first adopted the position that abortion would not be funded with federal funds. President Clinton rescinded the position. It was reinstated by President George W. Bush.

67. White House, Office of the Press Secretary, "Memorandum to the Director of the United States Agency for International Development—Subject: The Mexico City Policy," January 22, 2001.

68. Presidential debate between John Kerry and George W. Bush, Boston, Mass., October 8, 2004.

69. Presidential debate between John Kerry and George W. Bush, Tempe, Ariz., October 13, 2004.

70. Christopher Lee, "Bush Choice for Family Planning Post Criticized," *Washington Post*, November 17, 2006.

71. White House, Office of the Press Secretary, "President Bush Signs Partial Birth Abortion Ban Act of 2003," November 5, 2003.

72. Presidential debate between Vice President Al Gore and George W. Bush, Boston, Mass., October 3, 2000.

73. Gardiner Harris, "F.D.A. Approves Broader Access to Next-Day Pill," *New York Times*, August 25, 2006. See also Mark Kaufman, "Staff Scientists Reject FDA's Plan B Reasoning," *Washington Post*, June 18, 2004.

74. White House, Office of the Press Secretary, "President Discusses Stem Cell Research," August 9, 2001.

75. Schulman, *Undermining Science*, p. 130.

76. Sheryl Gay Stolberg, "First Bush Veto Maintains Limits on Stem Cell Use," *New York Times*, July 20, 2006.

CHAPTER 6: DICK CHENEY AND THE
BUSINESS-FRIENDLY PRESIDENCY

1. Cheney's concerns about an overly aggressive federal regulatory policy were discussed with Adam Meyerson for his article in the Hoover Institution's *Policy Review* in 1993. Cheney had just left his position as secretary of defense in January 1993, when the Clinton administration took office, and had taken a position as a Senior Fellow at the American Enterprise Institute. Among the questions posed to Cheney by Adam Meyerson in a wide-ranging discussion was "how would you lower the costs of environmental regulation without hurting environmental policy?" Cheney responded: "If you let the marketplace work, people will be amazingly creative in finding ways to make changes that are environmentally sound" (Meyerson, "Calm After Desert Storm," *Policy Review*, Summer 1993).

2. The term "the burden of government" emerged from the Heritage Foundation's planning for the 2000 transition. See *Priorities for the President,* ed. Stuart M. Butler and Kim R. Holmes (Washington, D.C.: Heritage Foundation, 2000), p. 79. Chapter 6 is titled "Burden of Government." In 1980, the Heritage Foundation produced *Mandate for Leadership* for the Reagan-Bush transition, with many of the same proposals for reining in regulations that in their view were a burden on business and industry.

3. White House, Office of the Press Secretary, "White House Press Secretary Meets with Reporters Friday," St. Louis, October 8, 2004. Bush also used the phrase "burdensome regulations," such as in a speech in 2004 on the benefits of private-sector innovation on the economy. According to Bush, "government has a way of imposing burdensome regulations" on the private-sector. See U.S. Department of Commerce, "Remarks by the

President on Innovation: High Tech Improving Economy, Health Care, and Education," June 24, 2004.

4. Joel Brinkley, "Out of Spotlight, Bush Overhauls U.S. Regulations," *New York Times*, August 14, 2004.

5. Center for Science in the Public Interest, "Letter to President Bush," March 7, 2001, www.cspinet.org.

6. Douglas Jehl, "E.P.A. to Abandon New Arsenic Limits for Water Supply," *New York Times*, March 21, 2001. See also Miguel Llanos, "EPA Drops Rule on Arsenic in Water: Clinton-Era Tighter Standard Questioned," MSNBC, March 20, 2001. Christine Todd Whitman, EPA administrator, released a statement saying, "I want to be sure that the conclusions about arsenic in the rule are supported by the best available science."

7. Jason K. Burnett and Robert W. Hahn, "EPA's Arsenic Rule: The Benefits of the Standard Do Not Justify the Costs" (AEI–Brookings Institution Joint Center for Regulatory Change, Regulatory Analysis 01–02, January 2001).

8. Congressman Henry Waxman, the ranking member of the House Committee on Government Reform, sent a letter to Christine Todd Whitman on April 20, 2001, seeking greater clarification for EPA's decision to ignore existing scientific data. The letter can be accessed at the web site of the House Committee on Oversight and Government Reform, www.oversight.house.gov.

9. "The Cost Is Too High: How Susan Dudley Threatens Public Protections," a Report by Public Citizen and OMB Watch, September 2006, www.ombwatch.org/regs/2006/dudleyreport.pdf.

10. Statement by Daniel Rosenberg, environmental attorney, Public Interest Research Group, "GE Identified as Worst Offender Nationwide," July 30, 1998, www.commondreams .org/pressreleases/July98/073098.htm.

11. House Committee on Oversight and Government Reform, "Committee Examines Political Interference with Climate Change," March 19, 2007, which can be accessed at the web site of the House Committee on Oversight and Government Reform at www .oversight.house.gov. See also Andrew C. Revkin, "Bush Aide Softened Greenhouse Gas Links to Global Warming," *New York Times*, June 8, 2005. Rick Piltz is quoted in Cullen Murphy and Todd Purdum, "Farewell to All That: An Oral History of the Bush White House," *Vanity Fair*, February 2009, www.vanityfair.com/politics/features/2009/02/bush-oral-history200902.html.

12. Tim Dickinson, "The Secret Campaign of President Bush's Administration to Deny Global Warming," *Rolling Stone*, June 20, 2007.

13. Jonathan H. Alder, "Post-Whitman EPA," National Review.online, June 2, 2003, www.nationalreview.com/adler/adler060203.asp. Whitman's treatment by Cheney is quoted from an interview with Rick Piltz, senior associate, U.S. Climate Change Science Program, in Murphy and Purdum, "Farewell to All That."

14. Michael Abramowitz and Steven Mufson, "Papers Detail Industry's Role in Cheney's Energy Report," *Washington Post*, July 18, 2007.

15. Dana Milbank and Justin Blum, "Document Says Oil Chiefs Met with Cheney Task Force," *Washington Post*, November 16, 2005.

16. Vice President Cheney, letter to President Bush, May 16, 2001, included in the National Energy Plan, www.whitehouse.gov/energy/national-energy-policy.

17. See National Energy Policy, Report of the National Energy Policy Development Group, May 16, 2001.

18. Speech at the annual meeting of the Associated Press, PBS Online, *NewsHour*,

April 30, 2001. This speech has been taken off of the vice president's official web site. See also "Bush Administration Policy: Outline of a New Energy Strategy," from an address by Vice President Richard Cheney, April 30, 2001, annual meeting of the Associated Press in Toronto, Canada, *Congressional Digest*, June–July 2001.

19. Darcy Frey, "Endangered Landscape," *New York Times*, June 30, 2002.

20. Michael Abramowitz and Steven Mufson, "Papers Detail Industry's Role in Cheney's Energy Report," *Washington Post*, July 18, 2007.

21. David Addington, letter to the Honorable Henry A. Waxman, January 3, 2002, available at www.house.gov/reform, the web site of the Committee on Government Reform in the House of Representatives.

22. *Walker v. Cheney*, 230 F.Supp. 2nd 51 (DDC 2002). Cheney refused to provide the GAO with either the names of the corporate advisors or the dates of the meetings with them. For a discussion of the court case, see Bruce P. Montgomery, "Congressional Oversight: Vice President Richard B. Cheney's Executive Branch Triumph," *Political Science Quarterly 120*, 4 (2005–6). See also Joel Aberbach, "The State of the Contemporary American President: Or, Is Bush Actually Ronald Reagan's Heir," in *The George W. Bush Presidency: Appraisals and Prospects*, ed. Colin Campbell and Bert A. Rockman (Washington, D.C.: CQ Press, 2004).

23. Immediately after the court's decision was released, the public affairs officer at the U.S. Department of Justice said that "allowing the GAO to sue the Vice President without legal authority would improperly interfere with the President's ability to formulate the best possible policies for the American people" (statement by Barbara Comstock, director of public affairs, Department of Justice, December 12, 2002, www.usdoj.opa .pr/2002December/02_as_703.htm).

24. The list of participants in the Energy Task Force that Abraham met with was provided from the secretary of energy's daily schedule that the Department of Energy released. See Don Van Natta Jr. and Neela Banerjee, "Bush Energy Paper Followed Industry Push," *New York Times*, March 27, 2002.

25. Executive Order 13212, May 18, 2001, stated that "it is the policy of this Administration that executive departments and agencies shall take appropriate actions, to the extent consistent with applicable law, to expedite projects that will increase the production, transmission, or conservation of energy." The Energy Task Force submitted its report to the president on May 16, 2001.

26. White House, Office of the Press Secretary, "Executive Summary of the Clear Skies Initiative," February 14, 2002, said that "the clear skies initiative will cut air pollution 70 percent, using a proven, market based approach that will save American consumers millions of dollars." In the business-friendly decisions being made on air pollution by the administration, a market-based approach was preferable to the regulatory approach. See also Katherine Q. Seelye, "E.P.A. and Energy Department War over Clean Air Rules," *New York Times*, March 27, 2002.

27. Edison Electric Institute, "New Source Review." See www.eei.org/industry_issues for more information on the electric industry's view of the new source review.

28. "Bush Administration Air Pollution Plan," Natural Resources Defense Council press release, February 27, 2002.

29. White House, Office of the Press Secretary, "President Announces Clear Skies Initiative," February 14, 2002.

30. Kari Lydersen, "Clear Skies Initiative Clouds the Issue," AlterNet.com, September 17, 2003.

31. Deborah Solomon, "Ah Wilderness: The Secretary of the Interior Talks About Her Problems with the Endangered Species Act, Falling Attendance in the National Parks, and Her Odd Job Title," *New York Times Magazine*, July 17, 2005.

32. Text of the testimony of Gale Norton before the Senate Energy and Natural Resources Committee, *New York Times*, January 18, 2001.

33. "Interior Secretary Makes Plans to Manage National Monuments," U.S. Department of the Interior, National Park Service news release, April 24, 2002, http://home.nps.gov/applications/release/Detail.cfm?ID=245.

34. On August 1, 2001, Griles signed a "statement of disqualification," which said "I hereby recuse myself for one year from my appointment as Deputy Secretary from any particular matter involving parties in which any of my former clients is or represents a party unless the Department of the Interior determines, pursuant to 5 C.F.R. 2635.502 (d) that the interests of the Government outweigh any appearance issue that may be present." Information on Griles's tenure at the Department of the Interior is available at the Friends of the Earth web site. See Friends of the Earth, "Watchdogging the Interior Department," September 25, 2002, www.foe.org/camps/eco/interior/902grilespr/html. See also Matthew Daley, "Nethercutt Joins Firm Led by ex-Cheney Energy Adviser," Associated Press, SpokesmanReview.com, January 31, 2005. Griles left the department in 2005 to form a lobbying firm with Andrew Lundquist, who had been the director of Cheney's Energy Task Force.

35. Sidney Blumenthal, *How Bush Rules: Chronicles of a Radical Regime* (Princeton, N.J.: Princeton University Press, 2006), p. 336.

36. Susan Schmidt and James V. Grimaldi, "Abramoff Pleads Guilty to 3 Counts," *Washington Post*, January 4, 2006.

37. "Former Interior Department Deputy Pleads Guilty to Lying to Congress," Office of Inspector General, Department of the Interior, www.doioig.gov/upload/griles5.txt. See also Douglas Waller, "Department of Billion-dollar Bungling," *Time*, September 16, 2006.

38. *Kentuckians for the Commonwealth, Inc. v. Rivenburgh*, 204 F. Supp 2d 927 (S.D. W. Va. 2002). "Some believe that reasonably priced energy from coal requires cheap disposal of the vast amounts of waste material created when mountaintops are removed to get at the natural resource," Judge Haden wrote in the opinion. He continued: "Congress did not, however, authorize cheap waste disposal when it passed the Clean Water Act."

39. During his confirmation hearings, Attorney General John Ashcroft promised to defend the roadless rule. But when U.S. District judge Edward Lodge in Idaho issued a preliminary injunction that allowed road building and logging in 2001, Ashcroft did not appeal. See *Kootenai Tribe v. Veneman*, 142 F. Supp. 2d 1231 (D. Idaho 2001).

40. U.S. Department of the Interior, Bureau of Land Management, Information Bulletin No. 2001-138, "Status of Bureau of Land Management's National Energy Policy Implementation Plan," August 15, 2001.

41. Margaret Kriz, "Working the Land," *National Journal*, February 23, 2002.

42. "Final Snowmobile Regulations," National Park Service press release, January 23, 2001. The regulations also allowed snowmobiles on the John D. Rockefeller, Jr. Memorial Parkway, which connects Yellowstone and Grand Teton National Parks.

43. *Greater Yellowstone Coalition v. Kempthorne*, 577 F. Supp. 2d 183 (D.D.C. 2008). Judge Sullivan said in 2008: "For the reasons stated above, the Court find that the Winter Use Plan, as codified in the Final Rule and explained in the 2007 ROD, is arbitrary and capricious, unsupported by the record, and contrary to law. In contravention of the Organic Act, the Plan clearly elevates use over conservation of park resources." Judge

Sullivan had reached a similar decision in 2003. See also "Judge Limits Snowmobiles in National Parks," CNN.com, December 17, 2003.

44. Environmental impact statements had been required for over thirty years following passage of the National Environmental Policy Act (NEPA) of 1970. The Bush administration was changing environmental regulations that had been in place since then. See Margaret Kriz, "Bush's Quiet Plan," *National Journal*, November 23, 2002.

45. Cindy Skrzycki, "Lining Up to Lobby for Rule Rescission," *Washington Post*, February 6, 2001.

46. Nicholas Thompson, "Dick Cheney's Dick Cheney," *Washington Monthly*, July–August 2001.

47. Frustrated by the pro-business orientation of the administration, the AFL-CIO sued the Department of Labor, arguing that the department had not issued rules requiring employers to pay for mandated safety equipment, such as helmets and face shields.

48. "EPA: Out of the Loop," *National Journal*, January 24, 2003.

49. Executive Order 12866 of September 30, 1993, as amended by E.O. 13258 of February 26, 2002, and E.O. 13422 of January 18, 2007. The 2007 amended E.O. states that "within 60 days of the date of this Executive order, each agency shall designate one of the agency's Presidential Appointees to be its Regulatory Policy Officer, advise OMB of such designation, and annually update OMB on the status of this designation." See also Margaret Kriz, "Thumbing His Nose," *National Journal*, July 7, 2007.

50. Senator Barack Obama (D-Ill.) sent the chairman of the Senate Commerce, Science, and Transportation Committee a letter on May 17, 2007, opposing Baroody's confirmation. Accessed at www.obama.senate.gov/press/070517-obama_raises_co/index.php.

51. Stephen Labaton, "White House to Offer Own Plan on Product Safety," *New York Times*, November 6, 2007.

52. Eric Lipton, "Safety Agency Faces Scrutiny Amid Changes," *New York Times*, September 2, 2007.

53. The President's Management Agenda was unveiled by OMB in August 2001. According to its web site, the President's Management Agenda was "an aggressive strategy for improving the management of the Federal government. It focused on five areas of management weakness across the government where improvements and the most progress can be made" (www.whitehouse.gov/omb/budgetintegration/pma_index.html).

54. Martin Kady II, "Congress Builds a Barrier to Bush Privatization Plan," *Congressional Quarterly*, October 11, 2003.

55. Jason Peckenpaugh, "OMB Sets New Targets for Management Agenda," GovernmentExecutive.com, May 21, 2003, www.govexec.com/story_page.cfm?filepath=/dailyfed/0503/052103p1.htm.

56. Angela B. Styles, the administrator of the Office of Federal Procurement Policy in OMB, which oversaw outsourcing, left in 2003 to go to the law firm of Miller and Chevalier, which specialized in helping contractors bid for federal jobs.

57. Philip E. Sakowitz Jr., deputy director, IMCOM, www.imcom.army.mil.site/plans/directstormsg.asp.

58. Jason Peckenpaugh, "Outlook Tall Order," GovernmentExecutive.com, July 1, 2003, www.govexec.com/mailbagDetails.cfm?aid=25975.

59. Jeremy Scahill, *Blackwater: The Rise of the World's Most Powerful Mercenary Army* (New York: Nation Books, 2007), p. 22.

60. Dana Priest and Anne Hull, "Soldiers Face Neglect, Frustration at Army's Top Medical Facility, *Washington Post*, February 18, 2007.

61. Paul Krugman, "Hired Gun Fetish," *New York Times*, September 28, 2007.

62. Neil King Jr. and August Cole, "Oversight of Blackwater Set," *Wall Street Journal*, October 6, 2007.

63. Jim Schaeffer, M. L. Elrick, and Todd Spangler, "Ready for a Fight," *Orange County Register*, October 14, 2007.

64. Leslie Wayne, "With Shuttle Program, an Intricate and Integral Partnership for NASA," *New York Times*, August 3, 2005.

65. Kimberly Palmer, "Bush Administration Official Downplays Reorganization," GovernmentExecutive.com, March 22, 2005, www.govexec.com/dailyfed/0305/032205k1 .htm

66. Professor Charles Tiefer, University of Baltimore Law School, "The Downside of Competitive Sourcing Initiative: Numerical Outsourcing Targets Under the Tilted New A-76" (testimony before the Senate Subcommittee on Oversight of Government Management, Restructuring, and the District of Columbia of the Committee on Governmental Affairs, July 24, 2003), http://hsgac.senate.gov/public/_files/072403tiefer.pdf.

67. Martin Kady II, "Congress Builds a Barrier to Bush Privatization Plan," *Congressional Quarterly*, October 11, 2003.

68. For a discussion of Joshua Bolten's memo on last-minute regulations, see Cindy Skrzycki, "Bush Wants Sun to Set on Midnight Regulations," *Washington Post*, June 3, 2008. For a discussion of Susan Dudley's actions at OMB, see Adriel Bettelheim, "Regulatory Official Says 'Midnight Rulemaking' Will Be Minimal," Congressional Quarterly Online News, December 10, 2008.

CHAPTER 7: WHAT HAPPENED TO THE DOMESTIC AGENDA?

1. White House, Office of the Press Secretary, "Inaugural Address of President George W. Bush," January 20, 2001.

2.. Stephen Goldsmith, "What Compassionate Conservatism Is—And Is Not" (speech delivered at the Hoover Institution, Stanford University, 2000).

3. Bush had been successful at creating policies that social conservatives embraced—such as abstinence education, faith-based programs, and expanded volunteer programs—and policies that fiscal conservatives embraced, such as pro-business environmental actions. The composition of the White House staff reflected this dual agenda. In the National Economic Council, for example, the senior member of the office was Lawrence Lindsey, a fiscal conservative. His deputy, Douglas Badger, was, however, a social conservative with a master's degree of divinity from Westminster Theological Seminary, where the core mission was to "form men for the gospel ministry."

4. John DiIulio interview, Washington, D.C., various dates; John Bridgeland interview, Washington, D.C., November 2007. Bolten had rented an apartment from Congressman Robert Portman (R-Ohio) in Washington, D.C., at one time, leading to a friendship that existed before the Bush campaign. Bridgeland worked for Portman in the House of Representatives and became friends with Bolten through Portman.

5. Nicholas Calio interviews, Washington, D.C., October–November 2007.

6. The 9/11 Commission Report: Final Report of the National Commission on Terrorist Attacks upon the United States, Section 10.1, "Immediate Responses at Home" (Washington, D.C.: Government Printing Office, 2004), p. 326. The Commission's members were Thomas H. Kean (chair), Lee H. Hamilton (vice chair), Richard Ben-Veniste, Fred F. Fielding, Jamie S. Gorelick, Slade Gorton, Bob Kerrey, John F. Lehman, Timothy J. Roemer, and James R. Thompson. Philip D. Zelikow was the executive director of the 9/11

Commission (he was named in 2005 as a counselor in the Department of State, working for Condoleezza Rice).

7. Frank Bruni, "A Nation Challenged: White House Memo—For President, A Mission and a Role in History," *New York Times*, September 22, 2001.

8. White House, Office of the Press Secretary, "President to Discuss New Citizen Corps Initiative," January 30, 2002. President Clinton signed the National and Community Trust Act in 1993, which created AmeriCorps, incorporating Volunteers in Service to America (VISTA) and the National Civilian Community Corps (NCCC). In the January 2002 State of the Union address, Bush highlighted the Citizen Corps and volunteerism and urged everyone in the country to give at least four thousand hours of volunteer service over their lifetimes.

9. White House, Office of the Press Secretary, "President Signs Landmark No Child Left Behind Education Bill," January 8, 2002. After the bill was passed by Congress, Bush signed it into law with great fanfare at Hamilton High School in Hamilton, Ohio, surrounded by students. Rove and Hughes had ensured that the bill signing would dominate the nightly news cycle with its fanfare to signal to the Republican Party's base that the administration had accomplished one of the central themes of its agenda for compassionate conservatism. Education would empower individuals, leading to economic independence, and would provide more time for civic engagement, both themes of compassionate conservatism.

10. When John DiIulio left the White House in August 2001, his replacement, James Towey, did not have the title of assistant to the president. Rather, the title was downgraded to deputy assistant to the president.

11. One of the few proactive policy initiatives was the White House Task Force for Disadvantaged Youth, created in December 2002, to assess how various programs within the federal government dealt with disadvantaged youth. In its 125-page report, the task force concluded that the federal government needed "better management" of existing programs, and that departments should "streamline" their responses to the problems faced by disadvantaged youth. It did not call for additional spending, but rather urged greater coordination among the "hundreds of federal youth programs" across the agencies. See "White House Task Force for Disadvantaged Youth—Final Report," October 2003. The report was commissioned December 23, 2002, under the direction of Margaret Spellings, assistant to the president for domestic policy, and John Bridgeland, director of the USA Freedom Corps.

12. Bush's belief that he was called upon by God was explained by a leader among Christian broadcasters, Jim Cody, who said, "It seems as if he is on an agenda from God," and continued with, "the Scriptures say God is the one who appoints leaders. If he truly knows God, that would give him a special anointing." Dana Milbank, "For Bush, War Defines Presidency," *Washington Post*, March 9, 2003.

13. White House, Office of the Press Secretary, "Personnel Announcement." Allen was appointed assistant to the president for domestic policy on January 5, 2005.

14. Timothy Noah, "Who Is Director of the Domestic Policy Council," Slate, January 15, 2003, www.slate.com/id/2077046. When Noah put the name Margaret LaMontagne in the White House web site search engine, it yielded only four entries. When he changed the search to her married name, Margaret Spellings, it yielded only seven entries.

15. White House, Office of the Press Secretary, "President Arrives in Alabama, Briefed on Hurricane Katrina," Mobile, Alabama, September 7, 2005. See also White House, Office of the Press Secretary, press gaggle with Scott McClellan aboard Air Force One, en route to Andrews Air Force Base, Maryland, August 31, 2005.

16. Brown resigned September 12, 2005. Soon after his resignation, he said that FEMA could not be blamed for the disaster response since FEMA was "not a first responder. It's a coordinator; it's an honest broker." More important, he said that "individuals must take personal responsibility for being prepared," which he believed absolved FEMA of some blame. Quoted in David Stout, "Former FEMA Chief Blames Local Officials for Failures," *New York Times*, September 27, 2005. Brown was replaced as director of FEMA by his deputy, R. David Paulison. In May 2006, Paulison was confirmed as FEMA director, after serving as acting director since Michael Brown's resignation. He paid $10,000 in a past-due federal tax bill before being sworn into office. Secretary of Homeland Security Michael Chertoff, however, brought a degree of professionalism to the disaster response when he separated operational responsibility for Hurricane Katrina by giving Vice Admiral Thad Allen, the Coast Guard's chief of staff, the lead role.

17. Paul Krugman, "All the President's Men," *New York Times*, September 12, 2005.

18. The opening blessing at the conference was given by Barry S. Black, chaplain of the U.S. Senate, a Seventh Day Adventist. Seventh Day Adventists oppose, for example, same-sex marriage, abortion, and the theory of evolution, and support strict adherence to biblical Scripture. See "Remarks by Barry S. Black, Chaplain of the U.S. Senate," Monday, December 12, 2005, Opening Plenary 2005 White House Conference on Aging, www.whcoa/press/speakers/remarks_barry_black.pdf. A transcript can also be found at kaisernetwork.org.

19. Karl Zinsmeister, interview by Ben Wattenberg, "Social Policy with Karl Zinsmeister," PBS Think Tank, aired June 15, 2006, www.pbs.org/thinktank/show_1232.html.

20. Dana Priest and Anne Hull, "Soldiers Face Neglect, Frustration at Army's Top Medical Center," *Washington Post*, February 18, 2007. Zinsmeister's proposals for dealing with Walter Reed were made six months later. See White House, Office of the Press Secretary, "Briefing via Conference Call by Karl Zinsmeister, Assistant to the President for Domestic Policy, on Wounded Warriors Reform," October 16, 2007.

21. Ron Suskind, *The Price of Loyalty: George W. Bush, the White House, and the Evolution of Paul O'Neill* (New York: Simon & Schuster, 2004), p. 119.

22. Bruce Barcott, "Changing All the Rules," *New York Times Magazine*, April 4, 2004.

23. Intergovernmental Panel on Climate Change (IPCC), Third Assessment Report, *Climate Change 2001: Synthesis Report*, vols. 1–4, available at www.ipcc.ch/ipccreports/assessments-reports.htm.

24. John B. Taylor, *Global Financial Warriors* (New York: Norton, 2005), pp. 144–45, which discusses Edson's role at the Genoa Summit, rather than in the IPPC discussion. Other material on Edson from an interview with John B. Taylor, Stanford University, November 2007.

25. John M. Bridgeland and Gary Edson, letter to Dr. Bruce Alberts, National Academy of Sciences, May 11, 2001, available at www.nap.edu.

26. National Academy of Sciences, "Leading Climate Scientists Advise White House on Global Warming," June 6, 2001, available at www.nationalacademies.org.

27. "Warming Up," interview of Dr. Ralph Cicerone on *NewsHour With Jim Lehrer*, PBS, June 7, 2001, www.pbs.org/newshour/bb/environment/energy/warming_6-7.html.

28. White House, Office of the Press Secretary, "President Bush Discusses Global Climate Change," June 11, 2001.

29. White House, Office of the Press Secretary, "Climate Change Review," June 11, 2001.

30. Jo Becker and Barton Gellman, "Angler: Leaving No Tracks," *Washington Post*, June 27, 2007.

31. Seth Shulman, *Undermining Science: Suppression and Distortion in the Bush Administration* (Berkeley: University of California Press, 2006), pp. 22–23. From an EPA internal memo, April 29, 2003; available as an appendix to Union of Concerned Scientists, "Scientific Integrity in Policy Making: Investigation of the Bush Administration's Abuse of Science," March 2004, www.ucsusa.org.

32. "Bush-League Lysenkoism," (editorial), *Scientific American*, May 2004, www .sciam.com/article.cfm?id=Bush-League-Lysenkoism.

33. Union of Concerned Scientists, "Scientific Integrity in Policy Making: Investigation of the Bush Administration's Abuse of Science," February 18, 2004, www.ucsusa.org. See also Union of Concern Scientists, "Atmosphere of Pressure: Political Influence in Federal Climate Science," February 2007, ucsusa.org.

34. Paul Recer, "Panelists Decry Bush Science Policies," *Los Angeles Times*, February 23, 2005. Criticism of the Bush administration at the meeting included the assertion that government scientists were often kept out of policy-making decisions by the administration's political appointees.

35. Chris Mooney, *The Republican War on Science* (New York: Basic Books 2005), and Shulman, *Undermining Science*, provide numerous examples of how the Bush administration ignored existing science, such as in global warming policy decisions.

36. Becker and Gellman, "Angler."

37. Dina Cappiello, "Bush Plan Would Limit Endangered Species Act," *Harrisburg Patriot-News*, August 12, 2008.

38. Editorial, "An Endangered Act," *New York Times*, August 12, 2008.

39. Claudia Dreifus, "A Conversation with Elizabeth H. Blackburn: Finding Clues to Aging in the Fraying Tips of Chromosomes," *New York Times*, July 3, 2007.

40. Wehner frequently sent e-mail from the White House to supporters across the country. This e-mail from Wehner is quoted by Michael Hilzik in his article, "Undoing the New Deal," *Los Angeles Times*, June 26, 2005. Wehner's e-mails to supporters were part of a discussion in an author interview, November 2007.

41. John Cogan, author interview, Stanford University, November 2007.

42. Sheryl Gay Stolberg, "In Bush's Last Year, Modest Domestic Aims," *New York Times*, November 24, 2007.

43. "The War at Home," *New York Times*, April 20, 2003.

44. Cullen Murphy and Todd Purdum, "Farewell to All That: An Oral History of the Bush White House," *Vanity Fair*, February 2009, www.vanityfair.com/politics/ fetures/2009/02/bush-oral-history200902.html.

CHAPTER 8: CHENEY'S PENCHANT FOR SECRECY

1. Charlie Savage of the *Boston Globe*, one of several commentators who discussed Cheney's secrecy in office on "Cheney's Law," *Frontline*, PBS, October 16, 2007, www.pbs .org/wgbh/pages/frontline/cheney. The secrecy with which Cheney operated was decried by others in the press. For example, an editorial in the *Miami Herald* had cautioned the year before that "[Cheney] and all other public officials should be mindful that, along with the power vested in them by virtue of holding public office, there is an obligation to undergo public scrutiny, and yes, even answer questions from pesky reporters from time to time" ("Under a Veil of Secrecy," editorial, *Miami Herald*, February 16, 2006).

2. Neal Peirce, "The Democratic Nominee . . . If I Were President," *National Journal*,

July 17, 1976. See also Erwin C. Hargrove, *Jimmy Carter as President: Leadership and the Politics of the Public Good* (Baton Rouge: Louisiana State University Press, 1988), p. 12.

3. James Mann, "The Armageddon Plan," *Atlantic*, March 2004. Mann lays out many of the details of the planning that Cheney and Rumsfeld did for the shadow government. The lengthy article provides new material on how deeply involved Cheney and Rumsfeld were in creating the plans for managing government in the event of a nuclear war during the 1980s.

4. Andrew Cockburn, *Rumsfeld: His Rise, Fall, and Catastrophic Legacy* (New York: Scribner, 2007), p. 85. Cockburn states that the budget of the National Program Office reached $1 billion by 1989. CNN noted that the budget reached $8 billion in 1982, largely spent on outsourcing a post–nuclear war communications system. See *Special Assignment*, CNN, November 17, 1991.

5. James Mann expanded on his *Atlantic* article on the continuity of government planning in *Rise of the Vulcans: The History of Bush's War Cabinet* (New York: Penguin Books, 2004), chap. 9, "In the Midst of Armageddon," pp. 138–49.

6. Ibid., p. 144.

7. Steven Emerson, "America's Doomsday Project," *U.S. News & World Report*, August 7, 1989, pp. 26–31. See also the CNN *Special Assignment*, November 17, 1991. Another discussion of Project 908, also known as the Doomsday Project and the Armageddon Plan, is found in Tom Shorrock, *Spies for Hire: The Secret World of Intelligence Outsourcing* (New York: Simon & Schuster, 2008), pp. 78–80.

8. Carl Cannon and Alexis Simendinger, "The Making of Team Bush," *National Journal*, September 22, 2001. On May 8, 2001, Bush assigned Cheney the role of overseeing the federal government's preparedness for a homeland terrorist attack. According to Bush, Cheney would head a task force to "ensure that all facets of our response to the threat from weapons of mass destruction are coordinated and cohesive." See White House, Office of the Press Secretary, "Statement by the President: Domestic Preparedness Against Weapons of Mass Destruction," May 8, 2001. At the same time, Bush announced that FEMA was establishing the Office of National Preparedness for terrorism. Cheney would be developing the guidelines, among other points, for the Office of National Preparedness. See also Frank Bruni, "Bush Taps Cheney to Study Antiterrorism Steps," *New York Times*, May 9, 2001.

9. Cheney's ability to influence policy was evident when Ridge took over as director of the White House Office of Homeland Security on October 29, 2001. He moved several of his senior staff with him from the governor's office in Harrisburg, including Mark Holman, Barbara Chaffee, and Becky Halkias. Abbot would have the institutional connections and working knowledge of current terrorism planning that Ridge and his staff lacked.

10. Richard A. Clarke, *Against All Enemies: Inside America's War on Terror* (New York: Free Press, 2004), p. 18.

11. Susan B. Glasser and Michael Grunwald, "Department's Mission Was Undermined from the Start," *Washington Post*, December 22, 2005.

12. The task force assembled by Card and Libby, known as the Group of Five, or G-5, consisted of Associate Counsel Brad Berenson, Deputy Budget Director Mark W. Everson, Card's deputy, Joel Kaplan, and Ridge staffers Major General Bruce Lawlor and Richard Falkenrath, a security expert. They met several times a week with DHS secretary Tom Ridge, Condoleezza Rice, Office of Management and Budget director Mitchell Daniels, Card, and Libby. See Susan B. Glasser and Michael Grunwald, "Department's Mission Was Undermined from the Start," *Washington Post*, December 22, 2005.

13. Ibid.

14. U.S. Department of Justice, National Security Division Program Report, April 2008. As a new supervision within the Department of Justice was being considered in 2005, the *New York Times* became the first newspaper to publish information on it. In its brief discussion, the *Times* raised concerns about such a powerful and largely secret division. "The idea [for the new division] amounts to a superdivision at the Justice Department, which is also likely to stir concerns from civil rights advocates and conservative libertarians who assert that the national antiterrorism law has already given the Justice Department too much power." See Eric Lichtblau, "A New Antiterror Agency Is Considered," *New York Times*, March 25, 2005. Lichtblau received the 2006 Pulitzer Prize for national reporting for his work on wiretapping. See also his book *Bush's Law: The Remaking of American Justice* (New York: Pantheon Books, 2008).

15. *Walker v. Cheney*, 230 F. Supp. 2d 51 (D.D.C. 2002). See also Don Van Natta Jr., "Cheney Argues Against Giving Congress Records," *New York Times*, September 28, 2002.

16. For an excellent overview of the litigation that emerged after the Energy Task Force had concluded its proceedings, see Bruce P. Montgomery, "Congressional Oversight: Vice President Richard B. Cheney's Executive Branch Triumph," *Political Science Quarterly 120*, 4 (2005–6). It is worth noting that George W. Bush appointed U.S. District Court judge John D. Bates to the bench in 2001. Bates had worked for Kenneth Starr's investigations of Bill Clinton. In 1997, Bates had been the deputy independent counsel under Starr, with responsibility for Hillary Clinton's discussions in the Whitewater land development investigation. Democrats in Congress were outraged at what they saw as the judge's political payback to the Bush administration.

17. *In re* Cheney, 365 U.S. App. D.C. 387, 406 F. 3d 723 (D.C. Cir. 2005).

18. *Natural Resources Defense Council v. Spencer Abraham*, 223 F. Supp 2d 162 (D.D.C. 2002).

19. Congressman Henry Waxman placed the letters from his committee to the vice president, which David Addington responded to, on the House Oversight and Government Reform web site, www.oversight.house.gov/investigations.

20. "Civics Quiz: Is Cheney Part of the Executive Branch?" ABCnews.com, June 26, 2007, http://abcnews.go.com/GMA/story?id=3316591&page=1.

21. Frank Rich, "When the Vice President Does It, That Means It's Not Illegal," *New York Times* (op-ed), July 1, 2007.

22. J. William Leonard, director, Information Security Oversight Office, National Archives and Records Administration, letter to David S. Addington, chief of staff to the vice president, June 8, 2006, www.oversight.house.gov/investigations.

23. The threat by Cheney's staff to have the Information Security Oversight Office abolished is repeated in a number of press stories and on the web site of the House Committee on Oversight and Government Reform, www.oversight.house.gov/investigations.

24. The letter from Fred Fielding and Stephen Bradbury's letter in the Office of Legal Counsel are available on the web site of the House Committee on Oversight and Government Reform, www.oversight.house.gov/investigations.

25. David Jackson, "Lawmaker Challenges Cheney on Executive Order," *USA Today*, June 25, 2006.

26. Kate Sheppard and Bob Williams, "Cheney Sidesteps Travel Disclosure Rules," Center for Public Integrity, November 16, 2005, http://projects.publicintegrity.org/lobby/report.aspx?aid=760.

27. David Addington, counsel to the president, letter to Marilyn Glynn, director,

Office of Government Ethics, February 25, 2005, web site of the House Committee on Oversight and Government Reform, www.oversight.house.gov/documents/20070621095027 .pdf.

28. Anne Kornblut and Ralph Blumenthal, "No End to Questions in Cheney Hunting Accident," *New York Times*, February 14, 2006.

29. Bill O'Reilly, "Dick Cheney's Quail Hunting Accident Affects No One," Foxnews .com, February 15, 2006, www.foxnews.com/story/0,2933,184933,00.html.

30. Michael Weisskopf, "Dick Cheney and His Invisible Guests," Time.com, May 31, 2007, www.time.com/time/nation/article/0,8599,1627051,00.html .

31. Associated Press, "Administration Asks to Keep Cheney Logs Secret," MSNBC .com, December 13, 2006, www.msnbc.msn.com/id/16194747.

32. *Citizens for Responsibility and Ethics in Washington v. Department of Homeland Security*, 527 F. Supp. 2d 76 (D.D.C. 2002). The case was brought by CREW against the Department of Homeland Security, of which the Secret Service is a part. Michael Abramowitz, "Secret Service Logs of White House Visitors Are Public Records, Judge Rules," *Washington Post*, December 18, 2007.

33. The decision by the U.S. Court of Appeals for the D.C. Circuit, written by Judge David Tatel, noted: "In this case, we disagree [with Cheney's position]. We find unpersuasive the government's argument that this case implicates the same separation-of-powers concerns [that were found in the Energy Task Force lawsuit]" (362 U.S. App. D.C. 259).

34. Charlie Savage, *Takeover: The Return of the Imperial Presidency and the Subversion of American Democracy* (New York: Little, Brown, 2007), p. 9.

CHAPTER 9: THE IMPERIAL PRESIDENCY

1. Jeffrey Goldberg, "Party Unfaithful: The Republican Implosion," *New Yorker*, June 4, 2007.

2. Office of the Vice President, the White House, "Interview of Vice President [in Cheney's office in the Old Executive Office Building] with Campbell Brown," January 28, 2002.

3. Dick Cheney was part of a panel discussion on "War Powers and the Constitution" sponsored by the American Enterprise Institute, December 6, 1983, held at its Washington, D.C. office. The panel was moderated by John Charles Daley and included Dick Cheney, Lee Hamilton, Charles Mathias Jr., and Brent Scowcroft.

4. Gerald R. Ford and Richard M. Nixon, "Two Ex-Presidents Assess the Job." Ford's part of the essay was entitled "Imperiled, Not Imperial." *Time*, November 10, 1980.

5. Arthur M. Schlesinger Jr., *The Imperial Presidency* (1973; Boston: Houghton Mifflin, 1989).

6. Arthur Schlesinger Jr. "The Imperial Presidency Redux," *Washington Post*, June 28, 2003. For an analysis of the expansion of presidential power in the Bush administration, see Andrew Rudalevige, *The New Imperial Presidency: Renewing Presidential Power After Watergate* (Ann Arbor: University of Michigan Press, 2005).

7. "Reports of the Iran-Contra Committees: Excerpts from the Minority View," *New York Times*, November 17, 1987.

8. Editorial, "Don't Veto, Don't Obey," *New York Times*, June 22, 2007.

9. For a discussion of signing statements, see Christopher S. Kelley, "The Significance of the Presidential Signing Statement," in *Executing the Constitution: Putting the President Back in the Constitution*, ed. Christopher S. Kelley (Albany: State University of New York Press, 2006).

10. Author interview with Jack Howard, deputy director, White House Office of Legislative Affairs, Washington, D.C., October 2007.

11. White House, Office of the Press Secretary, "President's Statement on H.R. 407, the 'Postal Accountability and Enhancement Act,'" December 20, 2006. See also response from the Center for National Security Studies, "President Bush Now Claims Authority to Open Mail Without a Warrant," www.cnss.org, and James Gordon Meek, "Bush Says Feds Can Open Mail Without Warrant," New York Daily News, January 4, 2007. The interpretation that the president had oversight over the postal service ran counter to the legislation itself. Passed in 1970, the Postal Service Act created an independent postal service intended to be free of political pressure or political actions. The postmaster general was removed from the president's cabinet at that time and employees of the postal service were given civil service protections. The interpretation that a member of the executive branch, such as the FBI or CIA, could open mail for national security reasons also seemed to run counter to the legislation that created the Foreign Intelligence Surveillance Court, which was specifically authorized by Congress to issue warrants in an expedited and veiled process if necessary for national security issues.

12. The Office of Legal Counsel opinion posted January 29, 2008, states that "Section 802(e)(1)'s direct reporting requirement need not be enforced in circumstances where its application would require the CPO to ignore the results of the President's review, through DHS, and OMBB, of a particular report. In such circumstances, the statute must yield to the President's exercise of his constitutional authority to supervise subordinate Executive Branch officers and their communications with Congress," www.u.doj.gov/olc/2008opinions .htm. See also Charlie Savage, "Administration to Bypass Reporting Law," New York Times, October 25, 2008.

13. Editorial, "Mr. Cheney's Imperial Presidency," New York Times, December 23, 2005.

14. Attorney General Edwin Meese had served as counsel to the president during the first term of the Reagan administration. At the start of the second term, Meese was named attorney general.

15. Charlie Savage, Takeover: The Return of the Imperial Presidency and the Subversion of American Democracy (New York: Little, Brown, 2007), p. 232. Savage, a journalist for the Boston Globe, provides detailed discussion of the evolution of signing statements in the Reagan Department of Justice under Edwin Meese.

16. Jess Bravin, "Judge Alito's View of the Presidency: Expansive Powers," Wall Street Journal, January 5, 2006.

17. Christopher S. Yoo, Steven G. Calabrisi, and Anthony Colangelo, "The Unitary Executive in the Modern Era, 1945–2004," Iowa Law Review 91 (January 2005), pp. 601–731.

18. Steven Calabrisi, a professor of law at Northwestern University who started the Federalist Society while at Yale Law School in 1985, said in an interview that he had intended it to be a "vehicle for bringing conservative and libertarian legal thinkers to campus to share ideas and counteract what he saw as a liberal bias." See Michael Fletcher, "What the Federalist Society Stands For," Washington Post, July 29, 2005. There are chapters of the Federalist Society at 191 law schools.

19. Jess Bravin, "Judge Alito's View of the Presidency: Expansive Powers," Wall Street Journal, January 5, 2006.

20. Curtis A. Bradley and Eric A. Posner, "Presidential Signing Statements and Executive Power" (University of Chicago, Public Law Working Paper No. 133, July 2006).

21. Quoted in John Herbers, "The 37th President; in Three Decades, Nixon Tasted

Crisis and Defeat, Victory, Ruin and Revival," *New York Times*, April 24, 1994. Nixon had just died, and the essay appeared on the obituary page.

22. Walter Dellinger, "A Slip of the Pen" (op-ed), *New York Times*, July 31, 2006.

23. President Bush urged Congress to enact a line-item veto for appropriations spending in 2006. See White House, Office of the Press Secretary, "Presidential Briefing on the President's Line Item Veto Legislation by OMB Director Josh Bolten," March 6, 2006.

24. American Bar Association, "Blue Ribbon Task Force Finds President Bush's Signing Statements Undermine Separation of Powers," July 24, 2006.

25. Jo Becker and Barton Gellman, "Taking on the Supreme Court Case: When It Came to Vetting the Potential Nominees, the Vice President Steered the Selection Process," *Washington Post*, June 26, 2007.

26. David Montgomery, "No Secrets Here: Federalist Society Plots in the Open; Conservative Legal Group Focuses on Judiciary to Come," *Washington Post*, November 18, 2006.

27. Elisabeth Bumiller, "Back at Work After Battle Prepping the Next in Line," *Washington Post*, November 14, 2005. See also Lois Romano and Juliet Eilperin, "Republicans Were Masters in the Race to Paint Alito; Democrats' Portrayal Failed to Sway the Public," *Washington Post*, February 2, 2006.

28. Bill Mears, "Specter: Alito Said He Will Respect Abortion Proceedings," CNN Washington Bureau, December 2, 2005. See also Carla Marinucci, "Governor's Team Adds Former Rove Protégé," *San Francisco Chronicle*, February 12, 2006. Soon after the Alito and Roberts hearings, Schmidt left Cheney's office to run California governor Arnold Schwarzenegger's reelection campaign in 2006. In 2008, Schmidt joined the presidential campaign of Senator John McCain; he was named a top strategist a few months later.

29. White House, Office of the Press Secretary, "President's Statement on Appointing Judge Charles Pickering to the Fifth Circuit Appeals Court," January 16, 2004. Judge Pickering's recess appointment expired at the end of the 108th Congress, at which time he retired. Because he was sixty-five years of age, he could have taken senior status on the appeals court without Senate confirmation. Bill Pryor was confirmed by the Senate on May 6, 2005. A discussion on the president's authority to make recess appointments is presented by Henry B. Hogue of the Congressional Research Service at the Library of Congress in "The Law: Recess Appointments to Article III Courts," *Presidential Studies Quarterly*, September 2004.

30. White House, Office of the Press Secretary "Statement on Appointment of William H. Pryor, Jr.," February 20, 2004.

31. The appointment of both Pickering and Pryor was framed in language typical of Cheney's drive to rebuild presidential authority. For Cheney, Congress had consistently used its own interpretation of the Constitution to limit presidential authority. The failure of Pickering and Pryor to win Senate confirmation, in spite of a Republican-controlled Senate, was a perfect opportunity to reinforce the guiding principle of the administration that Congress could not overstep its constitutional authority. The administration believed that the constitutional role of Congress was only to advise and consent and not to deny a presidential nomination.

32. Amy Bach, "Movin' Up with the Federalist Society," *The Nation*, September 13, 2001.

33. Steven Bradbury was nominated as director of the Office of Legal Counsel in the Department of Justice following the resignation of Jack Goldsmith.

34. Lawrence Wilkerson, author interview, Washington, D.C., April 2007. See also

Douglas Jehl, "Bolton Gets Unequivocal Backing from Bush, Not Powell," *New York Times*, April 26, 2005.

35. Byron York, "Democrats Sing in 'The Abuse of Power' Chorus," *The Hill*, August 3, 2005. The use of a recess appointment for John Bolton was called abuse of power by Senator Harry Reid, Senator Ted Kennedy, and Howard Dean (chair of the Democratic National Committee).

36. Rachel L. Swarns, "Democrats Criticize Appointment at Immigration Agency," *New York Times*, January 8, 2006.

37. Senator Patrick Leahy, chairman of the Senate Judiciary Committee, Statement on White House Claim of Executive Privilege, June 28, 2007, www.leahy.senate.gov .press/200706/062807.html.

38. *United States v. Nixon*, 418, U.S. 683 (1974). See also *In re* Bruce R. Lindsey, 148 F. 3d 1100 (D.C. Cir. 1998).

39. Bill Plante, "War on Terror: Bush Opposes 9/11 Query Panel," CBS News, May 23, 2002, www.cbsnews.com/stories/2002/05/15/attack/main509096.shtml.

40. Eric Lichtblau, "Former Prosecutor Says Departure Was Pressured," *New York Times*, March 6, 2007.

41. Dorothy Wickenden, "Never, Ever Land," *New Yorker*, "Talk of the Town," April 2, 2007.

42. White House, Office of the Press Secretary "President Bush Addresses Resignations of U.S. Attorneys," March 20, 2007.

43. Ibid.

44. White House, Office of the Press Secretary, "White House Counsel's Letter Regarding U.S. Attorneys," March 20, 2007.

45. Kyle Sampson and Monica Goodling, in particular, were in contact with the White House. The Department of Justice's inspector general concluded that "in addition, we determined that Goodling often used political or ideological affiliations. . . . Goodling's use of political considertions in connection with these details was particularly damaging to the Department because it resulted in high-quality candidates for important details being rejected in favor of less qualified candidates" (Department of Justice, Office of the Inspector General, Special Report, "An Investigation of Allegations of Politicized Hiring by Monica Goodling and Other Staff in the Office of the Attorney General," July 2008, chap. 8, "Conclusions and Recommendations," www.usdoj.gov/oig/special/s0807/chapter8/ htm). Evidence also surfaced that Goodling reviewed the credentials of nominees for judicial openings, including asking nominees to discuss their political affiliation and pursuing web searches of their political contributions. See Charlie Savage, "Vetted Judges More Likely to Reject Asylum Bids," *New York Times*, August 24, 2008.

CHAPTER 10: CHENEY'S WAR

1. Saddam Hussein's ability to use chemical, biological, and nuclear weapons against Iraq's neighbors was of great concern to the Clinton administration. In December 1998, President Clinton ordered military strikes against Iraq in Operation DESERT FOX. After the 70-hour attack, Secretary of Defense Bill Cohen noted that, "We've diminished his ability to wage war against his neighbors." In addition, Cohen said, "we have enforced the U.N. Security Council resolutions to contain Iraq from attacking its neighbors . . . and that containment policy continues." As Secretary Cohen asserted, Operation DESERT FOX was intended as a containment policy to ensure that Saddam Hussein did not "threaten the region again." There was no concern that Iraq had weapons of

mass destruction that could threaten the United States, as Cheney would assert in 2001. Secretary Cohen and the chairman of the Joint Chiefs of Staff were firm that U.S. forces had "degraded Saddam Hussein's ability to deliver chemical, biological and nuclear weapons" within the region. Cheney convinced Bush in 2003, when the decision was made to invade Iraq, that the Clinton administration had not completed the job, that Saddam Hussein continued to possess such weapons, that he could use them against his neighbors and, most important, he could use them against the United States. See Office of the Assistant Secretary of Defense (Public Affairs), "Presenter: Secretary of Defense William S. Cohen," December 19, 1998.

2. Glen Johnson, "Bush Fails Quiz on Foreign Affairs," *Washington Post*, November 4, 1999.

3. Judy Woodruff, "Bush Lacks Gore's Foreign Policy Expertise," CNN.com, June 24, 1999.

4. Quoted in Ron Suskind, *The Price of Loyalty: George W. Bush, the White House, and the Education of Paul O'Neill* (New York: Simon & Schuster, 2004), p. 80.

5. Transcript of presidential debate between Vice President Al Gore and Governor George Bush, October 3, 2000, Boston, Mass., Jim Lehrer, PBS News, moderator. See transcript at CNN.com.

6. Once in office and with the campaign behind him, Bush relied on the more experienced Dick Cheney to oversee national security policy. Although Cheney had independently taken responsibility for building business-friendly policies, the national security portfolio was clearly delegated to Cheney by Bush. This would be a formal role for Cheney, which would give him—as he wanted—a role of his own. Twenty-five years earlier, he complained that as Gerald Ford's chief of staff, he was just a "hired gun." "It's humbling—you're just somebody's hired gun," he said then, "and even if that somebody happens to be the president of the United States, there's not much you can do on your own" (T. R. Reid, "White House Staff Chief, in Love with Governing, Now Runs for Congress," *Washington Post*, August 28, 1978).

7. Treasury Secretary Paul O'Neill, who attended this NSC meeting, recalled: "Getting Hussein was now the administration's focus, that much was already clear" (Suskind, *Price of Loyalty*, p. 75).

8. Ibid., p. 83.

9. Lawrence Wilkerson, chief of staff to Secretary of State Colin Powell, recalled: "Cheney knew how to play to his [George W. Bush's] cowboy instincts" (author interview, Washington, D.C., April 2007).

10. David J. Rothkopf, "Inside the Committee That Runs the World," *Foreign Policy*, March–April 2005.

11. Ibid.

12. The Vulcans, as they called themselves, included Condoleezza Rice, Paul Wolfowitz, Richard Perle, Robert Zoellick, Stephen Hadley, Robert Blackwill, Richard Armitage, Donald Rumsfeld, and Dick Cheney. For more detail on the role of the Vulcans during the campaign and in the Bush administration, see James Mann, *Rise of the Vulcans: The History of Bush's War Cabinet* (New York: Penguin Books, 2004).

13. Karen DeYoung, *Soldier: The Life of Colin Powell* (New York: Knopf, 2006), p. 178.

14. Department of Defense, "Defense Planning Guidance for the Fiscal Years 1994–1999," February 18, 1992. Available in the PBS *Frontline* documentary "The War Behind Closed Doors," www.pbs.org/wgbh/pages/frontline/shows/iraq/etc/wolf.html See also

"Excerpts from Pentagon's Plan: 'Prevent the Re-Emergence of a New Rival,'" *New York Times*, March 8, 1992.

15. The term "access to oil" refers to national security policies that ensure that oil is available to the world markets (author interview with Major General William M. Matz Jr., U.S. Army, retired).

16. Jacob Heilbrunn suggests that neoconservative influence was in the ascendant in the first term of the George W. Bush administration, as it was in the first term of the Reagan administration, and that Bush had little in common with neoconservative principles until Cheney captured the national security policy process. Paul Wolfowitz, Douglas Feith, and Richard Perle were the architects of the response to the September 11, 2001, terrorist attacks, in Heilbrunn's view. See Heilbrunn, *They Knew They Were Right: The Rise of the Neocons* (New York: Doubleday, 2008).

17. Project for the New American Century, letter to the Honorable William J. Clinton, January 26, 1998, www.newamericancentury.org/iraqclintonletter.htm.

18. John Bolton entered government during the Reagan administration, where he served first with USAID and later in the Department of Justice.

19. Henry Kissinger regarded the USSR as a threat, viewed the United States as severely weakened by Vietnam and Watergate, and pursued détente to buy time.

20. Quoted in Mann, *Rise of the Vulcans*, p. 74.

21. Ibid., pp. 187–88.

22. The No Child Left Behind Act of 2001 was passed by the House of Representatives on May 23, 2001, and by the Senate on June 14, 2001. After revisions in the Conference Committee, the bill was finally signed into law on January 8, 2002. At the time of the September 11, 2001, terrorist attacks, Bush was on a nationwide tour of schools to reinvigorate attention to the No Child Left Behind bill, which remained in the Conference Committee.

23. *The 9/11 Commission Report: Final Report of the National Commission on Terrorist Attacks upon the United States* (Washington, D.C.: Government Printing Office, 2004), p. 325.

24. Air Force One left Barksdale Air Force Base and arrived at Offutt, where Bush went immediately to the U.S. Strategic Command Underground Command Center. After moving into the underground bunker, designed to withstand a nuclear attack, Bush talked via a teleconference call with Cheney, Rice, Rumsfeld, Tenet, Mineta, Armitage, and others.

25. Philip Shenon, *The Commission: The Uncensored History of the 9/11 Investigation* (New York: Twelve Books), p. 264.

26. Ibid., p. 266.

27. Ibid.

28. Richard Clarke, *Against All Enemies: Inside America's War on Terror* (New York: Free Press, 2004), p. 30. Clarke noted in an interview with Cullen Murphy and Todd S. Purdum that Rumsfeld said in the White House on the evening of September 11, 2001, "You know, we've got to do Iraq" (Murphy and Purdum, "Farewell to All That: An Oral History of the Bush White House," *Vanity Fair*, February 2009, www.vanityfair.com/politics/features/2009/02/bush-oral-history200902.html).

29. Bob Woodward, *Plan of Attack* (New York: Simon & Schuster, 2004), p. 77. Woodward also suggests in *Bush at War* that Rumsfeld believed that George H. W. Bush was a lightweight, more interested in friendships, public relations, and public opinion polls than substantive policy. Woodward added that Rumsfeld believed Bush had been a weak CIA director. See Woodward, *Bush at War* (New York: Simon & Schuster, 2002), p. 22.

30. *9/11 Commission Report*, pp. 334–35.

31. Ibid., p. 335.

32. Ibid.

33. Ibid.

34. Transcript of interview of Vice President Dick Cheney by Tim Russert on Sunday, September 16, 2001, on *Meet the Press*, which can be accessed at www.msnbc.msn.com and www.whitehouse.gov/vicepresident/news-speeches/speeches/vp20010916.html.

35. White House, Office of the Press Secretary, "President Discusses National Missile Defense," December 13, 2001.

36. DeYoung, *Soldier*, p. 360.

37. David Gray Adler, "The Law: Termination of the ABM Treaty and the Political Question Doctrine: Judicial Succor for Presidential Power," *Presidential Studies Quarterly* 34 (2004).

38. The Clinton administration was concerned about enhancing the U.S. missile defense system to protect against missile attacks from what were termed rogue states. In January 1999, President Clinton and Russian president Boris Yeltsin agreed to begin discussions on modifying the 1972 ABM treaty, but little had been accomplished by the time the Bush administration took office. However, as early as 1995, the Clinton administration had considered modifying the ABM treaty and had initiated an internal review for building the Alaska site. When Bush abrogated the treaty, plans were well under way for the Alaska site, even though little had moved forward in the bilateral discussions with Russia.

39. CNN Election 2000, George W. Bush's acceptance speech, www.cnn.com/ELECTION/2000/conventions/republican/transcripts/bush.html.

40. "Where Bob Dole Stands on Missile Defense," www.dolekemp96.org/agenda/issues/missile.htm. The material was also available at the Dole campaign web site, www.4president.org.

41. White House, Office of the Secretary, "President Discusses National Missile Defense," December 13, 2001.

42. Russ Feingold, "Senate Ignored on Treaty," *Capital Times* (Madison, Wis.), June 24, 2002.

43. Richard W. Stevenson and Adam Liptak, "Cheney Defends Eavesdropping Without Warrants," *New York Times*, December 21, 2005.

44. Charlie Savage, *Takeover: The Return of the Imperial Presidency and the Subversion of American Democracy* (New York: Little, Brown, 2007). See also similar charges made in Michael Isikoff and David Corn, *Hubris: The Inside Story of Spin, Scandal, and the Selling of the Iraq War* (New York: Crown, 2006).

45. Edward S. Corwin, *The President: Office and Powers* (New York: New York University, 1940).

46. Carlotta Gall, "A Nation Challenged: Taliban; Prison Sealed Off as U.S. Picks Inmates to Interrogate," *New York Times*, December 30, 2001.

47. Barton Gellman and Jo Becker, "A Different Understanding with the President," *Washington Post*, June 24, 2007. John Bellinger III, legal advisor to the National Security Council, and later to the secretary of state, said: "A small group of administration lawyers drafted the president's military order establishing the military commissions, but without the knowledge of the rest of the government, including the national security adviser, me, the secretary of state, or even the CIA director." Quoted in Murphy and Purdum, "Farewell to All That."

48. The issue of how nonstate prisoners of war are to be treated has been discussed for

years. "The international state system and its laws of war were not designed for, and did not contemplate, and still is trying to grapple with, the unprecedented reality of enemies who fall outside its legal purview," according to Dr. Charles Hill, a Yale scholar of international security studies (author interview, September 2008). Cheney's decision to deny the newly classified enemy combatants certain rights under the third Geneva Convention had been part of an ongoing discussion within the Departments of State and Defense that began well before the Bush administration took office. One issue was whether an enemy combatant who did not wear the uniform of his country was considered a civilian, and thus entitled to greater legal privileges than were prisoners of war.

49. For a long discussion of how William Luti operated in the Office of Special Plans, see Seymour Hersh, "Selective Intelligence," *New Yorker*, May 12, 2003.

50. Department of Defense, Deputy Inspector General for Intelligence, "Review of the Pre-Iraqi War Activities of the Office of the Undersecretary of Defense for Policy," February 7, 2007. Report No. 07–INTEL–04, p. ii.

51. U.S. Senate, Select Committee on Intelligence, 110th Cong., 2nd sess., "Final Phase II Report on Prewar Iraq Intelligence," June 5, 2008, http://intelligence.senate.gov/press/record.cfm?id=298775. Manucher Ghorbanifar was an expatriate Iranian arms dealer, whom the CIA had never trusted. Michael Ledeen was an academic/consultant who was serving at the time as a consultant to Douglas Feith in the Office of Special Plans (OSP). Ledeen set up a meeting with Ghorbanifar in Italy to discuss, among other points, possible regime change in Iran. The meeting, although sanctioned by OSP, was criticized by the State Department and the CIA. Neither was informed about it. The meeting was typical of Cheney (who clearly knew about it), since he had for two decades distrusted the CIA.

52. The term "rogue state" was most notably used to describe Mu'ammar al-Gadhafi's Libya, which was regarded as a threat to U.S. national security. After Pan Am Flight 103 was destroyed in the air by a bomb, widely thought to have been placed there by Libyans, over Scotland on December 21, 1988, the term was often repeated in reference to Libya. George H. W. Bush also regarded North Korea, Pakistan, Iraq, Iran, and Afghanistan as rogue states. The Clinton administration changed the label to "states of concern," but the term "rogue states" was revived in the George W. Bush administration. When the United States established an alliance with Pakistan after the September 11, 2001, terrorist attacks, official references to that country as a "rogue state" were dropped. Libya subsequently settled claims against it by relatives of those who had died in the downing of Pan Am Flight 103 and designation of it as a "rogue state" was also ceased. Afghanistan was removed from the list after the United States removed the Taliban-led government from power in 2001. By the time that George W. Bush delivered his January 2002 State of the Union Address, only Iraq, Iran, and North Korea were considered "rogue states."

53. The Anti-Ballistic Missile Treaty of 1972 was signed by President Richard M. Nixon and Soviet General Secretary Leonid Brezhnev at a summit in Moscow. George W. Bush, with the encouragement of Cheney, terminated the treaty, citing the dissolution of the USSR. Treaties between nations, they argued, are not valid when one of the signatories no longer exists.

54. White House, Office of the Press Secretary, "Address Before a Joint Session of Congress on the State of the Union," January 29, 2002.

55. White House, Office of the Press Secretary, "President Delivers State of the Union Address," January 28, 2003.

56. Thomas E. Ricks, *Fiasco: The American Military Adventure in Iraq* (New York: Penguin Books, 2006), p. 91.

57. Author interview, Lawrence Wilkerson, Gettysburg, Pennsylvania, April 2007. For additional material that Wilkerson noted about Cheney and his role in the buildup to the Iraq War, see Murphy and Purdum, "Farewell to All That."

58. Ibid.

59. White House, Office of the Press Secretary, "Secretary of State Powell Addresses the U.N. Security Council," February 5, 2003.

60. "We know that based on intelligence that he has been very, very good at hiding these kinds of efforts. He's had years to get good at it and we know he has been absolutely devoted to trying to acquire nuclear weapons. And we believe he has, in fact, reconstituted nuclear weapons," Cheney said in an interview with Tim Russert on *Meet the Press*, March 16, 2003 (www.msnbc.msn.com). For discussion of Cheney's assertions that Saddam Hussein had nuclear weapons, see also Mark Hosenball, Michael Isikoff, and Evan Thomas, "Cheney's Long Path to War," *Newsweek*, November 17, 2003 (www .newsweek.com/id/60579).

61. White House, "The National Security Strategy," September 2002, www.whitehouse .gov/nsc/nss/2002/index.html. For an expanded discussion, see Stephen Graubard, *Command of Office* (New York: Basic Books, 2004), p. 545.

62. Eric Lichtblau and Scott Shane, "A Defender of Bush's Power, Gonzales Resigns," *New York Times*, August 28, 2007.

63. Gonzales and his staff regularly supported the positions taken by Cheney and Addington, who "provided the intellectual framework for building up the power of an executive branch that they believed had been badly weakened by restrictions imposed after Vietnam and Watergate" (ibid.).

64. Yoo, another member of the Federalist Society, and a war powers expert, who was on leave from the University of California at Berkeley's Boalt Hall Law School, joined Addington in endorsing an expansive interpretation of presidential power. Although only a deputy in the Office of Legal Counsel, Yoo had extraordinary authority in the Office of Legal Counsel, which lacked a Senate-confirmed director. He was perhaps the most important member of the group, because he had the authority, within the OLC, to issue legal opinions that were binding on the executive branch. See Jack Goldsmith, *The Terror Presidency: Law and Judgment Inside the Bush Administration* (New York: Norton, 2007), pp. 22–23.

65. During the period that Yoo was making critical decisions on the rights of prisoners in Afghanistan, the Office of Legal Counsel had essentially been leaderless. A Senate confirmation fight kept a director from taking over until Thanksgiving, over two months after the terrorist attacks.

66. Nancy Kassop, "Bush and Cheney and the Separation of Powers Ledger: Will They 'Leave the Presidency Stronger Than They Found It'?" (paper presented at the American Political Science Association Annual Meeting, Chicago, August 30, 2007).

67. Ibid.

68. When Powell left the administration in 2005 at the start of George W. Bush's second term, Taft also left the administration and returned to the private practice of law in Washington, D.C. On September 12, 2006, along with twenty-eight other retired military or defense department officials, Taft co-signed a letter to the chairman and ranking member of the Senate Armed Services committee in which he stated his belief that the Bush administration's attempt to redefine Common Article 3 of the Geneva Conventions "poses a grave threat" to U.S. service members.

69. Goldsmith, *Terror Presidency*, p. 26. Goldsmith's interview with Gonzales and Addington was preceded by a meeting with a staffer in the outer office, who started

the conversation with, "Are you a Republican?" Goldsmith was then asked a series of other questions by the staffer, who had carefully reviewed his personal and professional background.

70. Alberto Mora, Navy general counsel, is quoted in Murphy and Purdum, "Farewell to All That." The memorandum authored by Yoo was similar to one on the acceptability of harsh interrogations techniques authored by Haynes, although did not carry the legal weight of one produced by the Office of Legal Counsel. Haynes's memo was strongly opposed by other members of the military establishment, including Mora. But Haynes ignored the objections, as did Rumsfeld, because they endorsed such techniques.

71. Goldsmith, *Terror Presidency*, p. 144.

72. White House, Office of the Press Secretary, "President Bush Welcomes Prime Minister of Hungary: Remarks by the President and Prime Minister Medgyessy of Hungary in Photo Opportunity," June 22, 2004, www.whitehouse.gov/news/releases/2004/06/20040622-4 .html.

73. Jan Crawford Greenburg, Howard L. Rosenberg, and Ariane deVogue, "Bush Aware of Advisers' Interrogation Talks: President Says He Knew His Senior Advisers Discussed Tough Interrogation Methods," ABC News interview by Bush with White House correspondent Martha Raddatz, www.abcnews.go.com/TheLaw/LawPolitics/ story?id=4635175.

74. James Risen, *State of War: The Secret History of the CIA and the Bush Administration* (New York: Free Press, 2006), p. 25. George Tenet does not mention any discussions with Cheney about interrogation techniques in his book. In fact, Tenet has only a few lines in his entire book on any interactions with Cheney. See George Tenet, with Bill Harlow, *At the Center of the Storm: My Years at the CIA* (New York: HarperCollins, 2007).

75. By the fall of 2005, there was growing discontent across the administration over the use of harsh interrogation techniques. The second Bush term had brought new faces to the cabinet and White House, and many of Cheney's supporters had left or changed positions. Within the White House, Alberto Gonzales and Harriet Miers were gone. Joshua Bolten, never a strong advocate of Cheney, had replaced Andy Card as the White House chief of staff. Cheney had few voices within the administration coming to his defense when he argued that the McCain bill, designed to end harsh treatment of detainees, should be blocked in Congress.

76. The Detainee Treatment Act of 2005, part of the Department of Defense Appropriations Act of 2006 (H.R. 2863, Title X).

77. Lawrence Wilkerson, interview by Dana Milbank, "Colonel Finally Saw Whites of Their Eyes," *Washington Post*, October 20, 2005. The full Wilkerson interview was posted online as part of the article, www.washingtonpost.com/wp-dyn/content/article/2005/10/19/ AR2005101902246.html.

78. Goldsmith, *Terror Presidency*, pp. 148–49.

79. Philip Shenon and Eric Lichtblau, "White House Renews Battle over Lawyer Who Signed Interrogation Memos," *New York Times*, January 24, 2008.

80. Goldsmith, *Terror Presidency*, p. 181.

81. James Risen and Eric Lichtblau, "Bush Lets U.S. Spy on Callers Without Courts," *New York Times*, December 16, 2005.

82. Dan Eggen and Walter Pincus, "Ex-Justice Lawyer Rips Case for Spying," *Washington Post*, March 9, 2006.

83. Elisabeth Bumiller, "Cheney Sees 'Shameless' Revisionism on War," *New York Times*, November 22, 2005.

84. David Abshire, author interview, Washington, D.C., October 2007.

85. The final report of the Iraq Study Group was released December 6, 2006 (www .usip.org/isg/iraq_study_group_report/report/1206/iraq_study_group_report.pdf). The United States Institute for Peace, an independent, nonpartisan organization funded by Congress, was the facilitating organization for the Iraq Study Group, with assistance from the Center for Strategic and International Studies, the Center for the Study of the Presidency, and the James A. Baker III Institute for Public Policy at Rice University. In addition to Baker and Hamilton, the members were Lawrence S. Eagleburger, Vernon E. Jordan Jr., Edwin Meese III, Sandra Day O'Connor, Leon E. Panetta, William J. Perry, Charles S. Robb, and Alan K. Simpson.

86. Jeff Zeleny, "Bush Iraq Plan Condemned by Senate Panel," *New York Times*, January 25, 2007.

87. According to Bob Woodward, Bush said to Cheney in early November 2006, "I've decided to replace Rumsfeld." Cheney replied, "Well, Mr. President, I disagree, but obviously it is your decision." Woodward, *The War Within* (New York: Simon & Schuster, 2008), photo no. 4, following p. 177. Cheney reinforced his opposition to firing Rumsfeld in an interview on Fox News Sunday, December 21, 2008, when he said that Rumsfeld had done "a good job for us. I did disagree with that decision" (www.foxnews.com/politics/2008/12/21/ cheney-mocks-biden-defends-rumsfeld-fox-news-sunday-interview.html).

88. Only weeks before Barack Obama was set to receive the Democratic Party's formal endorsement at the Denver Democratic Convention, Bolton sent a scathing op-ed piece to the *Los Angeles Times* suggesting that Obama "reveals failings in foreign policy that are far more serious than even his critics previously imagined." See John R. Bolton, "Obama the Naïve," *Los Angeles Times*, June 5, 2008.

89. Libby paid the fine of $250,400 with a cashier's check, which his spokeswoman said was taken from his personal funds. Speculation persisted as to the source of the money, particularly as to whether Cheney had arranged for or personally provided any funds to pay the fine. Libby also had substantial legal bills from his trial.

90. Cheney continued to argue that the war was necessary and that the president had exclusive authority to conduct it. In a letter to his grandchildren, he wrote that "the nation was engaged in a war with terrorists of global reach" and that "my principal focus as Vice President has been to help *protect the American people* and our way of life." The use of the phrase "protect the American people" reflected his insistence that the president had unfettered constitutional authority to protect and defend the nation. "What 'Acting' President Cheney Did," *Weekly Standard*, August 6, 2007.

91. Michael Duffy, "Dick Cheney in Twilight," *Time*, March 8, 2007.

EPILOGUE

1. Rachel L. Swarns, "Cheney, Needling Biden, Defends Bush's Record on Executive Power," *New York Times*, December 22, 2008.

Select Bibliography

Adler, David Gray, and Michael A. Genovese. 2002. *The Presidency and the Law: The Clinton Legacy*. Lawrence: University Press of Kansas.

Balmer, Randall Herbert. 2008. *God in the White House, A History: How Faith Shaped the Presidency from John F. Kennedy to George W. Bush*. New York: HarperOne.

Barnes, Fred. 2006. *Rebel-in-Chief: Inside the Bold and Controversial Presidency of George W. Bush*. New York: Three Rivers Press.

Bartlett, Bruce. 2006. *Impostor: How George W. Bush Bankrupted America and Betrayed the Reagan Legacy*. New York: Doubleday.

Black, Amy E., Douglas L. Koopman, and David K. Ryden. 2004. *Of Little Faith: The Politics of George W. Bush's Faith-Based Initiatives*. Washington, D.C.: Georgetown University Press

Blumenthal, Sidney. 2006. *How Bush Rules: Chronicles of a Radical Regime*. Princeton, N.J.: Princeton University Press.

Buchanan, Patrick J. 2004. *Where the Right Went Wrong: How Neoconservatives Subverted the Reagan Revolution and Hijacked the Bush Presidency*. New York: Thomas Dunne Books.

Burke, John P. 2004. *Becoming President: The Bush Transition, 2000–2003*. Boulder, Colo.: Lynne Rienner.

————. 2000. *Presidential Transitions: From Politics to Practice*. Boulder, Colo.: Lynne Rienner.

Bush, George W. 2003. *We Will Prevail: President George W. Bush on War, Terrorism, and Freedom*. Edited by National Review. New York: Continuum.

————. 1999. *A Charge to Keep*. New York: William Morrow.

Bush, George W., and Tom Freiling. 2004. *George W. Bush on God and Country*. Fairfax, Va.: Allegiance Press.

Butler, Stuart A., and Kim R. Holmes, eds. 2001. *Priorities for the President*. Washington, D.C.: Heritage Foundation.

Campbell, Colin, and Bert A. Rockman. 2004. *The George W. Bush Presidency: Appraisals and Prospects*. Washington, D.C.: CQ Press.

Campbell, Colin, Bert A. Rockman, and Andrew Rudalevige. 2008. *The George W. Bush Legacy*. Washington, D.C.: CQ Press.

Cannon, Carl M., Lou Dubose, and Jan Reid. 2003. *Boy Genius: Karl Rove, The Brains Behind the Remarkable Political Triumph of George W. Bush*. New York: Public Affairs.

Chandrasekaran, Rajiv. 2006. *Imperial Life in the Emerald City: Inside Iraq's Green Zone*. New York: Knopf.

Christie, Ron. 2006. *Black in the White House: Life Inside George W. Bush's West Wing*. Nashville, Tenn.: Nelson Current.

Clarke, Richard A. 2004. *Against All Enemies: Inside America's War on Terror*. New York: Free Press.

Cockburn, Andrew. 2007. *Rumsfeld: His Rise, Fall, and Catastrophic Legacy*. New York: Scribner.

Conason, Joe. 2007. *It Can Happen Here: Authoritarian Peril in the Age of Bush*. New York: St. Martin's Press.

Corwin, Edward S. 1940. *The President: Office and Powers*. New York: New York University Press.

Cromartie, Michael. 1996. *Caesar's Coin Revisited: Christians and the Limits of Government*. Washington, D.C.: Ethics and Public Policy Center.

Dean, John W. 2006. *Conservatives Without Conscience*. New York: Viking.

————. 2004. *Worse than Watergate: The Secret Presidency of George W. Bush*. New York: Little, Brown.

DeYoung, Karen. 2006. *Soldier: The Life of Colin Powell*. New York: Knopf.

Dorrien, Gary J. 1993. *The Neoconservative Mind: Politics, Culture, and the War of Ideology*. Philadelphia: Temple University Press.

Draper, Robert. 2007. *Dead Certain: The Presidency of George W. Bush*. New York: Free Press.

Fleischer, Ari. 2005. *Taking Heat: The President, the Press, and My Years in the White House*. New York: William Morrow.

Formicola, Jo Renee, Mary C. Segers, and Paul Weber. 2003. *Faith Based Initiatives in the Bush Administration: The Good, the Bad, and the Ugly*. Lanham, Md.: Rowman & Littlefield.

Fortier, John C., and Norman J. Ornstein. 2007. *Second-Term Blues: How George W. Bush Has Governed*. Washington, D.C.: American Enterprise Institute.

Freiling, Thomas. 2004. *George W. Bush on God and Country*. Fairfax, Va.: Allegiance Press.

Friedman, Murray. 2005. *The Neoconservative Revolution: Jewish Intellectuals and the Shaping of Public Policy*. Cambridge, U.K.: Cambridge University Press.

Frum, David. 2003. *The Right Man: The Surprise Presidency of George W. Bush*. New York: Random House.

Fukuyama, Francis. 2006. *America at the Crossroads: Democracy, Power, and the Neoconservative Legacy*. New Haven, Conn.: Yale University Press.

Gellman, Barton. *Angler: The Cheney Vice Presidency*. New York: Penguin Press, 2008.

Gerson, Mark. 1996. *The Essential Neoconservative Reader*. Reading, Mass.: Addison Wesley.

Gerson, Michael J. 2007. *Heroic Conservatism: Why Republicans Need to Embrace America's Ideals (And Why They Deserve to Fail if They Don't)*. New York: HarperOne.

Gold, Victor. 2007. *Invasion of the Party-Snatchers: How the Holy-Rollers and Neo-Cons Destroyed the GOP*. Naperville, Ill.: Sourcebooks.

Goldsmith, Jack L. 2007. *The Terror Presidency: Law and Judgment Inside the Bush Administration*. New York: Norton.

Gordon, Michael R., and Bernard E. Trainor. 2006. *Cobra II: The Inside Story of the Invasion and Occupation of Iraq*. New York: Pantheon Books.

Graubard, Stephen Richards. 2004. *Command of Office: How War, Secrecy, and Deception Transformed the Presidency from Theodore Roosevelt to George W. Bush*. New York: Basic Books.

Greene, John Robert. 2000. *The Presidency of George W. Bush*. Lawrence: University Press of Kansas.

————. 1995. *The Presidency of Gerald R. Ford*. Lawrence: University Press of Kansas.

Greenspan, Alan. 2007. *The Age of Turbulence—Adventures in a New World.* New York: Penguin Press.

Halper, Stefan A., and Jonathan Clarke. 2004. *America Alone: The Neo-Conservatives and the Global Order.* New York: Cambridge University Press.

Hargrove, Erwin C. 1988. *Jimmy Carter as President: Leadership and the Politics of the Public Good.* Baton Rouge: Louisiana State University Press.

Hayes, Stephen F. 2007. *Cheney: The Untold Story of America's Most Powerful and Controversial Vice President.* New York: HarperCollins.

Heatherly, Charles L., ed. 1981. *Mandate for Leadership: Policy Management in a Conservative Administration.* Washington, D.C.: Heritage Foundation.

Heilbrunn, Jacob. 2008. *They Knew They Were Right: The Rise of the Neocons.* New York: Doubleday.

Hughes, Karen. 2004. *Ten Minutes from Normal.* New York: Viking/Penguin.

Isikoff, Michael, and David Corn. 2006. *Hubris: The Inside Story of Spin, Scandal, and the Selling of the Iraq War.* New York: Crown.

Jacobson, Gary C. 2008. *A Divider, Not a Uniter: George W. Bush and the American People.* New York: Pearson Education.

Kagan, Robert. 2006. *Dangerous Nation.* New York: Knopf.

Kean, Thomas H., Lee Hamilton, and Benjamin Rhodes. 2006. *Without Precedent: The Inside Story of the 9/11 Commission.* New York: Knopf.

Kelley, Christopher S., ed. 2006. *Executing the Constitution: Putting the President Back in the Constitution.* Albany: State University of New York Press.

Kengor, Paul. 2004. *God and George W. Bush: A Spiritual Life.* New York: Regan Books.

Kuo, J. David. 2006. *Tempting Faith: An Inside Story of Political Seduction.* New York: Free Press.

Lichtblau, Eric. *Bush's Law: The Remaking of American Justice* New York: Pantheon Books.

Lind, Michael. 2006. *The American Way of Strategy.* New York: Oxford University Press.

Mabry, Marcus. 2007. *Twice as Good: Condoleezza Rice and Her Path to Power.* New York: Modern Times.

Mahler, Jonathan. 2008. *Hamdan v. Rumsfeld and the Fight over Presidential Power.* New York: Farrar, Straus & Giroux.

Mann, Brian. 2006. *Welcome to the Homeland: A Journey to the Rural Heart of America's Conservative Revolution.* Hanover, N.H.: Steerforth Press.

Mann, James. 2004. *Rise of the Vulcans: The History of Bush's War Cabinet.* New York: Viking.

Mansfield, Stephen. 2003. *The Faith of George W. Bush.* Lake Mary, Fla.: Charisma House.

Maranto, Robert, Douglas M. Brattebo, and Tom Lansford. 2006. *The Second Term of George W. Bush: Prospects and Perils.* New York: Palgrave Macmillan.

Margulies, Joseph. 2006. *Guantánamo and the Abuse of Presidential Power.* New York: Simon & Schuster.

Meacham, Jon. 2006. *American Gospel: God, the Founding Fathers, and the Making of a Nation.* New York: Random House.

McClellan, Scott. 2008. *What Happened: Inside the Bush White House and Washington's Culture of Deception.* New York: Public Affairs.

Mooney, Chris. 2005. *The Republican War on Science*. New York: Basic Books.

Phillips, Kevin P. 2004. *American Dynasty: Aristocracy, Fortune, and the Politics of Deceit in the House of Bush*. New York: Viking.

Reagan, Ronald. 1990. *An American Life*. New York: Pocket Books.

Renshon, Stanley Allen. 2004. *In His Father's Shadow: The Transformations of George W. Bush*. New York: Palgrave Macmillan.

Ricks, Thomas E. 2006. *Fiasco: The American Military Adventure in Iraq*. New York: Penguin Press.

Risen, James. 2006. *State of War: The Secret History of the CIA and the Bush Administration*. New York: Free Press.

Rudalevige, Andrew. 2005. *The New Imperial Presidency: Renewing Presidential Power after Watergate*. Ann Arbor: University of Michigan Press.

Runciman, Steven. 1987. *A History of the Crusades*. New York: Cambridge University Press.

Sammon, Bill. 2006. *Strategery: How George W. Bush Is Defeating Terrorists, Outwitting Democrats, and Confounding the Mainstream Media*. Washington, D.C.: Regnery.

Savage, Charlie. 2007. *Takeover: The Return of the Imperial Presidency and the Subversion of American Democracy*. New York: Little, Brown.

Scahill, Jeremy. 2007. *Blackwater: The Rise of the World's Most Powerful Mercenary Army*. New York: Nation Books.

Schlesinger, Arthur M., Jr. 1973. *The Imperial Presidency*. Boston: Houghton Mifflin.

Schweizer, Peter, and Rochelle Schweizer. 2004. *The Bushes: Portrait of a Dynasty*. New York: Doubleday.

Shenon, Philip. 2008. *The Commission: The Uncensored History of the 9/11 Commission*. New York: Twelve Books.

Shorrock, Tom. 2008. *Spies for Hire: The Secret World of Intelligence Outsourcing*. New York: Simon & Schuster.

Shulman, Seth. 2006. *Undermining Science: Suppression and Distortion in the Bush Administration*. Berkeley: University of California Press.

Smith, Gary Scott. 2006. *Faith and the Presidency: From George Washington to George W. Bush*. New York: Oxford University Press.

Suskind, Ron. 2006. *The One Percent Doctrine: Deep Inside America's Pursuit of Its Enemies Since 9/11*. New York: Simon & Schuster.

———. 2004. *The Price of Loyalty: George W. Bush, the White House, and the Education of Paul O'Neill*. New York: Simon & Schuster.

Tanner, Michael D. 2007. *Leviathan on the Right: How Big-Government Conservatism Brought Down the Republican Revolution*. Washington, D.C.: Cato Institute.

Taylor, John B. 2007. *Global Financial Warriors: The Untold Story of International Finance in the Post- 9/11 World*. New York: Norton.

Tenet, George, and Bill Harlow. 2007. *At the Center of the Storm: My Years at the CIA*. New York: HarperCollins.

Viguerie, Richard A. 2006. *Conservatives Betrayed: How George W. Bush and Other Big Government Republicans Hijacked the Conservative Cause*. Los Angeles: Bonus Books.

Warshaw, Shirley Anne. 2006. *Powersharing: White House-Cabinet Relations in the Modern Presidency*. Albany: State University of New York Press.

———. 1997. *The Domestic Presidency: Policy Making in the White House*. Boston: Allyn & Bacon.

Weiner, Tim. 2007. *Legacy of Ashes: The History of the CIA*. New York: Doubleday.

Williams, Walter. 2003. *Reaganism and the Death of Representative Democracy*. Washington, D.C.: Georgetown University Press.

Woodward, Bob. 2008. *The War Within*: New York: Simon & Schuster.

———. 2006. *State of Denial*. New York: Simon & Schuster.

———. 2004. *Plan of Attack*. New York: Simon & Schuster.

———. 2002. *Bush at War*. New York: Simon & Schuster.

Index

Note: Bush (the surname) appearing alone refers to George W. Bush (forty-third president of the United States) rather than George H. W. Bush (forty-first president of the United States).

National Preparedness Review Task
Force, 163
National Program Office (NPO), 162,
272n4
Natural Resources Defense Council
(NRDC), 113, 114, 115, 169
National Review, 90–91
National Sanctity of Life Day, 96
National Science Foundation, 156
national security. *See* Department
of Homeland Security; National
Security Agency (NSA); National
Security Council (NSC)
National Security Agency (NSA), 235–36
National Security Council (NSC): Cheney
influence, 137, 205; Cheney's national
security council, 66–67; continuity of
government plan, 162; Iran-Contra,
180; Iraq focus, 205, 207, 217, 218;
purpose, 136; Rove influence, 155
National Security Division (Department
of Justice), 167, 273n14
*National Security Strategy of the United
States of America*, 230
National Strategy for Victory in Iraq, 238
Natural Resources Defense Council
(NRDC), 112–13, 168–69
Neel, Roy, 37, 246
neoconservative influence, 279n16
NEPDG (National Energy Plan
Development Group), 110–14
New Orleans, 142–44, 156
Newsweek, 86
New Yorker, 201
New York Times, 47, 104, 144, 153, 215,
236
NIH (National Institutes of Health), 92
9/11: Bush evacuation and safe location,
164; Bush locations and security
measures, 213–16, 279nn22,24;
Cheney locations and activities, 213–
16; Cheney role in national security
management, 163–66; congressional
evacuations, 164; domestic policy
impact, 136–37, 140; executive
privilege, 197; long-term federal
budget impact, 157–58

9/11 Commission, 200, 215, 268n6
Nixon, Richard M., 2, 132, 160, 179,
180, 188, 199, 281n53
Nofziger, Lyn, 43
No Child Left Behind Act, 69, 135, 138,
140, 213–14, 269n9, 279n22
Nord, Nancy, 126
North, Oliver, 162, 180
Norton, Eleanor Holmes, 131
Norton, Gale, 53, 116–18, 120, 121

Obama, Barack, 125–26,
240, 241, 243–44
O'Beirne, James, 92–93
O'Beirne, Kate, 90–91
O'Connor, Sandra Day, 191, 284n85
O'Donovan, Kevin, 109
O'Neil, Paul, 75
Occupational Safety and Health
Administration (OSHA), 124
Office of Faith-Based and Community
Initiatives, 87–91, 146
Office of Domestic Policy, 145–54
Office of Government Ethics (OGE), 119,
122, 172, 173
Office of Homeland Security, 136, 163,
165–66, 272n9
Office of Information and Regulatory
Affairs (OIRA), 104–8, 124–25, 131,
132
Office of Legal Counsel (OLC), 184–85,
196, 224, 230–31, 239, 256n35,
275n12, 282n65, 283n70. *See also*
Addington, David; Ashcroft, John;
Bradbury, Stephen; Dellinger, Walter;
Goldsmith, Stephen; Gonzales,
Alberto; signing statements; Yoo, John
Office of Legislative Affairs, 184, 247.
See also Calio, Nicholas; Howard,
Jack
Office of Management and Budget
(OMB), 91, 123–32, 267n49,
267n56. *See also* Budget Review
Group; Cheney, Dick; Daniels,
Mitchell; Johnson, Clay; outsourcing;
President's Management Agenda
Office of National Preparedness, 163